SUBJECTS OF EMPIRES
CITIZENS OF STATES

SUBJECTS OF EMPIRES CITIZENS OF STATES
Yemenis in Djibouti and Ethiopia

Samson A. Bezabeh

The American University in Cairo Press
Cairo New York

The author and publisher are grateful to J.M. Coetzee for permission to use an excerpt from *Waiting for the Barbarians*.

First published in 2016 by
The American University in Cairo Press
113 Sharia Kasr el Aini, Cairo, Egypt
420 Fifth Avenue, New York, NY 10018
www.aucpress.com

Copyright © 2016 by Samson A. Bezabeh

All rights reserved. No part of this publication may be reproduced, stored in a retrieval system, or transmitted in any form or by any means, electronic, mechanical, photocopying, recording, or otherwise, without the prior written permission of the publisher.

Exclusive distribution outside Egypt and North America by I.B.Tauris & Co Ltd., 6 Salem Road, London, W4 2BU

Dar el Kutub No. 26165/14
ISBN 978 977 416 729 4

Dar el Kutub Cataloging-in-Publication Data

Bezabeh, Samson
     Subjects of Empires, Citizens of States: Yemenis in Djibouti and Ethiopia/ Samson Bezabeh.—Cairo: The American University in Cairo Press, 2016.
     p.   cm.
     978 977 416 729 4
     1.Yemenis—Ethiopia
     305.8092753363

1 2 3 4 5   19 18 17 16 15

Designed by Jon W. Stoy
Printed in Egypt

In memory of my mother Athen Tsehay Alemu

I [the Magistrate] was the lie that Empire tells itself when times are easy, he the truth that Empire tells when harsh winds blow. Two sides of imperial rule, no more, no less. But I temporized, I looked around this obscure frontier, this little backwater with its dusty summers and its cartload of apricots and its long siestas and its shiftless garrison and the waterbirds flying in and flying out year after year to and from the dazzling waveless sheet of the lake, and I said to myself, "Be patient, one of these days he [the Colonel] will go away, one of these days quiet will return: then our siestas will grow longer and our swords rustier, the watchman will sneak down from his tower to spend the night with his wife, the mortar will crumble till lizards nest between the bricks and owls fly out of the belfry, and the line that marks the frontier on the maps of Empire will grow hazy and obscure till we are blessedly forgotten." Thus I seduced myself, taking one of the many wrong turnings I have taken on a road that looks true but has delivered me into the heart of a labyrinth.

—J.M. Coetzee,
Waiting for the Barbarians (1980: 148–49)

Contents

Acknowledgments	ix
Preface	xiii
Maps	xxv
1. Introduction	1

Part I: Regulating Spaces

2. Disciplining the Natives	29
3. Nationalized Spaces: Yemeni Mobility in the Second Half of the Twentieth Century	57

Part II: The Shaping of Yemenis' Opportunities

4. Entrepreneurs, Laborers, and Smugglers: Yemenis in the Economy of States/Empires	83
5. Colonial Intermediaries, Emperors, Abettors, and Enemies of the People	105
6. State Vision, Imperial Hierarchies: Being a Muslim Yemeni	145
7. Conclusion	181
Notes	201
Bibliography	223
Index	243

Acknowledgments

Subjects of Empires/Citizens of States is the result of eleven years of academic research, beginning in 2004. Over this somewhat long period many individuals and institutions have generously supported my work. In the early days, Dr. Getachew Kassa Negussie, from the Institute of Ethiopian Studies at Addis Ababa University, raised my curiosity about the presence of Yemenis in the Horn of Africa and the Indian Ocean. Prof. Leif Ole Manger, from the University of Bergen, was instrumental in my coming to the Department of Social Anthropology, first as a master's student and later as a PhD candidate. Throughout the years that I have known him, Prof. Manger has been a source of inspiration. His constant urge to explore social complexities in their most minute detail is a rare instinct worth pursuing.

The preparation of this manuscript was generously funded by three institutions, to which I extend my deepest gratitude. My stay in Addis Ababa was funded by the Centre Française des Études Éthiopiennes, and was made pleasant by a number of individuals, chief among them Dr. Giulia Bonacci and Dr. Anaïs Wion. My time in Leiden was supported by the Afrika-Studiecentrum, which gave me a three-month fellowship. In Leiden, I would particularly like to thank Dr. Benjamin F. Soares, who was a very generous host who made my stay in the Netherlands memorable. My residency in Paris was made possible by a postdoctoral research grant from the European Commission and the Fondation Maison des Sciences de l'Homme. And special thanks go to Dr. Éloi Ficquet, my primary research contact at the École des Hautes Études en Sciences Sociales, where I was based during my time in Paris.

Various parts of this manuscript have been reviewed by a number of scholars. In this regard, I would particularly like to thank Dr. Anne K. Bang, an academic interlocutor since 2006, from the Christian Michelsen Institute in Norway. I have particularly benefited from the reading of Prof. Scott S. Reese from Northern Arizona University. His sharp criticism greatly helped me to reshape the original material. My thanks also go to Prof. Daniel Varisco from the American Institute of Yemeni Studies and Dr. Rita Abrahamssen from the School of International Development and Global Studies, University of Ottawa. Both have commented on parts of the manuscript and the insights I obtained from them have positively contributed in the shaping of the manuscript. I am also very grateful to Dr. Simon Imbert-Vier from the Université de Provence Aix-Marseille, who read the full manuscript. Dr. Imbert-Vier pointed out various gaps that would have been difficult for me to identify. I am also grateful to the two anonymous reviewers of this book, whose suggestions have greatly contributed to the improvement of the manuscript.

In addition to these individuals, I am indebted to Prof. Ulrike Freitag from Zentrum Moderner Orient in Berlin and Leila Harold Ingrams for helping me locate historical documents over the course of my research. Thanks are also due to those who provided the framework for intellectual exchange. In Bergen, the text writing seminars led by Prof. John Chr. Knudsen and the Middle Eastern cluster of the Department of Social Anthropology that Prof. Anh Nga Longva chaired provided excellent milieus for shaping the theoretical angle of this work. The many discussions and occasional talks I had with Dr. Bjørn Enge Bertelsen, Prof. Andrew Latas, Prof. Bruce Kapferer, Prof. Vigdis Broch-Due, and Prof. Nefissa Naguib were sources of inspiration. The interdepartmental meetings that brought together anthropologists based at University College London and the University of Bergen were also valuable encounters that helped in further shaping the argument of this book. The meetings were marked by intense debates and I was fortunate to be part of them. I would therefore like to extend my thanks to the coordinators, Prof. Knut Rio and Prof. Annelin Eriksen, and the fellow anthropologists present during those meetings, particularly Dr. Martin Holbraad, whose radical take on anthropology became a source of intense debate and hence helped in developing a specific argument that eventually found its way into this book.

In the field, I would like to extend my deep gratitude to the people who shared their stories, and who accepted me and introduced me to their friends. I would particularly like to thank those who directly facilitated my research. In Djibouti, I am indebted to former Prime Minister 'Abdallah Mohamed Kamil, Naguib 'Ali Tahir, Aref Mohamed Aref, Ambassador Muhammad 'Abdallah Hajar, Fathi Guelleh, Aman 'Abd al-Qadir, 'Adil Salah, Dr. Souad Kassim, Dr. Adawa Hassan 'Ali, Dr. Hibo Moumin Assoweh, Zaynab Kassim, Abu Baker Mohamed, Mohamed Ibrahim, Prof. Abdel Ghaffar Ahmed, and Saeed Rubah. In Ethiopia, I would like to extend my gratitude to Saeed Ba Zar'a, former Ambassador 'Abd al-Sala al-Awadi, 'Abd al-Basit al-Bedani, 'Isa Ahmed, 'Abd al-Rahman Ahmed al-Habshi, Salah Ba Naji, Taha al-Bar, Ruqayya Ba Zar'a, 'Ali Ba Zar'a, 'Abdallah Emmad, Abdo Ba Bedan, Husain Ezia, Mohamed Abdo Ramada, Mohamed and 'Ali Ba Hajeri, 'Abdallah 'Abd al-Rahman al-Qershi, Mohamed Hudeda, Tsega Sentayehu, Idris Mohamed, Najib Mehederi, Husain Mohamed, 'Abd al-Malik Mohamed, Mesfin Gebra, Zahab Mohamed, and Saeed Mohamed.

I would also like to thank my parents, Abebe Bezabeh and Athen Tsehay. My gratitude is deep and without your love and support I would not have reached this particular stage of my life. Thanks is also due to my three sisters: Sarah, Aster, and Rahel.

Last but not least I would like to thank my friends Zalila M. Ashetu, Aneley Engidawork, Sajan Thomas, Carmeliza Rosario, Thomas Mountjoy, Anne Straume, Jessica Mzamu, Melese Gatisso, Rita Cunningham, Thor Sortland, Jayaseelan Raj, Tord Austdal, Laura Adwan, Alexander Manuylov, Hanna Skartveit, Espen Helgesen, Reshma Bharadwaj, Kristine Fauske, Dean Kampanje Phiri, Endale Tsegaye Mohammed, Fasil Ayelegn Tassew, Harold Hazzang, Henos Kifle Tekle, Maria Njau, and Viviane Wei Wei.

Paris/Leiden
January 2015

Preface

The eminent anthropologist Claude Lévi-Strauss opens *Tristes tropiques* with a description of the sense of shame he feels in narrating a personal account of his travels. Convinced that such personal accounts have no place in the ethnologist's work, he observes,

> I hate travellers and explorers. Yet here I am proposing to tell the story of my expeditions. But how long it has taken me to make up my mind to do so! It is now fifteen years since I left Brazil for the last time and all during this period I have often planned to undertake the present work, but on each occasion a sort of shame and repugnance prevented me making a start. Why, I asked myself, should I give a detailed account of so many trivial circumstances and insignificant happenings? Adventure has no place in the anthropologist's profession; it is merely one of those unavoidable drawbacks (Lévi-Strauss, 1955/1992: 17).

While I was writing in the twenty-first century about the Horn of Africa, a field setting far from his Latin American context, Claude Lévi-Strauss's point produced a distant yet compelling echo to which I found myself listening. The present book, which is about the interaction of

Yemenis with states and empires, has not been written from the perspective of structural anthropology advocated by Lévi-Strauss, nor was I inclined to venture into the realms of the savage mind, or the symbology that was so dear to his heart. The basic act of undertaking fieldwork in a remote location, however, produces a relationship between a novice like myself and a distinguished master of the field such as Lévi-Strauss. The act of fieldwork makes his point of departure in *Tristes tropiques* relevant to the present book, as we have both been concerned with the personal stories in the field that enable the production of a monograph.

In current anthropological thinking, narrating the personal encounter of fieldwork is viewed both favorably and unfavorably. Narrating the presence of the anthropologist in the field servs as a strategy to justify one's presence and builds authority for the more objective discourse of the core chapters of the ethnography. Such an endeavor is critically regarded since the 1980s as anthropologist started focusing on textual strategies of ethnographic texts and question the claim of objectivity that ethnography text are making. On the other hand, giving an account of one's fieldwork is looked on as a significant part of the process, and in some circles anthropologists are encouraged to partake in a reflexive understanding of the processes of which they have been a part. Lévi-Strauss's position illustrates well the discomfort anthropologists feel in narrating these more personal accounts of fieldwork.

My own position reflects the anthropologist's ambivalence in this regard. Like Lévi-Strauss, I start from the assumption that ethnography should provide an objective account. Unlike Lévi-Strauss, however, I do not subscribe to the old idea of regarding reflexive engagement as a futile exercise that should not be included in the ethnographic description. Indeed, the fieldwork experience enlightens the debates about seemingly objective accounts of fieldwork.

In the case of this book it highlights the difficult balancing act that Yemenis must maintain in the Horn of Africa in dealing with states/empires—a subject this book sets out to explore. Drawing on ethnographic and historical research on the Yemeni diaspora community in two Horn of Africa countries, Djibouti and Ethiopia, this work aims to counter the hitherto dominant narrative that regards migrants across the Indian Ocean region as by-products of personal connections and an outcome of local oceanic systems. Any examination of such subjects of empires and citizens of states requires an analytical model that takes into account the relevance of those states/empires. Indeed, the present work shows that states and empires structure migrants' lives rather than vanishing as a result of migrants' networking acts that supposedly lead to hybrid cosmopolitan spaces. In view of this, it is relevant to narrate my personal journey within the context of the state in order to highlight the need to take the state/empire into account in any discussion of Yemeni diasporas.

In the Horn of Africa, Yemenis' existence is marked by the need to take into account the presence of state and empire. As with their lives, my fieldwork was based on a series of balancing acts that occurred within a state framework. This need of minding the state began as soon as I started my anthropological research. While preparing to go to Djibouti, I arranged to meet up with Tadios Assefa, a friend from my years at the University of Addis Ababa. I met Tadios to get some idea of the city; he had already traveled to Djibouti for trade purposes. I should say, however, that deep inside I met Tadios to gain some reassurance. Subconsciously, I wanted him to tell me nice things about Djibouti so that I could cope better with the anxiety that comes with every new anthropological field excursion. To my disappointment, Tadios was not a consoling buddy. In fact, he urged me not to go to Djibouti. His concern was the way the state was organized. According to Tadios, citizenship, or having the correct legal paperwork, meant nothing in face of the institution of the state and its officials. What counted were contacts. Djibouti, to use the parlance of anthropologists, is a state based on patron–client relationships. There is blanket exclusion of non-Somalis who do not control the state power structures. Although I had the required entry visa, Tadios was worried about the exclusion I would face as a result of being non-Somali. When I arrived in Djibouti, Tadios proved right.

Before leaving for Djibouti, because of the uncertainty in the region and the negative comments I had heard from people, I arranged through a friend of mine for someone to meet me at the airport. His name was 'Adil Saleh Sa'id. Before traveling, I spoke to him on the telephone. He assured me he would be at the airport on my arrival. Despite his assurances, I remained uncertain, not because I didn't trust 'Adil but because I didn't know anything about his ethnic background. The friend who put me in contact with him had not told me anything about his ethnic affiliation. Consequently, I assumed 'Adil would most probably be from one of the dominant ethnic groups of the country—'Afar or Somali. Being from the region myself, and given the nature of Horn of Africa politics, and especially the war between Somalia and Ethiopia, 'Adil's ethnic affiliation was a pertinent consideration. Being Ethiopian and going into a country dominated by ethnic Somalis, my preference was to be received by a non-Somali. Thus, I came to make a personal 'geopolitical analysis' of my situation and decided to also meet up with an Ethiopian. A friend of mine in Addis Ababa suggested I should meet Aman 'Abd al-Qadir. I called Aman and asked him if he was able to meet me at the airport; he agreed.

My first experience of the state-linked patron–client system in Djibouti started as soon as I disembarked from the plane. After exiting the Boeing 717 that flew me to Djibouti, the first thing I noticed was the all-engulfing heat; the second thing was my name being called out on the runway. At first I thought I was hearing things, but my name was being called repeatedly. I had to answer. I looked around and saw an Arab, about forty years of age, going around calling my name. I presented myself and the man asked me if I was Samson. Upon my affirmation he asked me to follow him. Once inside the terminal building he gave me an entry form and asked me to fill out the necessary information and return it to him when I had finished. I was completely taken aback by what was happening. As I did not understand what was going on, I could not help but occasionally stare at the man who was waiting for me. When I had finished filling out the form, I went to him and he started to tell me what I should do. He told me that when I reached the immigration window I should tell the officer that I would be living with him if asked where I would be staying in Djibouti. And almost immediately, without giving me a chance to speak, he took me to the officer. Luckily, I was not asked where I would be staying. I would have been in an awkward position if the officer had asked, as I was not prepared to inform him that I would be living with this man when I did not even know that man's name.

As soon as my passport was stamped and I was thus formally admitted to Djibouti, the man asked me if I had luggage to collect. When I said yes, he took my baggage claim ticket and proceeded through the airport. It was only when we were waiting for my luggage that I began to understand what was happening. The name of the man assisting me was Farouk, and I gradually learned that 'Adil had asked him to take care of me. This included getting me through immigration without being given a hard time by the entry officials or the customs office. And it worked. With Farouk at my side, I left the terminal without my bag being inspected. All that was said to me was *"Ahlan wa sahlen! Ahlan wa sahlen!* Hello! Hello!"

It was outside customs that I first met 'Adil Saleh Sa'id. Before departing, Farouk pointed him out to me, saying, "'Adil is the man with the green t-shirt." At first I was really surprised by 'Adil's appearance. Contrary to my expectations, he was not Somali or 'Afar. He was a fair-skinned, handsome Arab in his forties with small greenish eyes. At the same time, I also met Aman, the Ethiopian man I had asked to meet me at the airport. I had thought Aman would be closer to me in my micro-geopolitical analysis of ethnic affiliations, when in fact Aman looked more like a Somali. I learned later that Aman's father is from the Somali clan of Wardiqe. And despite being Somali, Aman was one of my closest companions during my research visit.

Unlike many anthropological fieldwork experiences, my first day in the field was not depressing. After I checked in to one of the good hotels in Djibouti, the Arab-owned Hotel Rayan, 'Adil recommended a sightseeing tour in an air-conditioned, United Nations–plated Land Cruiser. In the evening we went out with 'Adil to drink juice at Nugaprix, one of the city's best places for entertainment. During this outing, I learned that 'Adil Saleh was highly placed in the Djibouti Arab community. In fact, Aman told me on the same day that what I needed for my research was just such a person as 'Adil. The reason for 'Adil's status is that he married into a powerful Arab family—the Mouti family. The Mouti are historically powerful Yemeni families who built their wealth and political influence by selling slaves, arms, and ammunition at the beginning of the twentieth century. And it was indeed consoling to hear 'Adil promise his help on that first fieldwork night.

At the time, I did not fully understand the implications of 'Adil's offer, until the going got tough. After a few days, I was told that the Republic of Djibouti had stopped issuing visa extensions and that anyone needing a visa had to go back on a monthly basis to the Djibouti Embassy in Ethiopia. Given my financial and time constraints, it would have been impossible for me to go to Ethiopia every month.

Having heard about the policy change, I met 'Adil by chance in the central part of town, near Hotel Menelik, actually while I was thinking of telephoning him. 'Adil was heading home for lunch but he stopped his car in the middle of the road to inquire after my well-being. I took the opportunity and told him what had happened. He was surprised. I was still staying in the hotel he had taken me to on the first day, and he offered to come around in the afternoon. He said he knew somebody who could take us, if need be, to high-ranking officials.

The man 'Adil was referring to was Ziyad, an ethnic Somali. We went looking for him at the plateau, one of the open areas where Djiboutians play football. 'Adil guessed that he would be there and he was right. In the middle of the game 'Adil called him over. Ziyad arrived, sweating and breathing heavily. We told him briefly what it was all about and he asked us in a somewhat offhand manner to come to his office the next morning. Ziyad was working at the time at the Office National de l'Eau et de l'Assainissement de Djibouti (ONED). When we went as per our appointment, Ziyad was amazed by my visa concerns. He couldn't understand why I insisted on getting a visa when I knew a person like 'Adil. He said, "How can you be afraid when you have a friend like 'Adil? Even the street cats of Djibouti know him. Nothing will go wrong. And if there is a problem you can call me or 'Adil. If the police arrest you do not give them your passport. They do not even know how to read. Tell them you are Norwegian, a Yemeni, and an Ethiopian, it doesn't matter; and if they do not want to let you go just call me."

Even though Ziyad had confidence in 'Adil and the street cats knew him, I was unable to trust the informal system. Upon my insistence, we went to the then head of the Djibouti Immigration Office, Colonel Gonna, and later to the head of the Djibouti police force, Colonel 'Abdullahi Abdi Farah. Going to these offices and meeting the officials took almost three weeks. Colonel Gonna was not in his office every time we went to see him. When we finally managed to meet him he told us that I could not obtain a visa unless he got direct authorization from Colonel 'Abdullahi. On several occasions Ziyad tried to persuade him but failed to do so. Ziyad would play with him, make jokes, and address him as *mon colonel*, and then in the end he would say, "This is just a poor student who wants to do research." But none of it worked. So, taking his advice, Ziyad took us to meet Colonel 'Abdullahi 'Abdi Farah.

We met the colonel for the first time at the headquarters of the national police. Ziyad got us past the front desk, saying we were there to see the colonel. Obviously, Ziyad knew the guards, otherwise we would have been stopped or questioned. As soon as we reached the compound, Ziyad urged us to get out of the car quickly and follow him. Apparently, he had spotted the colonel in his car and was running to reach it. 'Adil parked the car and we started to run after Ziyad. We reached him when he was approaching the open window of the colonel's car, giving a military salute. During the next few minutes Ziyad spoke to the colonel, but apart from hearing that I am an Ethiopian there was almost nothing of relevance said. Important questions, such as where I came from and what I was doing, seemed to be irrelevant. Rather, Ziyad was talking about 'Adil and my relationship with him. Finally, as he was on his way to an important meeting, Colonel 'Abdullahi asked us to come back the following day.

Disappointed, I returned to my hotel room that day in a somber mood. By the time I met Colonel 'Abdullahi I had only one week left before my visa was due to expire. And in the twenty or so days that I had been there, I had been waking up every day only to wait for 'Adil and Ziyad to come and pick me up from my hotel to go and meet the relevant people. This waiting around was particularly agonizing. Sometimes I had to wait three or four hours before 'Adil and Ziyad would come to pick me up, as both of them had to get out of their offices. On what I would call the worst days, I would wait the whole morning only to realize that 'Adil or Ziyad would not make it that day. And given the fact that in Djibouti offices are open for only half a day because of the afternoon temperatures, I could not help but notice the countdown to the day my visa was due to expire.

I finally met Colonel 'Abdullahi for the second and final time, having gone fruitlessly to his office a couple of times with Ziyad and 'Adil. On the day we met him he was on his way to his office. As soon as he saw us he started to complain to Ziyad about the shortage of water at his house. It seems that Colonel 'Abdullahi was not able to get water to his home and he wanted Ziyad to fix the problem, as he was working with ONED. Ziyad was highly responsive, saying, "I will do it my colonel" every ten seconds or so. Colonel 'Abdullahi, as I later learned, has a reputation for being strict with Djiboutians, but he was a gentleman on his best behavior when he received us. After hearing my case he told us that he would make a telephone call to Colonel Gonna to resolve the matter. That day I went back to the hotel with a sigh of relief, after almost a month of seemingly unending bureaucratic procedures.

However, my relief was followed by reflection. In asking for a Djiboutian visa I was in fact trying to cross a line, a state-demarcated line that makes a distinction between those who are insiders and those who are outsiders. The problem was not per se the absence of a visa. If it were an absence of a visa sanctioned by law, I would not have been given one at all. My problem had arisen because I was among people the state did not embrace. Interestingly, this exclusion is based not on a criminal record but on my Ethiopian origins. Legally or not, a visa was not issued for an Ethiopian, while a French man coming to Djibouti could get a visa in a matter of minutes. Unlike the French, being of the 'wrong origin,' I needed the intervention of a patron who could bring me into the embrace of the state.

In the early days of my research the visa was not the only time I needed a person allied with the state. In the first few days of fieldwork, I was keen to consult back issues of *La Nation*, Djibouti's main newspaper. Doing so, I believed, would help me to understand more about the history of Djibouti, but also more about the history of the Yemeni community there. For the first few days I consulted the newspaper, including some of its back issues, at the Djibouti Chamber of Commerce. The issues available in that office were limited, however, and I was advised by the archivist, Girma, to examine other back issues in the archives of Radio Télévision de Djibouti (RTD), which also currently hosts the newspaper.

Determined to get access, I made a call to the number listed in the contact section of the paper. On the phone I spoke to Momina, who was in charge of the newspaper's commercial services. I explained who I was and what I was looking for. To better understand things, Momina asked me to come to the office.

The next day, I called Momina when I was close to the office and she was waiting for me in front of the main gate. A typical Djiboutian woman, Momina received me in her office with a smile and listened patiently to what I had to say, after which she asked me to draft a letter of application to the director of the paper. While I was doing so, Momina made a copy of the relevant letters that I had, and when I finished she told me that she would contact me when she had received a response from the director. While doing other research work I waited for her response for almost two weeks. Thinking that I had waited long enough, I called her in the second week to make an inquiry. To my frustration she told me that the director could not see me and that I could face logistical problems in accessing the back issues, as they had been relocated outside the city center. Basically, she was telling me not to pursue this path.

After this frustrating news, I happened to complain about the problem to a man called 'Umar Salam. 'Umar was a journalist and part of the press services team at the office of the president. As an Arab, 'Umar was interested in the research I was undertaking, and he promised he would personally call the director of the paper so that I would be able to gain access. Shortly after our meeting I received an email from 'Umar explaining that the director had been informed.

I went to the director's office without making an appointment. The director, 'Adil, was a tall man and quite pleasant to talk with. I sensed an uncertainty and a fear of taking responsibility, however, when we talked about my access to the archives. In the middle of our conversation 'Adil made a phone call to the president's press office and started to talk about me. From his conversation I learned that he was talking to Naguib 'Ali Tahir, the communications advisor to the president of Djibouti. Ever since I had arrived in Djibouti, I had heard about Naguib 'Ali Tahir. As an Arab who has unrestricted access to the president, Naguib is quite influential and famous in Djibouti. People like the then ambassador of

Yemen to Djibouti, Muhammad 'Abdallah Hajar, had on various occasions told me that I should try to contact him. However, as a high-ranking person, Naguib had been out of my reach. But to my surprise the director was talking to him as if he knew me—he referred to me as "the student you have sent." In the middle of their conversation the director handed me the phone and asked me to talk to Naguib. Although talking to a person I had never met left me feeling somewhat uncertain, I managed to introduce myself and explain what I was doing.

After listening to my explanations, Naguib asked me to go and see 'Abdallah Kamil, the former prime minister of Djibouti. He asked me to tell him that Naguib had sent me and added, "Although he is not an Arab he knows the history of Arabs better than the Arabs themselves." I had also heard about 'Abdallah Kamil. He had been mentioned by Girma, the archivist at the Chamber of Commerce. Girma had said that it would be useful if I met 'Abdallah Kamil. As I did not know where 'Abdallah Kamil could be found, upon my return from RTD I went to the Chamber of Commerce to ask Girma for the address.

Instead, Girma took me straight to 'Abdallah Kamil's office. The man I met was elderly, in his seventies, with penetrating eyes. After I introduced myself, I handed him a series of "to whom it may concern" letters written for me by the Yemen Embassy, the Yemen Association, and the University of Bergen. After reading the letters and hearing what I had to say, 'Abdallah Kamil proposed that we go to a *mabraze*, a room where Arabs meet to talk and chew the leaf of the mildly stimulant plant commonly referred to as qat. We made an appointment for Thursday of that week.

On the Thursday I realized that the high-profile connection I had managed to establish by meeting with 'Abdallah Kamil had been furthered by his decision to take me to the Arab *mabraze*, which was no ordinary *mabraze* but one where important Arab politicians met with each other. Although the person who established the *mabraze* had died, the people who used to chew with him still came every thursday afternoon. Of the *mabraze* I had seen so far, this one was the most artistically decorated and sophisticated. Fitted with the usual Arabian cushions, the walls were decorated with musical instruments and other artefacts. The photographs on the walls included one of the only Arab minister of the time, Rifki Ba Makhrama. A large poster of Djiboutian President Ismail Omar Guelleh posing beside the flag of Djibouti was displayed prominently on one wall. In one corner, a poster greeted newcomers with a political message: "THE PEOPLE OF DJIBOUTI SUPPORT THEIR PRESIDENT 100%."

The people in the *mabraze* were mostly Arabs who, as I later learned, are in the opposition party, although people such as Naguib 'Ali Tahir were also there. As I mentioned above, he was the president's communications advisor. There were also two 'Issa Somalis. Interestingly, one of them was Fathi Mohamed Guelleh, cousin of the president. An ex-comandant in the Djibouti police force, Fathi was among those accused of being part of a failed coup d'état in December 2000. When the coup failed, many of the participants were sent to the infamous Gabode prison in Djibouti. Apparently, Fathi was pardoned and released from prison after mediation with the president.

As soon as I entered the *mabraze* people were interested in what I was doing. Of the many people there, however, it was Fathi Mohamed Guelleh who was interested in establishing further contact. On that first day we exchanged phone numbers, and the next day Fathi called me, saying that he could assist me in my research. He has a lot of information on Djibouti as a result of being a one-time commander of the Djibouti police and secret service. He also reads widely and constantly researches both Djibouti and world affairs. As per his request, we met at one of the good restaurants in Djibouti, *Le Francolin*, for coffee. As a politically oriented person, Fathi was interested in talking about politics, although at the time I was not inclined to talk very much about this. Despite my reluctance, what Fathi had to say was interesting and worth paying attention to.

My brief association with Fathi and my overall research on Yemenis in a context where those in power were trying to maintain the hegemony of the Somali clan that dominated the state did not seem to be appreciated by some people in the Djiboutian government, however. I came to hear about this by chance when I went to the port of Djibouti to obtain an entrance permit. A Yemeni man was standing beside me as we waited in line. Unlike other people he was complaining loudly about the office procedures. As he was Yemeni, I was interested in getting to know him.

As I began to introduce myself he interrupted. He told me my name and details of my project in Djibouti. As I was not expecting this, the man's response came not only as a surprise but as a shock. I was even more shocked when I learned how he knew about me. Upon my inquiry, he told me that he worked at the presidential palace and that he knew about me because they had shown him my picture. As an average student only interested in documenting the presence of Yemenis in Djibouti, I listened to him in disbelief.

At the time, former prime minister 'Abdallah Kamil must have understood something about the situation in which I found myself. A few days after my encounter with the man at the port, he told me that I should come to him if I had any problems. He said some people might cause problems. People might say, "Why is this Ethiopian carrying out research on Arabs?" They might think that by writing about Arabs I will undermine their story. It might start with small talk, one thing might lead to another, and all of a sudden it would snowball. He said he hoped this would not happen. "But if it happens," he said, "don't worry. I am here and Naguib is also here."

From the airport to the prime minister, the story I have told in this preface speaks to both the complexity of living in the Horn of Africa and the constant balancing act required to survive the state framework. Through my fieldwork, I was privileged to gain a better understanding of the position of Yemenis living in this region. It taught me much about what it is to be a stranger in Djibouti. Because the Yemeni families there are diasporic groups living in a foreign land—they are strangers—they need to deploy a wide variety of strategies, many of which I will describe over the course of the book.

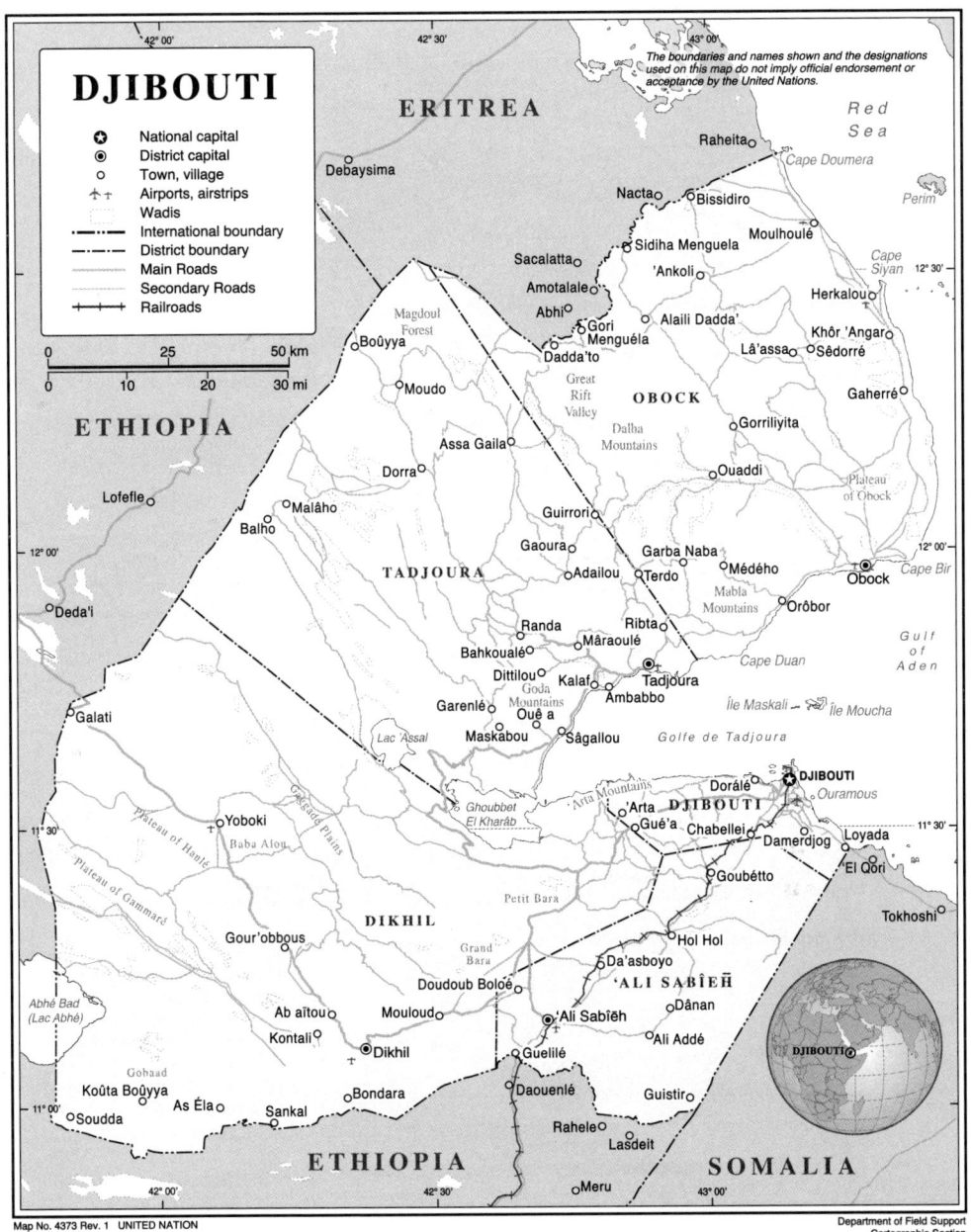

1. Introduction

In October 2004 I met 'Umar 'Ubayd Ba 'Aqil, my first Yemeni informant in the city of Dire Dawa in eastern Ethiopia. 'Umar was walking along the road to buy sweets from the Jabri Halawa Shop, near the main mosque of the city. I had come to the shop not to buy sweets but to find Yemenis who could tell me about the history of the Yemeni community. Upon my inquiry, the cashier sitting behind the counter told me that I was lucky, as the man who knew about the history of the Yemeni community was standing just behind me. That man was 'Umar.

But 'Umar did not seem to view our chance encounter as a good thing. He was visibly uncomfortable as he led me out of the shop to talk to me in private. I followed 'Umar to the bridge that divided the city into two halves. He told me that I should not speak about the topic of my research as it might get me into trouble. He then told me that his cousin had been shot on that very bridge while assisting a French academic who had come to study the history of Arabs in eastern Ethiopia in the early 1990s. To my horror, 'Umar told me that the French man had died, while his assistant, 'Umar's cousin, eventually recovered from his gunshot wounds. The killing of the unfortunate French academic, I later learned, was not an isolated incident. Back in the 1990s a number of foreigners were killed on the streets of Dire Dawa. The murders were believed to be the work of the Islamic Front for the Liberation of Oromia (IFLO), which at the time sought separation of the region of Ethiopia inhabited by ethnic Oromo.

For 'Umar, the cause of the trouble was not only a separatist organization. He also felt that the natives of Ethiopia did not want to see the history of the Arabs put on record by trained professionals. Although he was keen to help me, he wanted to be careful. As I learned later, 'Umar's anxiety came not only from the tragic events of the past but also out of personal problems. At the time, 'Umar was in trouble. He had been dragged through the courts on various charges. Every now and again he was picked up and taken to the police station. His crime was to have been caught with both a Yemeni and an Ethiopian passport: Ethiopia does not allow dual citizenship. When I first met 'Umar, he was fighting to remain in the country, and for that reason he did not want to identify himself publicly as Yemeni.

'Umar's story shows the relevance of the state. Of course, 'Umar was not the only Yemeni having problems with the state. A number of people whom I met had similar concerns. Like 'Umar, they worried about their presence within the state framework. The importance of the state is not only a contemporary matter but also one that existed in the past. French and British archives reflect the relevance of empire in the diasporic lives of Yemenis who were subjected to imperial control. Their political, social, and economic lives were defined by the presence of imperial powers. Just like 'Umar, Yemenis in the past tried to deal with imperial powers using different mechanisms.

Despite the clear relevance of state/empire in the life of Yemenis, Indian Ocean studies have largely failed to acknowledge the role that states and empires play in structuring the Yemeni diasporic community. Scholarly works on the Indian Ocean have, to a significant degree, taken their inspiration from the work of Fernand Braudel on the Mediterranean Sea. Braudel's (1972) aim was to look at how the region was united and how this unity was determined by the ecology of the Mediterranean Sea. Indian Ocean studies, by and large, have been bent on showing the presence of a Mediterranean-like unity, the ocean being a central factor for this supposed unity.[1] This tendency to see 'unity' is amply documented in scholarly work that focuses on the wider Indian Ocean, including that of Kirti N. Chaudhuri (1985; 1990) and Kenneth McPherson (1993), as well as in writings that examine how parts of the Indian Ocean have been linked to the broader Indian Ocean region, including that of Michael Pearson (1998; 2005) and Edward Alpers (2009). More recent research, for example by Thomas R. Metcalf (2007), has focused on how a particular state has been integrated into the broader Indian Ocean.

The intent of this book is to move away from a discussion that aims to demonstrate and document the unity/disunity of the Indian Ocean. The book does this by looking at how states and empires have interacted with diaspora groups. It questions the status accorded to diasporic groups in Indian Ocean studies. To date, scholars have largely looked for factors that have united the Indian Ocean. The ecology of the Indian Ocean, particularly the monsoon winds, has been identified as a key element in this unity (Chaudhuri, 1985; McPherson, 1993; Pearson, 2003). Thus, when in 2004 the western coast of Sumatra was hit by one of the most ruinous tsunamis in recent history, the effects of which were felt as far away as Somalia, scholars working on the Indian Ocean were happy to point out this ecological unity (Bose, 2006: 1–3). It was affirmed that the Indian Ocean is an ocean that is ecologically united.

There is, however, another factor that could be identified as key in this linkage: the diaspora. Chaudhuri (1985: 3–4), for example, identified diaspora groups as major unifiers of the Indian Ocean. A number of other scholars have viewed diasporic groups as links among places in the Indian Ocean (Alpers, 2009; Bang, 2003). This perspective is even accepted among scholars who contest the ecological unity of the Indian Ocean. Thus, Peregrine Horden and Nicholas Purcell (2006: 739), while they have attempted to refute the dominant narrative of Indian Ocean ecological unity, have nevertheless affirmed the role of diasporic groups as unifiers.

This view that the diaspora is a linking factor has led to a peculiar representation of diasporic communities in the Indian Ocean: namely, a representation that sees them as free and unhindered agents of change. This representation of the diaspora as having free movement and agency is particularly pervasive in studies of the Yemeni or Hadrami diasporic community, one of the main such communities in the Indian Ocean region. Scholars, both in the past and in the present, have focused on how Hadramis and Yemenis have been able to travel and then adapt in the diasporic environment by mobilizing their networks and cultural resources.[2]

Scholars who focused on documenting the role of the Sada, Yemenis who claim descent from the prophet Muhammad, have been particularly keen to document the community's networks and cultural capability. In these scholarly works it is common to read how a particular *sayyid* (singular for Sada) traveled to different places and enjoyed fruitful networking that often brought him close to power holders (Bang, 2003; Ho, 2006; Ho, 2002; Kathirithamby-Wells, 2009).

The Sada are indeed a peculiar class of Hadramis because of the genealogy they claim. One could claim that the representation of a freely moving diaspora community filled with networking and cultural capability is a consequence of the Sada being the descendants of the prophet Muhammad. This line of argument, however, will only take us a short distance in studies on Yemenis/Hadramis in the Indian Ocean. It is not only the *sayyids* but also other groups of Yemenis who are represented as having extraordinary cultural skills of interacting and moving around the ocean. Scholarly work that does not focus on the Sada makes a similar assertion and repeatedly tries to look at the question of diasporic linkage (Vianello, 2012; Walker, 2008; Walker, 2011; Walker, 2012; Beckerleg, 2009).

This book does not deny the presence of networks or the role of the diaspora community as links. Rather, it questions the pervasive role given to these networks and to cultural skills, and to the image of a freely moving diaspora community that follows from it. In doing so, this book aims to bring into play the role of empires and states and their structuring capacity.

In Indian Ocean studies, state and empire have certainly been addressed. The role that European empires had, including their impacts on the unity/disunity of the ocean, has been discussed at length (Alpers, 2014; Borsa, 1990; Bose, 2006; Bowen et al., 2012; Furber, 1976; Gupta, 2004; Hall, 1996; McPherson, 1993; Pearson, 2003; Prakash, 2004). How and when the Indian Ocean was integrated into the system created by the modern western empire has also been a subject of debate.[3] Following a geopolitical approach, scholars have analyzed past and present geopolitical contestations in the Indian Ocean (Anthony, 2013; Bouchard and Crumplin 2010; Cordner 2010). Indian Ocean studies have also looked at how states/empires have structured human mobility. In doing so, however, scholars of the Indian Ocean have been more interested in looking at the structuring role of empire and state in mobility in regard to indentured labor, prisoners, pirates, prostitutes, imperial careers, forcefully displaced people, imperial troops such as Indian soldiers, and slave trafficking.[4]

Diasporic groups, which are generated outside the direct involvement of empires, have not been looked at in terms of the structuring power of empire and state. This is particularly true in the case of Yemenis or Hadrami, the people who are the focus of this book. When the Yemenis or Hadrami are discussed in relation to state power, scholars most often take the perspective that members of the diaspora are essentially free agents. The dominating and structuring role of empire is made to give way to the capacity and capability of the Yemeni diaspora community.

Perhaps the best example of the point that I am making here is the seminal work of Engseng Ho, particularly his article "Empire through Diasporic Eyes: A View from the Other Boat" (2004). Writing in the post-9/11 context, Ho seeks to historicize the role of Osama bin Laden in al-Qaeda attacks. He argues that Bin Laden is a historical continuation of past Hadrami militants who challenged western powers in the Indian Ocean region. Ho asserts that western imperialists were threatened by Hadramis, who moved from place to place mobilizing the Islamic community in the Indian Ocean against the West. The perspective that Ho puts forward is not only a polarized one in which so-called Islamic diaspora leaders are positioned against empires but also one that overtly and overly emphasizes the agency of diaspora militant leaders.

The two militant figures Ho uses as an example are Osama bin Laden and 'Abd al Rahman b. Muhammad al Zahir, a Hadrami born in the 1830s. Zahir became a militant actor during the Dutch conquest of Aceh in Sumatra. In Ho's telling, the two men are seen traversing the various corners of the Indian Ocean mobilizing Muslims against western empires. Thus, the diasporic group is once again represented as being free and endowed with extraordinary capabilities. But Ho does not tell us how Osama bin Laden was constrained by states and empires in the Indian Ocean. We do not read, for example, how the mobility of Osama bin Laden, including his jihad against the Soviet Union in Afghanistan, was facilitated by the United States in the 1980s. Nor do we learn about the complicated relations Osama bin Laden had with the Republic of Sudan, which hosted him from 1991 to 1996 but later considered handing him over to Saudi Arabia or the United States during the Clinton administration. We do not learn how Osama bin Laden's communications were restricted by Mullah 'Umar during his time in Afghanistan (National Commission on Terrorist Attacks upon the United States, 2004: 56–65; Khalid, 2010: 496).

Ho's emphasis on Yemeni agency is not an isolated instance. It is common for scholars to look at the role Yemenis have played in local state politics as well as in the international arena. For example, a volume edited by Ulrike Freitag and William G. Clarence-Smith (1997) contains a section on the political role of Hadramis. This relation between Yemenis and 'the political' is however mostly described in a unidirectional manner. It is common to read about Hadrami establishing themselves in a particular state or region and playing a significant political role.

Needless to say, not all writing on Yemenis' interactions with states and empires adopts the perspective of Yemeni agency. There are works that have looked at how imperial powers have treated the diaspora communities in the Indian Ocean region. Kees van Dijk (2002) and Huub de Jong (2002; 1997), for example, show how the Arabs of southeast Asia were controlled and put under surveillance by the Dutch empire. Again from southeast Asia, we also have the writing of Kris Alexanderson (2014), which looks at the fear the Dutch colonial authority had toward pan-Islamism and Hadramis. The work of Leif Manger (2010) equally shows how Hadramis came to be affected by state and imperial power. There are also writings that try to show how Yemenis were affected by the process of decolonization and nationalism that swept the third world (Brennan 2008; Bang 2008).

Nevertheless, Indian Ocean studies have persisted in a traditional representation of romanticized figures, of a diasporic group that freely traverses the ocean and creates linkages as it does.[5] The latest publications in the field, including that of Sheriff and Ho (2014), Jonathan Miran (2012), and Sheriff (2010), are good examples of the hegemonic place that the network model, rather than the state/empire model, has in our understanding of diasporic processes. Miran outlines the ways in which the Indian Ocean region in general and the northwestern Indian Ocean region in particular have been viewed to date:

> [The] premise of this collection is that beyond its role in connecting the Mediterranean with the Indian Ocean through long-distance trade, the particularly narrow bodies of water in the Red Sea and Gulf of Aden constitute an arena of circuits and connectivities characterized by brisk flows and criss-crossing of people, goods, and ideas across this area. In other words, while like other maritime spaces the Red Sea may be understood as an innately fractured, fragmented, and unstable arena, the host of regional, translocal, and trans-marine cross-Red Sea commercial circuits, labor flows, and religious networks that animated it produced spaces (social, economic, political) and features (cultural) of varying degrees of coherence and integration (2012: xi).

Similarly, the back cover of Sheriff and Ho's 2014 work emphasizes the dominant paradigm of the Indian Ocean:

> The Indian Ocean was the first venue of global trade, connecting the Mediterranean and South China Sea. Inspired by the insights of Fernand Braudel, and by Michaell Mollat, who saw it as a 'zone of encounters and contacts ... a privileged crossroad of culture', this volume explores two inter-related themes. The first, on oceanic linkages, presents the diversity of the people who have traversed it and their relationships by tracing their tangible movements and their connections. The second, on the creation of new societies, revisits better- known socio-historical phenomena—such as slavery, indentured labour, the Swahili language and Muslim charity—which tie the genesis of these social formations to the seascape of an interconnected, transcultural ocean.

This book aims to present a more nuanced understanding by actively looking at the structuring capacity of state/empire. The intent is not to dismiss the relevance of networks or the agency of diasporic communities, but to show how this agency and capacity fundamentally existed within states and empires and how the role of the state is not only present in extraordinary moments such as decolonization but also before and after, both in moments of calm and in periods of dynamic change that are not necessarily linked to the state.

In addition, rather than seeing the diaspora community as being united against state, *Subjects of Empires/Citizens of States* shows how diasporic communities are actually engaged in a balancing act that constantly takes into account state/empire. The place where Bin Laden was eventually found and killed is telling, and much more in line with the perspective this book is advancing. Rather than being a lone figure who was moving from place to place in the process of galvanizing the Muslims of the Indian Ocean, Osama bin Laden was a man pacing the length of one small room in a house that was not near a mosque or the Indian Ocean but a hundred feet from a major Pakistani military facility. In and of itself, the end of bin Laden is very important in any attempt to question and reassess how we conceive diaspora mobility and existence in the Indian Ocean region in relation to the power of states and empires. This is the core problem this book aims to shed light on.

In calling for a perspective that reassesses the role of the diaspora in the Indian Ocean and the interaction of Yemenis with state/empire, this book also implicitly asserts the need to qualify not only our representation of diasporic groups in the Indian Ocean but also the time and the methodology used to describe the life of the diaspora in the Indian Ocean. Indian Ocean studies that focus on Yemenis, and are bent on showing how the Indian Ocean unity/continuity has been affected through them, have led to a perspective that sees these Yemenis as a throwback. In the case of the Yemeni diaspora, time is seemingly of no importance, as the current diasporic communities in the Indian Ocean region are described as being linked to those of a century ago. It is because of this freezing of time that Ho can make a confident comparison between an Osama bin Laden of the twenty-first century and 'Abd al Rahman b. Muhammad al Zahir of the nineteenth century, or Anne Bang can assert that Ahmad ibn Sumayt is "a descendant of the Prophet Muhammad through the Hadrami *ashraf* known collectively as the Ba (Bani) 'Alawi" (2003: 1). This desire to represent Yemenis as throwbacks, as people who somehow activate the unity of the past in the present, requires an extensive study of its own.

One of the factors that has contributed to this representation is the methodology that Indian Ocean studies use to study the Yemenis. Part of that methodology heavily relies on the extensive genealogies and biographies that Yemenis have created over time. This emphasis on genealogy and biography, and the overenthusiasm shown for text written by the Sada, as in the case of Ho (2002; 2006), has led to not only an overreliance on these genealogies but also the representation of Hadrami using a language of continuity. Added to this is the general tendency of Indian Ocean studies to use the *longue durée* approach of Braudel (1972), who focuses on the continuity of civilization. The lives of Yemenis have been so entangled with texts and genealogies that their present-day existence appears to support an unbroken cycle, a continuum, a connection with the past.

This strategy of looking at genealogy and biography forgets the dynamics present on the ground as it emphasizes those absent (yet present) migrants, the ancestors, whose influence persists once their worldly physical existence has ended. Focused on the absent migrants and the genealogies and text that have been handed down to their descendants, the strategy sidelines the power dynamics and the changing nature of state/empire on the ground. For example, it prevents us from looking at the changing nature of class, and how Hadramis have been part of these changes. Relying on the genealogical account of the Sada also omits recognition of how space has evolved over time. Seen from a genealogic model, space is constructed through genealogies. Ho (2002) tells us how Hadrami genealogy, which is spatially expansive, heavily contrasts with the state model, which is rooted in a bounded territory. Hadrami genealogy, according to Ho, engulfs and brings different places together under one domain; it does not create a state based on exclusion and inclusion. As proof of this, Ho quotes from medival texts written by Hadramis, as well as biographies. He tells us how, in those texts, we can see an imagined society that is akin to what Benedict Anderson (1983) described in his now classic book on nationalism.

Indeed, relying on genealogies and textual biographies easily leads us to see the unity of place. But the matter of space and time is much more complicated than what we can see through the genealogical model. The nature of space is that it changes, and the space that Hadramis have constructed through the means of genealogy cannot be conceived exclusively outside the space of state/empire that Ho polarizes. No space is neutral. In Indian Ocean studies, including the work of Ho, there is a tendency to see space as neutral and natural, something through which identity is constructed (see, e.g., Camelin, 2004; Serjeant, 1978). The Indian Ocean is also conceived as an arena in which Yemenis engage unproblematically in politics that range from mere integration into the state to reconstructing the state (see Freitag, 2003).

The very premise of the Indian Ocean contributes to this neutralist perspective on space in which the diaspora freely operates. Indian Ocean studies emphasize the way different spaces are connected without adopting a radical perspective that looks at space as an entity formed by power structures. When it comes to space, the emphasis has been on seeing the connection/overlap that exists between different spaces—that is, issues of translocality. This has entailed looking at the interplay between the coast and the hinterland, the local and the translocal, and the intercivilizational contact (both in its material and its immaterial forms) that flows within these interlinked spaces (see, e.g., Ghazal, 2010; Ghosh and Muecke, 2007a; Kresse, 2007; Larson, 2009; Machado, 2014; Moorthy and Jamal, 2010; Prestholdt, 2008; Subrahmanyam, 2005). As Bang (2014) recently put it, this emphasis on translocality forms the very premise of Indian Ocean studies. In this prism, the making of the local through a process of spatial connection, the traveling of texts, narrations, knowledge and people, becomes important for creating a history that places the ocean at its center and for generating what Ulrike Freitag and Achim von Oppen (2010) call a southern perspective on globalization.

We should not forget that spaces are entities that are power-laden and shaped by the application of force. As they have a juridico-political order, they do not easily allow a free construction of genealogies.[6] Nor can we have spatial connections that are devoid of the influence of state/empire. The very logic of state making and building empires involves a process of naming, defining, classifying, and controlling space. And the diaspora moving from one locality to the other cannot be just restless travelers who are unhindered in their journeys. Both in the past and in the present borders matter, and not all people travel through them at will (Smart and Smart, 2008; Donnan and Wilson, 2010; Cunningham and Heyman, 2004). Despite the presence of "time–space compression" (Harvey, 1989), current neoliberal globalization creates tensions that center on space (Gupta and Ferguson, 1997a; Gupta and Ferguson, 1997b; Kalb and Talk, 2005).

It is the firm belief of this author that we do not only need to resort to an explanation that views the Indian Ocean as a fluid space marked by the intense connection/interaction of its people to have a southern perspective on globalization. The South can be effectively explained by taking into account elements from the North/West, such as capital, empire, and the modern nation-state, which scholars working on the diaspora in the Indian Ocean region regard as exogenous. Unfortunately the exogenizing of western factors such as state and empire has only led to the exoticization of the ocean and its people.

In Indian Ocean studies, the self-ascribed task of writing the translocal history of the region partly comes in reaction to critiques directed at globalization studies. Authors such as Frederick Cooper (2001) have posed questions regarding the relevance of generalized discussion for societies in the South. Globalization theories have been deemed insensitive to local dynamics and other forms of globalization that come without taking the West as a reference point. It is to narrow the perceived research gap that Indian Ocean studies in part embarked on studies of translocality. This attempt to fill the gap came with its own drawbacks, however, as it overtly forgot to document the active presence of states and empires.

Given their deep and often shattering effects as well as the connection that diasporic groups foster with states and empires, there is a need to reintroduce, in a much elaborated manner, state/empire into our discussion of Indian Ocean diasporic communities. For the many advocates of translocality and/or local forms of globalization, this call for *bringing in* states and empires might look like a step backward. The call is in fact a step back that is only taken to step forward. At present, Indian Ocean studies are saturated by projects that focus on documenting translocal connections of all sorts. Although these studies have without doubt been useful for our understanding of migration in the region, when our understanding was scant, the documenting of translocal connections has now been fully explored.

In view of this, the book argues for taking the relation of space and state/empire seriously and calls upon research to move from a network to a state/empire model. It is only through such a move, which places Yemenis in the realm of the concrete and not the imagined, that we can see a Yemeni diaspora community that is not frozen in time but is responsive to dynamics generated by state/empire and expressed in space.

Beyond engaging in further developing models that better capture human mobility, as Ned Bertz (2003) suggests, one possible way of taking account of state/empire is to look at hierarchical processes generated by state and empire within the spatial configurations they came to form. Indian Ocean studies have examined Yemenis in terms of hierarchical societal processes. The important works of Abdallah Bujra (1967; 1971) on systems of stratification among Yemenis and the many studies that followed are examples. These attempts to take hierarchies at the societal level into account have by and large been studies that confine their analysis of hierarchy to the societies under study without taking into account hierarchies generated by state/empire. The justification that Bang (2014) gives demonstrates this lack of attention to hierarchical processes generated by state/empire. In an attempt to defend the network model's inherent incapacity to accommodate hierarchical processes, Bang argues that Sufi networks have their own form of hierarchies that "transcend political, cultural and ethnic boundaries, and which thus became embedded in different hierarchies at different times" (2014: 18). Rather than accepting the limits of the network model, here the attempt has been to circumnavigate the issue by indicating the presence of an internal hierarchy that exists as a result of the 'simultaneous' interaction of people and ideas that exist in different places, in other words, networks.

A shortcut approach such as this is not helpful, however, as the people engaged in the act of networking do not live in a vacuum, and certainly not in other times, but rather in a context shaped by state/empire, whose effect remains even if one turns a blind eye to it. Constructing an academic narrative of connection and travel by simultaneously looking at what happened in different places does not erase the effects of state/empire. Such scholarly narratives remain academic constructions embedded within the politics and poetics of a specific time framework that is influenced by global power configurations. Paradoxically, they do not fully document the presence of the states and empires of their time or of the recent past as they privilege travel over fixity, network over power, and internal hierarchies over the hierarchy that states and empires generate. This book calls for a revision of the Indian Ocean studies approach to hierarchy and space, and in its concluding section extensively discusses the implication of state-generated hierarchies such as class, ethnicity, and citizenship.

This focus on state/empire does not mean, however, that we are not entitled to or should not speak about Hadrami networks and cultural capabilities. An account of the experience, existence, and adaptive strategies of Yemenis is indeed possible, but it should be done in a way that recognizes the changing nature of states and empires and of the Yemeni community. Nevertheless, looking at an overarching system that goes beyond the diasporic network and its genealogies should not also mean advancing a perspective that represents Yemenis as helpless victims merely embedded in these structures. This book demonstrates how narrating the life of Yemenis cannot and should not be done in a simplistic manner, using explanations that rely on either network or sociocultural traits to explain the paths taken by members of the Yemeni diasporic community.

The presence of Yemenis is marked not only by the control exercised by state/empire but also by Yemenis' ability to adapt to and trespass on attempts by state/empire to control their mobility, as well as their economic, political, and religious existence. Some Yemenis have been wholly affected by the regularizing power of state/empire, while others have benefited by forming alliances with state/empire. In other circumstances, Yemenis themselves have acted as a sovereign power and repressed other subjects of empire and state. There have also been points at which Yemenis tried to revolt against the political system into which they were integrated.

In view of this complexity, Yemenis are not simply free and peaceful agents of change or social and cultural interlocutors who bring cosmopolitanism and a cultural mix to the region, as some within Indian Ocean studies have asserted. They are not merely a diasporic community that plays a role in the withering of state and empire. Neither are they the cosmopolitan hero or the villain. Rather, Yemenis are engaged in a constant process of balancing the shifting contexts that see the coming and going of empires and the rise and fall of the different state governments that empires have created.

Focus and Purpose

This book examines Yemeni interactions with states and empires in the Horn of Africa, focusing on the port of Djibouti and the hinterland of Ethiopia. Migrants from South Arabia have traveled to this region for centuries, if not millennia. Archaeological records attest to migration from present-day South Yemen in ancient times.[7] In the Middle Ages, around the sixteenth century, people from South Arabia, particularly Hadramis, also traveled to the region and participated in the war between the Ethiopian highland Christian kingdom and the Muslim sultanate of ʾÄdalə.[8] Reverse movement, including the colonization of Yemen by Ethiopia, is also well documented in historical records. The two regions also share common legends. Both Yemenis and Ethiopians assert that the legendary Queen of Sheba,[9] mentioned in both the Bible and the Qurʾan, was the ruler of their lands. There is also the story of how the western Indian Ocean was created by the miraculous act of Dhu al-Qarnayn.[10] He is said to have transformed a small river in South Yemen into the Red Sea, separating Ethiopians and Yemenis, who were constantly at war with each other.[11]

While there is a long history of movement of people within the framework of state/empire, this book focuses on Yemeni migration in the twentieth century. This movement occurred during the period when European powers began to colonize the region. The aim here is to show how states/empires were relevant from the beginning of the twentieth century to the present.

In doing so, this book documents what is largely a forgotten period in the history of Yemeni migration. The movement of Yemenis to the Horn of Africa, and their interactions with state/empire, has remained undocumented, despite this region being one of the earliest destinations for Yemenis in the Indian Ocean region. *Subjects of Empires/Citizens of States* contributes to the growing literature that notes the role of Africa in the Indian Ocean region. East Africa has traditionally not been considered of importance to the rest of the Indian Ocean. Chaudhuri (1985) famously argued that Africa was irrelevant to the region. This has been strongly challenged by the excellent writing of Michael Pearson (2005), Edward Alpers (2009), John Middleton (1992), Justin Wills (1993), Abdul Sheriff (1987; 2010), and Kai Kresse (2007). This book aims to build a greater understanding of the very important role of Africa in both the history and the future of the Indian Ocean region.

This book is also important for its reflections on globalization. Often, globalization is considered as a process of flow where people unproblematically cross borders and participate in an open system. As noted by Ronen Shamir (2005), however, in the process of globalization there are regimes of power that structure/limit the mobility of people. This book examines the role of empires and states in structuring human mobility across space. In doing so, it illustrates how in the western Indian Ocean the process of globalization has been a structured phenomenon.

The book advances a perspective on transnational migration and the formation of diasporic communities. In examining transnational border crossing, mobility studies have often focused on elite travelers and their ability to consume difference and hence create cosmopolitanism. This has resulted in a scholarly discourse that is agentless and frictionless (Schiller and Salazar, 2013), which has emphasized diasporic communities' ability to create linkages across national borders (see, e.g., Hall, 1991; Gilroy, 1993). Anthropological works also focus on the role diasporas play in globalization (for example, Appadurai, 1996). Scholars, particularly in cultural studies and social anthropology, refer to diasporic groups in terms of creolization and hybridity. There is also a tendency, among left-leaning scholars, to categorize these groups as part of a new working class (Ong, 1999). In this framing, diasporic groups pose a challenge to the capitalist system. Because of their networks outside the nation-state, they are seen as having the potential to destabilize the state and hence accelerate its collapse (Bhabha, 1990; Clifford, 1994; Gilroy, 1993). For leftist scholars, the very mobility of diasporic groups is seen as a factor that could contribute to the end of empire (Hardt and Negri, 2000; 2004).

Subjects of Empires/Citizens of States examines not only the agency of the diaspora but also, using empirical material, the structuring and constraining role of state and empire. This is important for Indian Ocean studies, which historically have focused on matters of hybridity and cultural networks, understating, or even ignoring, the constraining role of empires and states. As recent trends in the social sciences have advanced an explanation that is based on actors and networks, the perspective this book puts forward is also useful for reflecting on current social science theorization.

This book adds to knowledge of Djibouti and Ethiopia. In scholarly works, Djibouti has occupied a marginal position. This is particularly true when it comes to scholarly works in the English language. The last book-length English-language publication on Djibouti's history and society, by Virginia Thompson and Richard Adloff, was published in 1968, when Djibouti was still under French colonial rule.[12] In view of this, a book on Yemenis in that country enriches our understanding of the history of Djibouti.

This is also true in the case of Ethiopia. Although the number of publications about Ethiopian history and society far exceeds that about Djibouti, there are few that focus on the presence of Yemenis. These include two short articles by Hussein Ahmed (1997; 2000) and a book chapter by Manger (2010).[13] Standard history books describe Ethiopia as a Christian nation and only note the presence of Yemenis in passing. Yemenis are often portrayed as minor shop owners who are not in any way connected to power holders.[14] This book is one step in correcting our understanding of Ethiopian society and history, including the role of Yemenis.

Even though this work focuses primarily on Djibouti and Ethiopia, the discussion also takes readers to 'other lands' such as Palestine, Syria, Israel, Lebanon, Saudi Arabia, Yemen, and the United States of America. Events that took place in those countries have impacted on the interaction of Yemenis with states and empires in the Horn of Africa. As a result, it is also appropriate to give full attention to these seemingly distant places. This book's discussion of Yemenis' interactions with states and empires occurs with a full awareness of geopolitical contestations and power struggles that surpass the immediate context of Djibouti and Ethiopia.

The Horn of Africa: Empires and States

Since this book focuses on Yemenis' interactions with states and empires in the Horn of Africa, this section offers a brief historical overview of the involvement of empires and the formation of the state. The Horn of Africa has seen the emergence of many different empires and states over millennia. In the ancient period, the region witnessed the rise of the kingdoms of Punt, Damat, and Aksum.[15] In the Middle Ages, the territory that is now Djibouti and Ethiopia was dominated by a centralized Abyssinian Christian kingdom located in present-day northern Ethiopia, and by a number of Muslim sultanates along the Red Sea, the Gulf of Aden, and south of Ethiopia.[16] Starting from the mid-nineteenth century, this area went through a series of political developments that eventually resulted in the region's present form.

One of the major political reconfigurations that took place in the mid-eighteenth century was the unification of the Ethiopian kingdoms into a centralized kingdom under Emperor Tewodros II.[17] This period also witnessed expansion by a number of imperial powers. The major external powers were the Ottoman Empire and Egypt. In 1849, the Ottomans took control of the regions of Suakin and Massawa. By 1864, they also controlled Zayla'.[18] This Ottoman control was strengthened by the Egyptians. Under Khedive Ismail, Egypt expanded southward, resulting in the incorporation of northern Sudan.[19] On the Red Sea coast, Egypt effectively controlled the ports of Massawa and Suakin.[20] Farther south, Egypt occupied the port of Berbera in 1874 and Tajura in 1875. From their territory in Zayla', Egyptians sent out forces to occupy the medieval town of Harar.[21]

The Egyptian presence in the region is an early example of an imperial power structure, which was later followed by European colonial powers. The European presence began with a series of agreements made with local rulers. For example, on March 11, 1869, Giuseppe Sapeto bought land from a local ruler in present-day Assab in the name of Navigation Rubattino, an Italian company. In 1882, this land was formally incorporated by the Italian government.[22] In addition, through a series of agreements with local leaders, the Italians were able to gain a foothold in Somalia.[23]

The French and the British made similar moves. The British also signed a series of agreements in Somalia. In the territory of Djibouti, the French mariner Henry Lambert sailed to the region to join his brother, Joseph, who had established himself as a planter in Mauritius.[24] Henry Lambert made a number of attempts to sign an agreement with one of the local leaders, Abu Bakr Pasha.[25] Although he managed to convince Abu Bakr Pasha to give up Obock and Ras 'Ali for 10,000 thalers, Lambert failed to get an agreement signed. Although he corresponded with higher authorities on the matter,[26] he was killed while traveling on an Arab boat from Hudayda to Mukha.[27] After his death, on March 11, 1862, Dini Abu Bakr, a cousin of the pasha of Tajura, signed away the agreed area after being taken to Paris on a warship that had been sent to investigate Lambert's death.

Through such means, European powers gradually expanded their control over the region. In the north, the Italians moved further inland and established the colony of Eritrea. The French, originally situated in Obock (a port in present-day northern Djibouti), enlarged their territory in what is now known as Djibouti through a series of agreements with local rulers.[28] Similarly, the British and the Italians to the south of Obock turned their initial agreements into colonies: British Somaliland and Italian Somaliland. The Ethiopian kingdom, meanwhile, started the process of unification in the mid-nineteenth century. This was consolidated by the end of the nineteenth century, under Menelik II, who moved southward and eastward, annexing a number of territories through brutal military campaigns.[29]

The arrival of the western powers was marked by competition, and outright conflict, but these were eventually settled through a series of border agreements. The first border was the result of an agreement signed between the British and the French on February 8, 1888.[30] At the same time, Britain and France agreed to leave Harar as neutral territory, although neither side renounced the right to oppose attempts on the part of another power (other than Ethiopia, which at the time controlled the region) to acquire or assert any rights over it.[31]

On December 13, 1906, France, Italy, and Britain signed an agreement on the status of Ethiopia.[32] In the first article of the agreement the three powers pledged to maintain Ethiopia's territorial integrity as well as the status quo. They agreed not to interfere in Ethiopian affairs of state in the event of internal conflict. Concomitantly, in the fourth article of the agreement, the three nations identified a zone of influence or interest where they would intervene in the event of internal turmoil. Thus, France took the hinterland area adjoining Djibouti, Britain (as a result of its involvement in Egypt) identified the Nile basin as its priority zone, and Italy claimed the hinterland beyond the occupied territory of Eritrea.

Alongside these developments, the imperial powers oversaw the construction of a number of facilities in the areas under their control. The Italians started to build port and railway facilities. The French relocated their capital from Obock to the southern region, which came to be referred to as Djibouti (Péroz, 1907: 21–22).

A company created by Alfred Ilg and Léon Chefneux, La compagnie impériale des chemins de fer éthiopiens, reached an agreement with Emperor Menelik to construct a railway line that would connect Djibouti with the Ethiopian interior.[33] Although the company faced financial difficulties and was eventually put under French government control, construction of the railway line continued. In December 1902, the line reached what was to become the first station, at Dire Dawa (a city created as a result of the construction of the train line).[34] Eventually, in 1915, the line reached Addis Ababa, the capital of Ethiopia.[35]

The Yemenis who migrated during this period were men who came to settle in the regions occupied by imperial powers. In the initial phase, most were economic migrants, setting off on solitary journeys in a bid to escape harsh conditions caused by drought, poverty, conflict, and the tyrannical rule of leaders in their home countries. They were attracted by the opportunities created by colonial construction of the railway line and port facilities. The ports of Massawa, Mogadishu, and Djibouti became the focal points of migration.

This study primarily focuses on Yemenis who settled in the port of Djibouti and eventually moved inland, following the train line to Dire Dawa and Addis Ababa. Without assuming that their mobility was unproblematic, I document how their inland movement and their residence in city spaces was structured. Beyond documenting how Yemenis moved into those spaces, I also show how their economic, political, and social lives were structured by state/empire in those spaces.

Figure 1. Early Picture of the Franco-Djibouti Train Line (Source: Archive of the Ethio-Djibouti Railway Enterprise).

This book does not consider the state as being composed of a set of institutions. Rather, adopting a contemporary reading of the state, it sees the state as built in socioeconomic and spatial arenas.[36] The state is about space.[37] It is also about economy,[38] politics, and worldview, a certain vision that creates divisions in society.[39] Thus, one can speak of the state in an overlapping manner as state/space, state/economy, state/politics, and state/vision or mentality.[40] The four fields this book is concerned with are therefore regarded as part of a state's domain.

This study also conceives of the state and empire as overlapping. The state, such as the colonial state of Djibouti, was not a state that stood on its own but rather was part of an empire. It is therefore more fruitful to speak about state/empire than state and empire, to note the overlapping nature of the two. This overlapping nature, however, is not something that ends with the independence of former colonial states. Like the colonial state, the postcolonial state is part of an imperial network. The nature and form of imperial rule constantly evolves from one based on colony to one based on empire without colony.[41] The empires of our time are characterized by the latter, and this is an outcome of the changing nature of the global capitalist structure, from a situation where capital was limited to the nation-state to one in which capital has transformed itself to an extent where its presence is not limited to a particular state and its colonies.[42]

In contemporary Africa, former colonies are still part of a network of power of former colonizing powers, which continue to function as empires without formal colonies. France, for example, controls its former colonies because of a number of agreements signed at the threshold of independence. These agreements guarantee France continued linkage with her former colonies, including monetary and defense linkages (see Gregory, 2000). Djibouti, unlike the former French colonies in West Africa, stopped using *Communauté Financière Africaine* (CFA) currency with the introduction in 1949 of the Djibouti franc, which is based on the United States dollar. But the defense agreement signed by Djibouti and France on the eve of decolonization guarantees the deployment of French soldiers in the country. France is not, however, the single most important imperial presence in the region. Other global powers without colonies operate in the territory, including the United States. Since 9/11, the United States has maintained a naval base at a former French military camp, Camp Lemonier.[43]

The case of Ethiopia is somewhat ambiguous, as Ethiopia was never colonized. Ethnonationalist scholars, such as Bonnie K. Holcomb and Sisai Ibssa (1990), categorize Ethiopia as an imperial power engaged in a similar process of colonizing during the 'scramble for Africa.' This assertion comes as a result of the southward expansion of the Ethiopian state. This book does not characterize Ethiopia as an imperial power, as the label 'empire' requires the incorporation of multiple spaces. France was an empire with colonies and is now an empire without colonies, as it has involved itself in multiple spaces. The United States' global power can be characterized as that of an imperial power because there are only a few corners of the world where it does not have significant involvement or influence. Ethiopia's expansion was not in any way imperial, as the country's spatial expansion was not multiple and involved only the immediate region. Adopting such a perspective is not in any way an attempt to ignore the suffering and injustices committed by Ethiopian emperors in their march southward.

Ethiopia, however, can be characterized as the earliest African country under neocolonial domination. Ethiopia is, of course, officially independent, and the preferred representation of Ethiopia among pan-Africanists is that of a polity that has existed as an independent nation-state for centuries. This perspective is tempting but it omits or sidelines recognition of foreign involvement in that country. Since it emerged as a modern nation-state, Ethiopia has been dependent on foreign powers. These powers agreed to respect Ethiopia's independence but the various Ethiopian regions were recognized as their spheres of influence, in which they could interfere in any way they considered appropriate, such as in wartime. It was this process that saw the creation of Ethiopia as a semi-dependent, neocolonial state that would go on to commit atrocities in connection with its southern expansion.

The façade of sovereignty and the rhetoric that surrounds Ethiopia, and other so-called postcolonial African states such as Djibouti, should not prevent us from seeing that imperial connections of the past continue to be present today. It is for this reason that I refer to Ethiopia using the term 'state/empire,' just as I do for Djibouti, even though Ethiopia was not colonized in the formal sense of the word.

Outline of the Book: Chronology, Themes, and Arguments

The book's timeline begins at the end of the nineteenth century. As a work of anthropology rather than history, the book follows a thematic approach in which Yemenis' interaction is examined within a specific domain, such as space, economy, politics, and religion. In each of these domains I take a chronological look at how Yemenis have interacted with states/empires from the colonial period up to the present time. Each thematic area therefore begins with the colonial period and ends in the twenty-first century. For a historian this might be a disappointment, as the historical timelines are contained within each chapter rather than applied to the entire book. This book remains true to an anthropological usage of history, however, in which history is employed to understand contemporary issues rather than written for the purpose of demonstrating events of the past. In short, the focus of this book is not to narrate the history of Yemenis per se but to demonstrate an argument by combining historical material and contemporary issues.

In presenting the argument of the book I have prioritized the theme of space over other themes, such as economy or politics, as space is the first element in which empires/states organize and interact with their populations. Composed of chapters two and three, the first part examines the interaction of Yemenis with space in states/empires. The chapters show that space is not just a location but an arena in which states and empires apply power. In particular, these chapters explore how Yemeni movement has been regularized by empires/states from the end of the nineteenth century onward. They examine how people's mobility changed following the emergence of colonial empires and the formation of modern nation-states. The chapters detail the various regulatory mechanisms employed for controlling mobility and, ultimately, expelling or including people categorized as bad or good according to the empire and/or the state. This part also explores the ways in which war and nationalism affected Yemeni mobility both in the inland territory and across the Gulf of Aden region. It particularly focuses on various wider developments, such as the Second World War and the emergence of nationalist movements and pan-Arab ideology, as well as on the United States' more recent 'war on terrorism.'[44]

The second part of the book, which starts with chapter four, focuses on how opportunities for Yemenis have been shaped within the space created by state/empire. Here, the focus is Yemeni interaction with state/space in the fields of economy and politics, and the more intangible field that relates to state mentality. Continuing with this examination of the interaction of Yemenis with state/empire, the chapter discusses the ways in which Yemenis have interacted with the economic field. It particularly looks at how their economic existence was restructured by colonial power and the formation of enclosed boundaries in the region. It also traces how this relationship has changed over time, taking into account the changing nature of state and capital.

Chapter five looks at the interaction of Yemenis with states/empires from a political perspective. It documents the processes of exclusion and inclusion that Yemenis have encountered since the arrival of European powers in the region. The work here focuses on how Yemeni interactions with states/empires developed in the context of dynastic changes, the introduction of citizenship rights, the formation of political parties, and the emergence of independence politics, socialism, and neoliberal democracy.

Chapter six turns to the field of religion within the state/empire framework. This chapter gives an account of how the various states and empires in the Horn of Africa regarded Islam and how that view structured the existence of Yemenis. This chapter also examines the role of social attitudes that are directly and indirectly linked with the state.

In the core chapters of the book, the discussion begins with Yemeni interactions with state/empire in the Djiboutian context before moving to a consideration of similar interactions in the hinterland countries of Ethiopia. In academic terms, 'hinterland' may be understood in a number of different ways (Bird, 1971). It can refer to a place where a specific type of commodity is shipped. It can also refer to the immediate environs of a port, particularly the area over which a port has direct influence. The concept can also be used to signify the hegemonic relationship that a port has with a region. In the latter sense, an area is a hinterland if the majority of its imports arrive through the port. Currently, Djibouti holds a hegemonic status vis-à-vis Ethiopia; in history, it exercised a hegemonic status over the eastern part of Ethiopia. Given this, I discuss the 'hinterland' not only in terms of the immediate region adjoining the port but also in relation to the entire area of Ethiopia.

A word is also due regarding my use of the term 'Yemeni.' Traditionally in Indian Ocean studies, and also during the colonial period, 'Yemeni' has been used to refer only to northern Yemenis. Southern Yemenis, particularly those from the region of Hadramawt, have been referred to as Hadrami. In Ethiopia and Djibouti, on the other hand, both Yemeni and Hadrami have commonly been referred to as 'Arabs.' As this book explores the stories of both northern and southern Yemenis, for the sake of simplicity and given the absence of another appropriate term I employ the term 'Yemeni' broadly and also describe southern Yemenis in this way. It is an imperfect designation, however, as it does not indicate the geographical, administrative, and national differences between northern and southern Yemenis.

Throughout, this research refers to Djibouti. In the present context, Djibouti denotes the city of Djibouti as well as the country, which is formally referred to as the Republic of Djibouti. Historically speaking, the present-day Djibouti area was not referred to as Djibouti. In the early days, the French, for example, used the term Territoire d'Obock, and later referred to the area as the Côte Française des Somalis. Later this was modified, and the present-day Djibouti area was referred to as Territoire Français des Afars et des Issas (TFAI). The correct procedure would be to employ the official name of the country within the appropriate time period. However, I found that such a strategy hampered the flow of my discussion to an unreasonable extent. Because of this, I have employed 'Djibouti' to describe the Republic of Djibouti both in history and in contemporary times, irrespective of the political or official denomination of the time.

Part I:
Regulating Spaces

2. Disciplining the Natives

[Allah said to the sea] "I have created thee and designed thee as a carrier for some of my servants, who seek my bounty, praising me, worshiping me, magnifying me and glorifying me, and so how wilt thou act towards them?" Said the Sea: "My Lord, then I shall drown them." Said the Lord: "Begone, for I curse thee, and will diminish thy worth and thy fish." Then the Lord inspired into the sea of Al Iraq [the Indian Ocean] the following words, and it said, "My Lord, in that case I shall carry them on my back, when they praise Thee I praise Thee with them, and when they worship Thee I worship Thee with them, when they magnify Thee I magnify Thee with them." Said the Lord: "Go, for I have blessed thee, and will increase thy bounty and thy fish." (al-Muqaddasi, [985]2001: 15)

The above text, quoted from the ninth-century Arab geographer al-Muqaddasi, shows that travel and movement on the Indian Ocean is an ancient affair that started before the arrival of European powers. Scholarly works that examine the technical aspect of this travel show how ocean-going vessels were built and made use of the Indian Ocean's monsoon winds.[1] Accounts by Arab travelers such as Ibn Battuta (1966) leave no doubt that there was regular travel between different parts of the Indian Ocean coast.

European travelers who came to the region, including Vasco da Gama and the first French explorers of the Red Sea, de la Merveille and de Champloret who came to the region in 1708, benefited from this ancient knowledge of navigation in the Indian Ocean. Both men were at some point in their travels guided by Arab sailors who knew the ocean routes.[2]

During the nineteenth century, prior to the arrival of French and other European colonial powers in the region, we see contact and mobility in the western Indian Ocean region, including Djibouti and its hinterland. Mansfield Parkyns (1853; 1966) traveled on the Red Sea in the 1850s using an Arab boat. He described in detail both the ship he boarded and the knowledge required to travel in the port spaces of the Red Sea. Another traveler of the time, Rev. Dr. Lewis Krapf (1860), wrote that Arab ships traveled only during daylight hours due to the threat of underwater rocks and shallow waters along the shores of the Red Sea and the Gulf of Aden.

In the precolonial period we read not only about the presence of travelers but also about foreigners who came to establish themselves in the port spaces and hinterland. The French traveler Arnauld d'Abbadie came to the area at the turn of the nineteenth century. He wrote at length about his encounters in the port of Tajura (located in present-day Djibouti) with a certain Saber whose family originated from Yemen and worked transporting people to the hinterland. Further south, in the port of Berbera, Major M. Cornwallis (1844) reported the presence of various native people both local and foreigners, including Arabs and Banians. The famous travel writer Richard Burton (1856) also wrote in great detail about foreigners. In the port of Zayla', near the border with Djibouti in Somalia, we learn from Burton (1856: 33) that the one-time governor of the port city was a Hadrami by the name of Sayyid Muhammad al Bar. We also learn of a large contingent of Arab mercenaries stationed in this port city under the command of a Hadrami. Burton was one of the first Europeans to visit the walled city of Harar; there, as well, there were many Arabs (Burton, 1856: 33).

These travel accounts document the presence of foreigners in the port and hinterland spaces of present-day Djibouti, leaving no doubt that human mobility and interaction were a long-standing affair, predating the arrival of Europeans. These interactions are also well documented in Indian Ocean Studies, establishing in no uncertain terms the presence of communication and contact in the region. This chapter aims to show how this human mobility during the colonial period was structured by imperial power, an aspect that I argue has been neglected in Indian Ocean Studies.

This chapter examines how the mobility of Yemenis during the first half of the twentieth century was structured in three spaces, namely the sea, port spaces, and the hinterland. To dispel the myth of free travel, and also not to create a false dichotomy between a precolonial period marked by the free movement of people and a colonial period marked by increased control, this chapter first looks at the structures of control used to regulate the movement of people in the precolonial period. In the section that follows I provide a brief account of precolonial regulatory mechanisms. I then look at Yemeni interactions with this process, under the influence of state/empire, beginning from the end of the nineteenth century.

Precolonial Movement

In the precolonial period, the coastal region of the Horn of Africa, where present-day Djibouti is located, was connected to the Ethiopian hinterland by caravan trade routes, linking the sea with major cities in the interior. The ports of Zayla' and Berbera were key starting points for caravan trade routes. Moving in an easterly direction, the caravans connected the ports with eastern and southwestern Ethiopia. The city of Harar was a major point along the interior caravan route. Other caravan routes started from the coastal town of Massawa in present-day Eritrea, connecting the port with northern and central Ethiopia.

In the precolonial period movement from ports into the interior was not completely free, permitting a comparison between this period and the colonial era. In the earlier period, movement was determined, in part, by navigational considerations and the sea itself. Arab boats traveled on the Red Sea only during the day as there were hazards, including rocky shores. As in other parts of the Indian Ocean, seafarers relied on the monsoon winds that for centuries if not millennia powered vessels crossing the Indian Ocean. Major W. Cornwallis Harris, on a visit to the port of Berbera, noted the temporal nature of the port activity because of the monsoon winds. The port was deserted between October and March, as the monsoon winds did not reach the region (Harris, 1844: 38–39).

The port space of this region, however, was not only structured or regulated by the natural force of the ocean and the underlying structures of the port space. The ports were managed by the amir al-bahr (commander of the maritime frontier), a system that had existed for many centuries.[3] Several precolonial European travelers were subject to regulations enforced by the amir al-bahr or other local authorities who were in control of port spaces and to which the amir al-bahr answered. The first French travelers to the region, de la Merveille and de Champloret, mention the amir al-bahr at the port of Mocha, when they attempted to travel to the coast of of Tajura in present-day Djibouti (De la Roque, 1732: 39-56). Arnauld d'Abbadie came to Djibouti at the beginning of the nineteenth century. He wrote of being denied access to the port of Tajura by one of the local rulers of the time, Sharmarke (d'Abbadie, 1808: 581).

The hinterland caravan trade routes were also structured spaces. Each section of a route was controlled by the ethnic group that inhabited the territory. Along the traditional caravan routes that connected Djibouti to the interior, Afar and Somali ethnic groups controlled different sections, and moving between Afar- and Somali-controlled zones was not an easy affair. Traveler Jules Borelli (1890: 3), for example, informs us that travelers had to change their guide *(ābanǝ)* when switching between these two zones because escorting people in zones outside one's own region could trigger outright conflict. These hinterland trade routes were also highly securitized by the authorities who controlled the port spaces to which they were linked. The sultan of Tajura's sons, for example, maintained an extended network of informants to ensure that their father was constantly informed of events that could affect trade and security (Borelli, 1890: 37).

Major cities, both along the coast and in the hinterland, were also structured spaces. The port of Zayla', built in the shape of a parallelogram, was a gated city where people were instructed to wear their weapons under their clothes (Bardey, 1897; Burton, 1856: 45). The major interport area of Harar was also a gated city where the coming and going of foreigners was controlled (Christopher, 1844: 103). Burton, for example, notes that at the time of his arrival a dozen petty Arab peddlers were barred from entering the city (1856: 329).

Starting from the end of the nineteenth century the local authorities of gated cities such as Harar gave way to colonial power. In Djibouti and its hinterland, colonialism led to the demise of the trade route system. This was caused by the construction of a railway connecting the port of Djibouti with Addis Ababa, established by Emperor Menelik in 1886. Harar's economic importance fell while Dire Dawa became a key trading city. The railway lines were faster and more reliable than the old caravans. Within a short time, traffic was drawn to the newly built areas. Diasporic groups, including Yemenis, traveled by train to the interior. It was not just the pattern and direction of mobility that changed but also the way that movement was governed, as is discussed in the remaining pages of this chapter.

Seascapes and Movement during the Colonial Period

The French arrived with their own notions about seascapes and quickly changed the navigation practices in the Gulf of Aden. In the earliest period of colonization, one of the first acts by the French was to divide, name, and effectively appropriate the seascapes and port towns. In Obock, one of the areas first colonized by France, the port, now named the port of Obock, was divided into three banks: le Banc de Curieux, le Banc de Clocheterie, and le Banc du Surcouf. They also designated two port areas: le Port du Sud and le Port du Nord (Poydenot, 1889: 68).

In addition to being named and divided, port spaces were incorporated into the symbolic regime of international maritime law. In this respect, one of the first tasks was to illuminate *(éclairage)* and another was to signpost *(balisage)* port towns (Poydenot, 1889: 69). In Obock, French colonial administrators installed a red light for guiding ships coming from the direction of Rasə Birr. The Banc du Surcouf came to be indicated by a red rubber ring, while they placed a black ring to indicate the Banc de Clocheterie. The port was also lit up by three lighthouses. At night, two lighthouses glowed red, while the other had a green beam for guiding ships traveling in the dark (Poydenot, 1889: 69).

In addition to the use of new technologies, the French colonial authorities required all ships sailing in the area to display a specific symbol to aid in their identification. On September 1, 1884, the French passed a decree that made it illegal for vessels to sail without appropriate identification, Règlement Concernant les Règles établies pour Prévenir les Abordages. This decree detailed for the first time the rules of navigation both in France and in its overseas territories (Poinsard, 1894: 36–37). The regulation distinguished between traditional vessels and those powered by steam engines and specified in detail the symbols and lights that must be used at night. Ships had to use a sign that enabled port authorities to determine whether they were powered by steam or not. The regulation also made it mandatory for boat owners to display a signal that indicated the direction in which the boat was traveling. In case of emergency, the law also required ships to indicate the hazard by sounding a specific alarm, such as a siren in the case of steamships and bells and drums in the case of smaller traditional boats. To enforce the decree, a law stipulating various penalties was passed on March 10, 1891 (Poinsard, 1894: 36–37).

Regularized Port Spaces

The arrival of the French saw the regulation not only of vessel traffic but also of the port space itself. The port space was measured, and the limiting and defining of what was and what was not port space was now of utmost importance. These efforts to measure, and thus enclose, the port space ended traditional practices that had kept the port relatively open and unbounded. In the specific case of Djibouti these changes were institutionalized through the order (*arrêté*) of November 14, 1889.[4] The order was aimed at fixing and limiting the port of Djibouti, and explicitly prescribed the areas where boarding and deboarding was allowed. Article one of the order states that all disembarkment and embarkment, unless there was a special authorization, could be made only at the quay established in the old harbor and the surrounding water. The article goes on to specify the depth of the water: "This embarkment and disembarkment is only possible in water (in this harbor) within 60 meters north of the quay and 30 meters south of the quay."[5] The order also made all disembarkment and embarkment outside the defined zones illegal.[6] In the subsequent period the limits of the port were further modified and fixed through regulations such as order 112 of February 15, 1943.[7]

As port spaces became limited through specific measurement of the area, access to these spaces also became regulated. Order 297 of November 1916, published in the *Journal Officiel de la Côte Française des Somalis*, was the chief instrument used to regulate port spaces.[8] Article 2 of the decree stated that all vessels, including small vessels and those carrying passengers, could not leave the port of Djibouti before six o'clock in the morning.[9] The same article forbade the movement of vessels after eight o'clock in the evening.[10] The only exemptions were for government vessels in possession of a special pass from the customs authority. The order of November 10 specified the time of departure from the designated port space and advised that vessels must leave the port space within a specific time defined by the order. Article 4 states that at the time of departure a customs service agent, accompanied by an *'askari* (native soldier), will board the vessel to inspect the documents of all travelers and the goods aboard.[11] Violation of the *arrêté* was punishable by five days in prison and a fine ranging from one to fifteen francs.[12]

The French colonial government took further measures of control, including the establishment of the port police force through a decree passed on June 30, 1889, and further decrees passed on November 14, 1889, and May 3, 1900 (Angoulvant and Vignéras, 1902: 286). Linked to the formation of the port police, another decree passed on August 18, 1900 established port customs duties. Vessels at the port of Djibouti were exempt from paying duties related to the lighthouse, anchorage, and signposting. However, vessels were now required to pay a fee for the process of loading and off-loading cargo (Angoulvant and Vignéras, 1902: 286).

These new rules affected Yemenis living in the region. They had to follow the various regulations, including signposting. Yemenis had to deal on a daily basis with the changes introduced by the colonial rulers. The spreading French control meant that Yemenis were now living under a regime that did not always support their interests.

The Yemeni community wrote two letters to the head of the Chamber of Commerce, Paul Marill. The first letter detailed the problems they faced with the customs officer and the *'askari*, who now had the right to board and inspect vessels. The letter, written by those aboard one such boat, claimed that money found on the vessel had been confiscated by the agents of the state. After attempting to recover the money, only a small portion of the total sum had been returned. In the letter the Yemenis, characterizing themselves as ignorant foreigners who did not have knowledge of the law, implored Marill to intervene so that they could get their money back.[13] The second letter, written on July 28, 1917, has to do with the problem Yemeni dhow owners faced as a result of the regulation of time in port spaces. It was also addressed to the head of the Chamber of Commerce:

> We, the undersigned, owners of the dhows that set sail at Djibouti, have the honor of bringing the following to your attention:
>
> As a result of the very marked decline in this area, we find ourselves obliged to wait either at the end of the pier or in the harbor with the rising tide until we can maneuver our dhows. And as the flood tide comes only after 6 o'clock in the evening at present, as a result of the new law that forbids us from entering or exiting the harbor after 6 o'clock in the evening our dhows are forced to stay where they are indefinitely, and cannot move on pain of a fine. Thus, recently two of us were heavily fined because, benefiting from the rising tide after 6 o'clock in the evening, one had tried to move his dhow into the harbor and the other had tried to move his out, loaded, to the end of the pier in order to set sail the following morning. We would be grateful, Sir, if you would ask the honorable Governor to authorize us on this very particular matter . . . to allow us to maneuver our dhow. . . . We thank you in advance and are honored, Sir, to send you our greetings. Dhow owners.[14]

The regulation of port spaces and time indeed had a direct effect on Yemenis using the port spaces. The regime of control that was established by the colonial authorities, however, was not limited to those already mentioned. In fact, one can say that limiting the space and time of the port space of Djibouti acted as the framework for a much more intense control focused on the movement of people. Under the French, people traveling into the area were required to have a health certificate and to pass through quarantine centers. Those who failed to do so were detained in health centers, something that had never occurred during precolonial times.

It was for this purpose of checking and detaining unhealthy people that a zone of quarantine was first established on the nearby island in 1899. The colonial authorities eventually built a hospital/police center in Djibouti, known as Police Sanitaire Maritime-Lazaret. Administratively speaking, the Police Sanitaire Maritime-Lazaret was under the control of a member of the medical staff.[15] An *agent sanitaire indigène*, a native sanitary agent, worked with the chief medical officer.[16] The Police Sanitaire Maritime-Lazaret was responsible for inspecting war ships and postal vessels. Although not on a daily basis, this body was also mandated to investigate other kinds of ships.[17]

The arrival of people into the territory was also an issue. In addition to creating the port police, the French colonial authorities passed decrees relating to immigration. While mobility was regulated in the precolonial period, this was a more formal and much more intrusive form of control. One of the earliest orders on immigration, issued on August 15, 1903, states that an individual cannot be received in the protectorate unless he is the owner of an establishment or employed by an establishment.[18] It further states that an employed person must show proof of a formal contract.[19] If the immigrant did not have a contract he needed to prove that he had two hundred francs.

The French colonial power also sought to better control the territories and inland regions. When they first arrived at Obock, the French established a prison and garrison staffed by Sudanese and Senegalese soldiers.[20] Later, through a decree passed on August 28, 1900, they formed an urban police force (Angoulvant and Vignéras, 1902: 222–23) and organized "un cadre local d'agents indigènes de la police", (a native service composed of native agents who work as a police force).[21] This force was charged with policing the urban and suburban areas of the colony, as well as the prison. Placed directly under l'Administration Chargée de la Police et la Justice Indigène, the administrative structure that controlled the police and the native justice system, this force was made up of Arabs, Gadabursi, Habr Awal, Sudanese, Abyssinians, and 'Issa.

Besides the native service, the *agents indigènes*, a year later, on June 1, 1901, the colonial authorities created a rural police force, the primary purpose of which was to protect the railway.[22] This force manned eight posts along the train line (at kilometers 19, 27, 37, 52, 56, 70, 75, and 90).[23] At each post, staff included one brigadier and a number of police.[24] This arrangement, as well, was unlike the precolonial traditional system. As we saw in the previous section, caravan routes before the establishment of the train line operated under a system of localized control. There were always authorities who watched over the area and the movement of people within it. The caravan was itself hierarchically organized and travel from Afar- to 'Issa-controlled zones required knowledge of the terrain and the people. The French system brought control to the new railway line. This further curtailment of people's freedom of movement presented a challenge to Yemenis who wanted to move from the coast to the hinterland.

The new trains and the regulation of movement were not welcomed by Yemenis, bringing new challenges to their lives in Djibouti. This was especially true when it came to relations between Yemenis and the *'askari*, the native soldiers employed to control and tax people at checkpoints. Hoping to address this problematic relationship with the *'askari*, a group of Yemeni and Indian traders wrote a letter of complaint.[25] From what they wrote, passengers and travelers daily faced problems with the *'askari* connected to the customs office. A merchant particularly noted that instead of demanding that he open his luggage to show whether he was carrying any prohibited items, the *'askari* asked him, before making any inspection, to list all items contained in his luggage. If the *'askari* found one or two articles that the passenger had forgotten to mention, the merchants noted, the *'askari* would take the passenger to the head of the customs office, who would then make him pay a large fee, well above the required fee for the particular items.

After briefly detailing some other problems they had encountered, the writers of the letter continued, "We demand the termination of all discrimination against us Indians and Arabs so that we will not be attacked by the police and we will be free like the other foreigners."[26] Despite such protests and demands that the unfair police treatment stop, the situation for Yemenis did not change. Aboard trains, Yemenis were relegated to a space reserved for natives. This space, referred to as *3ème classe* (third class), was located at the end of the train and was for use by natives, who were regarded as inferior compared to white people, who occupied *1ère classe* (first class). In contrast to the first-class carriages, third-class compartments were congested and lacked facilities appropriate for longer journeys. The company put more passengers into third class, and Arabs and Indians suffered discomfort on the twelve-hour journey.[27] Sometimes travelers were forced to stand as there were too few seats.[28] Neither did the third-class carriage have toilets. We learn from correspondence written[29] during that time that passengers were reluctant to get off the train to relieve themselves, fearing that the train would leave without them.[30]

The French authorities also divided the territory into different zones that functioned not only as administrative areas but also as zones of control. In the initial phase of colonization, posts were placed at the entrance to the town of Djibouti, to mark the city limits. As the colonization process continued, however, the territories were divided into different zones. On December 29, 1899, an order was issued to divide the colony's territory into three broad categories: urban, suburban, and rural.[31] The French authorities later divided the territory into two broader districts, namely Danakil and 'Issa.[32] Later, various administrative and territorial districts were formed within these areas, leading to the subdivision of Djibouti into five administrative areas, each with a leader responsible for representing the population.[33] These districts, quarters, and segregated areas came to be divided along racial lines. For example, cities such as Djibouti were composed of a European quarter, Ville Européenne, and a separate quarter for native people.[34]

In the subdivisions, the colonial administration was keen to regulate the movement of natives. A police regulation from June 23, 1900, for example, was explicitly concerned with the movement of people in the territory.[35] Article 64 of the decree stated that movement by unaccompanied Europeans posed risks to the individual.[36] All Europeans were forbidden from going to the rural areas without a guide or men bearing arms.[37] At the same time, the law instructed natives wishing to enter the city to turn their daggers, spears, and sticks over to a checkpoint established in Ambouli (Frennelet, 1894: 223).

The process of disarming native people within particular spaces affected their everyday activities. On August 4, 1921, Hassan Safi, Hamid al Bar, and Hassan al Bar wrote a letter describing how their daily lives had been affected by the decree.³⁸ We read that the public enforcement officer seized even their walking sticks. Noting that they carry a small stick rather than a big stick, which they say was the kind actually forbidden, they asked the relevant authorities if they could be allowed to retain the use of the smaller sticks.

Aside from everyday inconveniences, there were greater consequences of the zonal control of Djibouti. It brought with it arbitrary punishment. Yemenis, as well as other natives of the territory, were subjected to various administrative (as opposed to legal) measures. A decree passed on September 30, 1912 was concerned with discouraging crime among natives by *voix disciplinaire*, which entails the giving of repressive judicial power to colonial administrators in order to swiftly deal with infractions committed by the natives.³⁹ The order, which was similar to previous orders issued in other colonies, allowed colonial administrators, officers, and functionaries, as well as the governor of the territory, to take measures against the natives. Without any recourse to the courts, the colonial authorities were allowed to imprison any native found to have committed an offense for fifteen days.⁴⁰ They could also impose fines up to five francs. Acts by natives considered an offense that could be dealt with outside the court were many, but most related to movement and contact between natives and the authorities in areas designated as legitimate zones of control.

Yemenis wrote yet another protest letter in December 1927 to the district attorney. Written six years after the above-mentioned letter, the writers of this letter complained at length about the mistreatment and excessive control they had endured since the foundation of the colony.⁴¹ This letter clearly shows Yemenis' dire situation. I quote it here in full:

> Notable Arabs who have commanded the respect of the public and that of the French authorities do not have the right to go on board ship to see their friends or their family members without acquiring authorization from the district head and the head of the police. . . . For a simple paper that the wind has brought before one's house; for a few minutes' delay after ten at night; for sitting in front of one's door taking fresh air, we are treated like common criminals.

The 'askaris make degrading comments and arrest us and take us to the police station, too happy to inflict this humiliation. In the police station the police do not make any distinction. A common criminal who frequents the prison and the Arabs who live by hard work are treated equally. . . . If we want to send our wives to their families in Arabia we need to obtain three days in advance authorization from the district chief so that the police can issue a travel permit. There is no justification for these vexatious measures. . . . The most innocent things must be submitted for the approval of the authorities.[42]

Indeed, the colonial structure established by France intensely structured the lives of Yemenis. As this letter points out, the laws placed the most natural things under the control of colonial authorities. When it came to punishing Yemenis, the French penal system recommended severe treatment. A decree of March 3, 1886 regarding condemned natives specifically mentions the use of hard labor for individuals of Arab origin (Frennelet, 1894: 114). Thus, an Arab in Djibouti was not only a person whose scant belongings could be confiscated at will but also the target of a decree issued to punish those of Arab origin.

Apart from the new laws relating to the police and the penal system, Yemenis came under the disciplinary powers of the French administration through the immigration law. In fact, the immigration decree had a section that specifically related to Yemenis. Article 4, sections C and D, stated in explicit terms what Yemenis coming from Yemen and Djibouti should do. In section C, relating to Yemenis coming from the state of Yemen, the decree indicated that they should have a travel permit issued by the governor of Aden. If Yemenis were disembarking at the port of Djibouti, it was mandatory for them to have a travel permit, which in this case had to be certified by the British embassy in Djibouti. Section D concerned the Arabs of Djibouti and stated that they should have a valid travel permit with a visa from the British diplomatic agency in Djibouti in order to travel to Aden.

While Yemenis' movement was controlled by the French following colonization of the area, it should be noted that in the early part of the twentieth century traditional authorities also controlled the movement of people in the region. Observations made by Henry de Monfreid in the 1930s are, in this regard, revealing. In *Aventures de Mer* (1932: 56), Monfreid writes that he was met by soldiers of the amir al-bahr, who formally inquired as to from where he came. We also read that during one of his several trips to the port of Yemen, the passengers Monfreid was transporting were confronted by the old system of restricting people's movement: fearing an ambush by a rival, Monfreid dropped his passengers off on a remote shore, outside the port. The passengers who were Yemeni did not object to the unplanned disembarkation. In his account, Monfreid says that during their inland journey, "they will always have to pay for right of passage, because every tribe considered itself as a state. If they have no money, they will pay in kind: he who is a builder will build a wall for the sheikh whose territory he wants to cross; the carpenter will make doors or windows for one of his houses ... and so it will go in every territory, some of which are barely the size of a county" (1932: 50; author's translation).

Thus, up to a certain point of time the traditional system coexisted with the new, more regulated system introduced by the French. The latter had considerably more force, through the process of colonization. Behavior that previously was seen as natural and legal was now subjected to the constraints of an arbitrary colonial structure. This affair of layering previous systems of mobility within a much more 'modern' form of control that was intense and pervasive was not, however, limited to the formal spaces of Djibouti. It was also implemented and exercised in the hinterland. The following section examines the control Yemenis encountered when they moved toward the hinterland region of Ethiopia. Yemenis, following the construction of the train line, settled primarily in the town of Dire Dawa, the first stop on the line that would eventually reach Addis Ababa, some 350 kilometers away. My analysis focuses on the experience of Yemenis in Dire Dawa and Addis Ababa.

Hinterland City Spaces
In the first three decades of the twentieth century the differential access to space that Yemenis encountered under the French empire was extended to Dire Dawa, the railway's first major terminal. Administratively

speaking, Dire Dawa was divided into two broad sections: Gazira and Ville Indigène (the latter was also referred to as Mägala). Until 1929, Gazira was administered by the French while Mägala was administered by Ethiopia (Bekele, 1989: 91–92).

As the etymology of the names of these two parts of the city indicates, beyond their physical aspects Ville Indigène and Ville Européenne were racial spaces. Ville Européenne was occupied by French personnel, most of whom worked for the railway. It also housed a number of other white settlers, including Greeks, Italians, Armenians, and Germans. Yemenis who came to Djibouti by train and remained in Dire Dawa on a temporary or a permanent basis were relegated to the space reserved for the supposedly inferior native people. Compared to the space the Europeans lived in, the Ville Indigène lacked basic urban amenities. From a European perspective, the area was overcrowded and full of dangerous criminals (Bekele, 1994: 612–14).

Dire Dawa featured regulatory measures deployed to control the movement of people. As in the case of Djibouti, the regulatory power that structured the city's space used a state-organized police force to enforce its rules. In the early days of Dire Dawa, the European part of the city was administered by the railway company's guards while Mägala's security was the responsibility of a police force organized by the Ethiopian government (Bekele, 1989: 106–109). Apart from carrying out standard policing duties, the Dire Dawa police were involved in controlling how natives moved around at night. Yemenis and other native people were required to carry a lantern if they wanted to be on the streets after nine o'clock at night. White foreigners were free from this enforced visibility. In a letter to his father, written from Dire Dawa on September 6, 1911, Monfreid wrote about this practice. "The police in Dire Dawa," he wrote, "are incredible. At 9 pm any native walking around without a lantern is thrown into the block and shot if he tries to run away. The only free people are the Europeans, and they have nothing to fear from the *'askari*s. If they did that in Paris there'd be fewer of the Apaches gang" (2007: 34; author's translation).

As one moved from Dire Dawa and its hinterland to Addis Ababa, the dynamics present in Dire Dawa changed. As a capital city ruled by

Ethiopians and hence free from European colonial administration, Addis Ababa provided a sharp contrast to both Dire Dawa and Djibouti. Yemenis moving to Addis Ababa were not confined to specific spaces designated for native people and lived among the Ethiopian community. In the first three decades of the twentieth century, rather than being divided on the basis of state-enforced racial spaces, Addis Ababa was compartmentalized into spaces referred to as *säfär*s. *Säfär*s were residential areas formed as a result of the settlement of people involved in particular occupations. *Säfär*s were also formed by the presence (in a particular locality) of an important military chief and his (usually) large army and retinue. The *säfär*s of Addis Ababa were also formed around the main palace of Emperor Menelik II of Ethiopia, who was the founder of the city. At the time, rather than race, as the etymology of the *säfär*s of Addis Ababa shows, the *säfär*s reflected the type of people residing within them, such as *serategnoche säfär*s (workers' quarters), Warjih *säfär*s (quarters of the Warjih ethnic group), and Arab *säfär*s (Arab quarters) (Zewde, 2005: 124–25; Zewdu, 1995).

Bureaucratized Hinterland Spaces

Yemeni settlement in the *säfär*s of Addis Ababa went unchecked by the imperial government of Ethiopia. However, this was soon to change as a result of the introduction of a modern bureaucratic system and a series of decrees intended to formalize the informal controls on movement in traditional Ethiopian society. The new system began with a declaration arising from a concern that the European powers were interested in the country. Urged by European consular personnel in Addis Ababa, Emperor Menelik II introduced a modern bureaucratic system that later came to affect the free movement of people. As part of this modernization, he appointed a number of ministers in a decree passed on October 10, 1900 (Nogno, 1989: 83).

This was followed by more specific legislation directly concerning foreign residents. Fearing the growing number of immigrants and the uncontrolled nature of their entry, Menelik's government issued a decree that required all foreigners to register with the Ethiopian authorities or their respective legations. The decree noted the presence of many men from foreign countries, the consulates of which were not known. In view of this the directive urged all those who had not registered with their legation, or even identified with a particular legation, to do so (Nogno, 1989: 83).

This decree was further consolidated in an official notice that came out on October 10, 1928.[43] This notice, according to United States embassy personnel in Addis Ababa, came about because "the country has become the residence of a number of alleged undesirable characters mainly from the Levant, who are thought to be a menace to social as well as to official law and order."[44] It instructed all foreigners to have their passports stamped with a visa. Failure to do this would mean not only rejection at the border but also deportation of all those found in the country without a visa.[45] This notice was modified following a protest by the foreign legations, which were concerned about the clause stipulating the summary deportation of foreigners without a visa.[46] In the modified version, which came out on December 13, 1928, this clause was substituted with a clause requiring all foreigners to deposit a sum of one hundred thalery.[47] The modified notice also obliged foreigners who frequently traveled by train to present a certificate issued by their consulate to the Ethiopian Ministry of Foreign Affairs, which would give them a certificate valid for one year.[48]

In addition to the above developments, the Ethiopian government signed a treaty with France on January 10, 1908 for the establishment of a consular court for foreign subjects.[49] Following this treaty, France passed a law on November 16, 1909, which declared the application of the law in civil and criminal cases.[50] The treaty between Ethiopia and France delegated all disputes between French and Ethiopian subjects to the Ethiopian magistrate, who was to be assisted by the French consul or his representative. How the law was applied differed, however. For French subjects, French law was used, while for Ethiopians it was Ethiopian law that was used. If there was disagreement between judges, the treaty allowed the case to be taken to the court of the Ethiopian emperor. The treaty stated that the territorial authority had the right of searching and arresting French subjects who committed crimes. It also stated, however, that investigations and arrests should immediately be reported to the French consul and that the criminals should be transferred to the consul.[51]

Initially it was standard practice for other colonial powers to extend and use the treaty with France in matters concerning their subjects.[52] Eventually, however, they sought to establish their own arrangements in Ethiopia. For example, on December 19, 1913, the Royal Court of Great Britain ordered the establishment of a system of consular courts in Abyssinia.[53]

The establishment of the provisions outlined above meant that Yemenis were formally distributed among the colonial legations in Addis Ababa. As Yemenis originated from north Yemen, the British-controlled area of Aden and its hinterland, and the French-administered area of Djibouti, the new regulation divided Yemenis into three legations. Yemenis who came from Djibouti were French subjects and placed under the control of the French consul. Those from Aden and the British protectorate were registered under British control. Through an agreement with the Imam of Yemen, the Ethiopian government took responsibility for Yemenis originating from the northern part of Yemen.

This allocation to different legations became not only permanent but also a matter of routine. Yemenis were asked to register annually. Part three of the order of the British Royal Court, which established the system of consular courts in Ethiopia, stated that a "register of British subjects shall be kept in the office of every consulate in Abyssinia. Every British subject resident in Abyssinia, being of the age of 21 years or upwards, or being married, or a widower or widow, though under that age shall in the month of January of every year register himself or herself at the consulate of the consular district in which he or she resides."[54] Yemenis now also needed railway passes and permits for entering and leaving the country.

In terms of the bureaucratization of the Ethiopian empire, perhaps the most crucial element of control established at the time was the police force, which was at first under the leadership of Rasə Mäkonənə, who in 1882 was the governor of the eastern province of Harärge. Composed mainly of Somali recruits and men trained in Turkey, the police force was central to the control of movement within the city. Similar to the Dire Dawa police, the Addis Ababa police force was established in the early days of the city and referred to as Däwariä. An important part of its work was to enforce curfews on native people, including Yemenis residing in the town. Enforced from six o'clock in the evening, when a whistle was blown to indicate the start of the curfew, this practice confined people to the 'security' of their homes against their will (Täkəlämariyamə, 2006). The task of regulating native movement in Addis Ababa by use of police whistles later became more sophisticated. Police-approved movement control permits, which had to be periodically renewed, were issued. Yemenis were given a paper known as an Ethiopian Police Force Movement Control Permit. This permit included the holder's full name, his race, the place he was going to move to, the reason for his movement, the mode of transport to be used, and the expiration date of the permit.

The effect of this bureaucratization of space is seen in the experience of Sheikh Sa'id Ba Zar'a, a Yemeni who migrated to the hinterland of Ethiopia and become one of the first Yemeni to settle in Addis Ababa. I interviewed the Ba Zar'a family in 2006—they were my host family during my research in Addis Ababa. Currently, the Ba Zar'a family is located in multiple spaces: they live in Addis Ababa, Saudi Arabia, and Mukalla. This situation is not new; previously they lived in a variety of spaces ranging from East Africa to Mumbai.

The Ba Zar'a family was primarily settled in Djibouti, Addis Ababa, and Dire Dawa. Interestingly, it was their history of settlement and movement that first alerted me to the changing nature of movement following the establishment of borders, lines, and checkpoints. Until recently, the oldest member of the Ba Zar'a family was Abd al-Hamid Sa'id Ba Zar'a, who died in 2006 at the age of ninety-seven. Abd al-Hamid was the eldest son of Sheikh Sa'id Ba Zar'a, the first family member to come to the region. As Monfreid (1938: 82) noted, Ba Zar'a was famous for his wealth and the influence he commanded in Djibouti and its hinterland. During my interview with Abd al-Hamid, shortly before his death, it became clear that Sa'id Ba Zar'a's traveling had been marked by incremental changes in formal control (outlined above and further explained below). Travel by other family members had also been marked in this way.

Sheikh Sa'id Ba Zar'a originally came from the province of Wadi Du"an in Hadramawt, South Yemen. His journey started in the last part of the nineteenth century, in the period when the frontiers were still in the making. The movements of Sheikh Sa'id Ba Zar'a involved less bureaucracy than later family migrations. Starting from Wadi Du'an, Sa'id Ba

Zar'a traveled first to Aden, where his relatives were already living. From Aden, apparently with the encouragement of his family, he moved to the other side of the Gulf of Aden by dhow. Once there, Sa'id Ba Zar'a settled in the coastal region and then moved inward, to the Ethiopian hinterland, without encountering any formal hindrance.

This state of affairs, however, was soon to change, for both him and his son, Abd al-Hamid, whom he brought from Yemen. The key factor in this change, which can be seen from evidence provided by the family in the form of interviews and documents, was the emergence of the imperial powers that were forming colonial states in the region and controlling the movement of people. Sa'id Ba Zar'a's movements seem to have been increasingly regulated as a result of his incorporation into a political and social order whose division was made spatially visible.

In the case of Sa'id Ba Zar'a, the new order and the consequent spatial restructuring was made visible in the form of travel documents. In the first part of the twentieth century, the French authorities in Djibouti issued Sa'id Ba Zar'a with a permit that allowed him to move between Ethiopia and Djibouti. On the Ethiopian side of the border, the newly formed Ethiopian Ministry of Foreign Affairs also issued him a pass. This document, issued by Belata Geta Heruy, was valid for one year and described Sa'id Ba Zar'a as a resident trader of Addis Ababa, from the country of Wadi Du"an, and as a subject of Great Britain. His son Abd al Hamid, whom I was interviewing when this information came to light, was also issued with the appropriate papers. His document, which was an old passport, was entitled "Passport of the State of Shihr and Mukalla." Valid for two years, it identified the passport holder as Abd al-Hamid Sheikh Sa'id Ba Zar'a, resident of Addis Ababa, who was traveling from Mukalla to Addis Ababa via Djibouti. He was described as a subject of Qu'ayti.

Transformed from 'free' migrants, the Ba Zar'a family by the middle of the twentieth century became part of the order constructed by imperial powers. They were correct/legal men who moved across territories using passports. They became identified with a certain legation and a particular nation-state.

Apart from colonial processes/structures that affected Yemenis like Sa'id Ba Zar'a, the many wars waged between colonial powers were

Figure 2. Sheik Sheikh Sa'id Ba Zar'a (Courtesy of Saeed 'Abd al-Hamid Ba Zar'a).

another factor that affected the movement of people in this corner of the world. As part of their war effort, the colonial powers attempted to control movement in and out of port spaces. In extreme cases this took the form of blockades against enemy territory. Such blockades put restrictions on the movement of native people in and out of port towns, as well as restrictions on food supplies and other essential goods. In view of this, it is important to document how imperial war came to structure the mobility of Yemenis and other native people in the port of Djibouti and its hinterland. The following section deals specifically with this issue.

War and Controlled Spaces
Movement during the Ottoman–British conflict

In the northwestern Indian Ocean region, territorial blockades were an ongoing problem for native people and migrants, including Yemenis. One of the first such blockades in the first part of the twentieth century was carried out by the Ottoman and British empires before and during the First World War. Ottoman forces, then stationed in northern Yemen,[55] occupied a large area of the Red Sea coastal region, with the exception of 'Asir, which was pro-British and under the authority of Sayyid Muhammad al Idrisi.[56] The British were relegated to the Aden protectorate. In the context of the war, the two powers tried to block each other's ports and cut off the movement of people and goods. In 1913, the Ottoman authorities blocked the Yemen littoral zone to stop supplies of goods and ammunition to Sayyid Muhammad al Idrisi (Shipman, 2006). This resulted in a prohibition against the movement of ships and boats, as well as the confiscation of goods on ships coming from Djibouti.[57]

Similarly, the British attempted to block ports and territories under the control of the Ottoman Empire. As part of these blockades, and to secure the area, the British placed two naval patrols along the coastline held by the Ottoman Empire. One such blockade was placed along a line from Suez to Jeddah, while the navy patrolled the area from Jeddah to Aden. In 1916 the British further stepped up their efforts to block the ports in the eastern part of the Red Sea region by allowing ships to travel only to Yemeni ports that were under the control of 'Asir, such as Midi and Djayzan (Shipman, 2006).

Yemenis in the northwestern Indian Ocean region were affected by this imperial battle. Not only were they deprived of essential supplies, they were also unable to move from one area to another. Many of their small traditional boats operating in the area were sunk by the British because they were suspected of smuggling goods to the territory controlled by the Ottoman Empire. This blockade did not only affect Yemenis, of course;

it also affected the French colony of Djibouti, which was deprived of the Yemeni laborers who were the main workforce.

The effects of the British blockade on Djibouti and its Yemeni population are discussed by Monfreid (1932). He relates that the French authorities had informally permitted him to travel to Arab shores in a bid to obtain workers. This move was also intended to stimulate and encourage the movement of Arabs between Djibouti and the blockaded Arab shores. This is how he describes the situation at that time:

> Governor Simonin was worried to see that the native laborers of Djibouti are making more and more defaults because the Arabs of Yemen constituted almost the entire workforce of Djibouti. In addition the commerce that used to attract a lot of small vessels from Yemen has been totally ruined. In this situation it was necessary to reassure the Arab pilots who were terrorized by the menace of the British by showing them that it was in fact easy to break this famous blockade. . . . The customs officer who has obtained the necessary instruction to give me the necessary papers by turning a blind eye gave me a patent stating that I am heading to Assab on the western side of the sea. . . . Even though the imports I made were modest, they nevertheless helped to reduce the price of foodstuffs in Arabia and the merchandise escorted by the Cowajee was no longer the mysterious galleons filled with gold. A large number of Arabs, encouraged by my success, came with their Zaragous and an intense traffic was established. The English complained to the governor, who responded by saying that he is not responsible for the blockade of the coast of Arabia. We were at the critical moment where the Yemenis have expelled the Turks from all of their territory. On top of that the English wanted to "help" this country and indirectly they were blocking our colony by mercilessly sinking sailing ships heading to Djibouti. Dozens of Arab ships that do not have the English flag (they used to give them in Aden on condition that they would come to the port for supplies or for buying merchandise) were sunk and lost for good. (1932: 114–15; author's translation).

Territorial blockade: Dynamics of the Second World War

The Arabs were also affected by another blockade—in Djibouti. Following the outbreak of the Second World War, France, after six months of resistance, was defeated by the Nazi regime, which led to the occupation of Paris by the German army.[58]

Soon after this defeat, Philippe Pétain declared the establishment of the Vichy government, following a vote of the French National Assembly on July 10, 1940. The establishment of this government, which intended to make peace with Germany, led to the division of France into two zones referred to as the occupied German territory, which lay mostly in northern France, and Vichy France, which consisted mostly of territories in the southeast.[59] However, French rule was contested by General Charles de Gaulle, who aligned himself with the Allies and proclaimed the establishment of the Provisional Government of the French Republic in June 1944.

The distant but important colony of Djibouti aligned itself with the Vichy regime, although as a matter of policy the territory had declared itself neutral in the war. The British, hoping to reduce the power of the Vichy government and, by association, Nazi Germany, sealed off the Gulf of Tajura in October 1940, thereby isolating the territory from any outside contact.[60] General Archibald Wavell, who was responsible for this blockade, justified the action of Great Britain to the governor of Djibouti on the grounds that France had allowed Germany to use its airfields in Syria.[61] The British feared that the same thing could happen in Djibouti if Nazi Germany found it in its interest to ask. The British, represented by General Wavell, refrained from any diplomatic negotiation.[62] They persisted in maintaining the blockade until the governor declared his willingness to join England in support of the Allied forces.[63]

As in the case of the 1916 blockade, the 1940 blockade of Djibouti meant further curtailment of movement for Yemenis. There were many Yemeni ships engaged at this time in transporting food, ammunition, and general provisions to Djibouti and Ethiopia, breaking the British blockade by using their small boats. But the majority of Yemenis were stranded in Djibouti for nearly a year, and shared the hard times experienced by others throughout the area. One story that shows the vulnerability of Yemenis, and their inability to move around in the face of the British blockade, is that of a group of Yemenis who attempted to return from Djibouti to Yemen. On September 26, 1941, taking advantage of a temporary opportunity offered by the British for travel to Port Said, Yemeni notables in the territory and the French government organized free transport for some 192 Yemenis, most of whom were women and children.[64]

The passengers were all from the district of Obock and were accompanied by a doctor and a nurse.[65] They were also followed by a Red Cross boat commanded by a lieutenant of the national navy.[66] After around eleven hours at sea the vessel was intercepted by two British warships. An officer went aboard the ship and rallied the navy vessel "Hindoustan," from which the order was immediately given to the convoy to make a detour to Zayla'.[67] Confirming the order, a group of armed British marines went aboard the ship, under the direction of an officer, and commanded the ship to Zayla'.[68]

Mobility in occupied Ethiopia

The war dynamics that affected Yemenis in Djibouti had repercussions in the hinterland region. From 1935, beginning as a clash between Ethiopian and Italian forces, an Italian invasion led to the occupation of major Ethiopian cities. The Italian occupation affected the Yemeni population positively and negatively. At the beginning it was a source of anxiety in both Djibouti and Ethiopia. Fearing the possible annexation of the small territory by Italy, the Djibouti government was concerned about the implications of the invasion. Reflecting the government's position, Yemenis in Djibouti held a demonstration affirming that the territory within the boundary of Djibouti was French.

According to "Une manifestation musulmane signative" in the French journal *Correspondance d'Orient*, the demonstration was carried out by Arabs and Somalis after Ramadan in 1937 :

> After the great prayer, notables and sheikhs from the tribes of Dankils, Somalis, and Arabs came in a single procession to the Government Palace and requested the head of the colony to firmly inform the Colonial Secretary and the Government about the unwavering commitment of the population to France; the Qadi of

Djibouti has declared that France was an ally and supporter of Islam, and that it is much better than the Duce's statement proclaiming itself on African soil as the "Sword of Islam." The Ethiopians have realized that if he came to them with a sword in his hand it was the sword of Rome and this did not represent anything good for Islam.

Whether or not the manifesto demands were government-induced or a true expression of Arab and Somali sentiment, the manifesto shows that Yemenis in Djibouti were embedded in the problematic of possible space reconfiguration that might occur as a result of the occupation of Ethiopia by a colonial power other than France. However, in the case of the major towns of Ethiopia, and particularly Addis Ababa, the anxiety was real and immediate. Shortly before the occupation of Addis Ababa by the Italian army, the imperial family, assisted by British forces, fled to Djibouti by train. They eventually boarded a British ship headed for Jerusalem, and later went on to England.[69] The departure of the emperor resulted in chaos in Addis Ababa.[70] We are told that "Addis Ababa was the scene of some serious incidents. The city was plundered after the departure of the king and the disappearance of regular troops."[71]

In this atmosphere of chaos, Yemenis who had been residing in Addis Ababa fled from the city to rural areas where things were calmer. A large majority of Yemenis went to East African port spaces and eventually moved back to their homeland and other Arab countries. Thus, the initial period of Italian occupation resulted in a voluntary and involuntary displacement of Yemenis. This displacement was reversed, however, after the Italians managed to bring order to the major urban cities.

In the meantime, in 'stable' occupied Ethiopia, Yemenis encountered a new way of classifying people. Obsessed with the formation of cities and towns, which they saw as being a sign of civilization, the Italian occupying force made a point of constructing new cities and redesigning old Ethiopian ones. The Italians were interested in meticulous town planning; they were particularly concerned about building urban spaces that had a geometrical order (Antonsich, 2000: 330). They viewed Ethiopians as "people with no towns and no houses" (Cortese, 1938) and were keen to build a city where native people were segregated from the white occupying population. In this regard, Addis Ababa, the capital city of Ethiopia, became a clear example of Italian segregationist policies. The city was divided into a space for native people and a space reserved for white citizens. The former was called Mercato Indigino while the latter was organized around an old market, Arada, which was renamed Piazza. In Dire Dawa, the Italians reinforced the division between the Ville Indigène/Mägala and the Ville Européenne/Gäzira. But the Italians largely failed to enforce the policy. Yemenis continued to live in Dire Dawa, despite policies supporting racial segregation.

The changes that Yemenis faced because of the Italian occupation were not confined to segregation in urban spaces. Yemenis living in Ethiopia also came under scrutiny from other major powers, particularly the British. A key reason was the pro-Muslim rhetoric adopted by Italy. The Italians considered Arabs to be more civilized than native people. And because of their involvement in Libya, the Italians were keen to portray themselves as champions of Islam. They tried to assert power through the old colonial tactic of divide and rule. Italy's support for Arabs meant that Yemenis came under suspicion. In particular, members of the British legation at Addis Ababa became worried and contemplated putting Yemenis under surveillance. An official from the Addis Ababa British Legation wrote to a counterpart in Aden, putting forward his concerns and making some recommendations:

> In view of the active Arab policy adopted by the Italians I suggest it would be advantageous to keep close watch on movements between Abyssinia and Yemen and other parts of Arabia of all Italians, Yemeni and other Arabs, Hararis and other Moslem Abyssinians, Syrians. Such information could, I would suggest, most usefully be coordinated by you and if you agree I would instruct His Majesty's consuls here at Harar and at Djibouti to forward it regularly to you. I realize of course that movement except via Aden will largely escape us but so far I can offer no suggestion how this could be observed. I shall be interested to learn if you received any information of steamship services being established between Massawa (or any other port in Italian hands) and Hudaydah (or any other Arabian port).[72]

This quotation shows that Yemenis in Djibouti faced a systematic process of increased control over space. During the first part of the twentieth century, the population was arranged in a systematic way. From railways to cities, Yemeni movement was subject to control and compartmentalized into spaces. State power holders sought to document, check, and confirm the movement of Yemenis. Colonial powers also tried to contain and order Yemenis and other natives according to now discredited racial ideologies. This was something that continued in the second half of the twentieth century.

3. Nationalized Spaces: Yemeni Mobility in the Second Half of the Twentieth Century

The end of the Second World War brought tremendous change to the French empire in general and to Djibouti in particular. At the end of the war the empire engaged in political reform.[1] The focus was to provide more political space for inhabitants of French colonies. The French National Assembly passed a series of legal reforms that enabled the colonies gradually to participate in politics.[2] Following this, a number of political parties emerged, often representing a colony's different ethnic groups, as well as independence movements that used both violent and nonviolent tactics. In a number of colonies, referenda were held to determine people's aspirations for independence.

Immediately after the Second World War, the Horn of Africa was composed of different territories. These included the previous Italian colonies of Eritrea and Italian Somaliland, which came to be administered by the British and eventually sanctioned by a United Nations mandate.[3] British Somaliland expanded to incorporate the region of the Ogaden and the Haud (as in the case of Eritrea and Italian Somaliland, this territory was also given to the British following a decision made by the United Nations).[4] The still-independent Ethiopian state made a historical claim to the British-administered area of Eritrea and the Ogaden.

At the time, these areas were engulfed by political processes and movements that affected both internal and regional issues. In British Somaliland, political movements such as the Somali Youth Club envisioned incorporation into one territory of all Horn of Africa areas inhabited by ethnic Somalis.[5] The political movement in British Somaliland formed a republic in 1960, incorporating only the former Italian Somaliland. In Ethiopia, the postwar period saw the incorporation of the British-administered region of the Ogaden and the Haud.[6] After a considerable period of deliberation, the United Nations stipulated the annexation of Eritrea into Ethiopia as a federal state.[7]

Internally, the Ethiopian state was undertaking major political reform. In 1961 some of the top military and political officers in Ethiopia attempted a coup against Emperor Haile Selassie while he was on a visit abroad.[8] Although the coup failed, political movements (and especially Marxist student movements that attempted to abolish the position of emperor) became more widespread over the following decade.[9] This widespread movement against the imperial house led to the overthrow of the regime and the takeover of state power by a military junta, the Derg, which was aligned with the Soviet Union.

At the regional level, in the thirty years following the Second World War the Horn of Africa witnessed much contestation. Somalia and Ethiopia were embroiled in a major power struggle that led to war in 1977.[10] The dispute between the two countries was primarily over the Ogaden territory, which had been added to Ethiopia by the British. Moreover, Somalia and Ethiopia were striving for regional hegemony. After the establishment of the state of Somalia, one of the areas affected by the power struggle between Somalia and Ethiopia was Djibouti. As around half of Djiboutians were ethnic Somalis, the Somali government used all possible means, including the Organization of African Unity, to try to place Djibouti within the already-formed territory of Somalia. They sought to do this under the banner of 'Greater Somalia,' or Soomaaliweyen, an idea initially proposed by Lord Bovin, the foreign secretary of Britain, as a key idea for safeguarding the interests of Great Britan in the region (see Barnes, 2007: 281). In the meantime, Ethiopia was doing what it could to prevent the takeover of Djibouti by Somalia.[11]

At the same time, apart from this competition among states, the region saw the arrival of new powers interested in reshaping and dominating the area. In 1952, Egypt came under the leadership of President Gamal Abdel Nasser, who, along with the Syrian Baath Party, advocated pan-Arabism. In the Horn of Africa, this call from Nasser and his political allies received a positive response from many segments of society. In northern Ethiopia, in the newly incorporated territory of Eritrea, the appeal led to the emergence of a small separatist movement (Erlich, 1983). Financially backed by Arab nations, and having obtained military training in places such as Aleppo, the separatist movement claimed that Eritrea was Arab land, a claim also made by the Syrian Baath Party (Erlich, 1995: 130–52).

In addition, the region was affected by the Cold War, divided as it was between ties with the United States and its allies on the one hand and the Soviet bloc on the other. Initially, the United States maintained a close relationship with Ethiopia's imperial regime and maintained a military base in the country's north. The Soviets backed Somalia, which became pro-Soviet, while the French clung to the small territory of Djibouti. Over time, however, the alliances were reshuffled. Following Haile Selassie's overthrow by the Derg, the United States withdrew its support from Ethiopia. Within a few years the Derg, proclaiming itself to be Marxist, joined the Soviet bloc, strengthening ties with the Soviet Union and Cuba. Meanwhile, the Soviet Union, during the Ethiopian-Somali war of 1977, withdrew its support from Somalia in favor of Ethiopia, while the United States tacitly started to support Somalia.[12] As the only European country with an active force in Djibouti, France managed to secure a place for itself in the Horn of Africa by entering into a defense pact with the newly independent nation of the Republic of Djibouti, which led to the continued presence of French soldiers on Djibouti territory (Legum and Lee, 1979; Tholomier, 1981: 129–147).

Intense Control: Independence Movements, Elections, and Yemeni Mobility

The reshuffling of the political system in the Horn of Africa, and the emergence of an independence movement influenced by pan-Arabism and eventually the postcolonial nation-state, presented new forms of control for people living in the region, including Yemeni Arab residents. In Djibouti, the first effect of this post–Second World War reconfiguration, particularly the emergence of pan-Arabism, was marked by increased control over the movement of Yemenis. The French authorities suspected Yemenis of spreading pan-Arabism and began monitoring prominent Yemenis who were vocal or were suspected of opposing French rule. One person put under intense surveillance was Sa'id 'Ali Coubèche. As we will see in later chapters, Coubèche was one of the few Arabs involved in politics in the region. In this regard, the Djibouti secret service wrote an intelligence report regarding Coubèche's activities on October 14, 1953.[13] The secret service accused Coubèche of having a warm relationship with the Arab League and advancing a pan-Arabist ideology through secretly writing anti-France articles in Arab periodicals.[14]

Beyond these surveillance tactics and attempts to control specific individuals, mass expulsion of Yemenis became a norm. The authorities in the colonies suspected foreigners, particularly Yemenis, of being the main agitators spreading ideas of anticolonialism and pan-Arabism. From 1947 to 1957 the names of some five hundred Yemenis expelled from Djibouti were published in the territory's official journal (Imbert-Vier, 2011: 336). Given the intense focus on Yemenis, the consul general of the Yemeni consulate in Djibouti wrote a letter to the governor of Djibouti on April 24, 1956, demanding an explanation. Referring to three cases, the consul complained that the security services had not stopped mistreating Yemenis, despite a previous communication to the governor. This treatment, the consul wrote to the governor, singled out Yemenis from all other nations based in Djibouti and subjected them to expulsion. It allowed their passports to be confiscated and occasionally their foreign residency permits to be taken away in a bid to force them out of the country. This call of the Yemeni consul did not bring any change. In fact, things got worse in the 1960s as a result of the intensification of African independence movements that led to the emergence of independent states such as Somalia. In Djibouti, the first effect of this was an extension of the use of curfews. As a result of the violence and conflict that emerged with the independence movement, Yemenis and other local people increasingly saw the establishment of curfew regimes that inhibited their movement for a specified period of time. In Djibouti, a key change in the curfew regime took place following a visit on August 25, 1966 by French president Géneral Charles de Gaulle. This was the first visit of a French president to the territory, and the government invited the people of Djibouti to come and greet him. The gathering of the people was expected to show support and admiration but it turned into a violent anti-France and more generally anti-colonial demonstration that lasted for days. In light of the anti-French demonstration that he had witnessed, upon his return to France de Gaulle declared that the peoples of Djibouti must know what they want and must negotiate it democratically. In Djibouti, some of the key political opposition parties called for calm in the city (Thompson and Adloff, 1968: 86–87; Coubba, 1993; 105–107).

Despite this call for calm, the continuing violence posed a danger to the French colonial administration. On September 14, 1966, the population turned on Ethiopians residing in the city of Djibouti. In Quartier 2, Ethiopian restaurant owners were attacked and a number took refuge in the compound of the Ethiopian community.[15] In view of these continuous challenges to French rule, which took the form of street action, Governor Louis Saget (who took up his post shortly after de Gaulle returned to France) took legal action:

> Tonight there have been incidents in the city. When I arrived in this country less than three days ago, I confirmed that the French government had decided to examine as broadly as possible the territory's possibilities for development. I will not accept attempts that aim to smother the voice of the people. The people have the right to live in peace and to determine their future in tranquillity. Today I am making some arrangements so that trust will be reborn in respect for the law and protection ensured by the legitimate authority.[16]

The legal action to which the governor was alluding was the indefinite imposition of strict restrictions on the movement of people. Declared as Order No. 1478 of September 14, 1966, a curfew was put in place from seven o'clock in the evening to five o'clock in the morning across the city of Djibouti.[17] Two days later, the starting time of the curfew was adjusted from seven to eight o'clock.[18] Order 1478 also forbade the assembly of more than five people in public spaces.[19] The public was informed that "the beginning and the end of the curfew will be announced every day by clarion calls."[20]

The immediate effect for Yemenis and other native people residing in the city was an incremental increase in control and the curtailment of movement. Following the establishment of the curfew, an operation to check identity cards was undertaken and neighborhoods were sealed off.[21] On September 15, neighborhoods known for their anti-French sentiment were cordoned off and residents were required to show their identity cards. In this operation, some 5,500 people were stopped and, eventually, 331 people were expelled from Djibouti.[22]

This situation would not have been particularly memorable but for the consequences of the action. Indeed, such measures might have been regarded as just some among many of the increased controls on people if they had not triggered a whole series of further controls that resulted in considerable curtailment of movement and the deaths of many native people.

Following the imposition of the curfew, the French colonial administration was not only intent on blocking access to certain neighborhoods in order to check identity cards, it also decided to seal off the city of Djibouti from the neighboring rural areas using barbed-wire fences. Following the establishment of the curfew, *Le Réveil de Djibouti*, the colony's main newspaper, noted that the area commandant informed people that starting from September 14, 1966, "until a new order comes into place, a barrage will be placed around the city of Djibouti to forbid the entrance of foreigners who have played a key role in the disorder."[23] The 14.5 kilometers of wire erected were used for the strict control of the coming and going of people. Only those with the required papers issued by the French colonial government were allowed access and the French military was apt to fire on those who did not respect the system of control.

At the time, the confinement of the native people in the area was highly controversial. Periodicals in the metropolis reported negatively on the morality of the practice and its deadly consequences. Despite this, the French authorities were unwilling to concede the point and in fact gave a statement justifying these inhumane control. French president Georges

Pompidou visited Djibouti in 1973, and events surrounding his visit illustrate the French government's position on the matter.[24] Coming five years after de Gaulle's visit, which started the protests in the first place, Pompidou in a press interview reflected on the events:

> I read somewhere that I was going to a kind of "concentration camp" in Djibouti, although it's the opposite for this barricade. It's not about preventing people from leaving, it's about channelling entry. It's precisely the proof that this territory holds a sort of allure for its neighbors—something of which we have reason to be proud—that is a major disadvantage when it translates into an uncontrolled inflow and creates problems, particularly employment problems.[25]

Pompidou omits any mention of the general suffering the fence caused. His comments also obscure what was actually happening inside the barrier, where daily life was far from peaceful. On a 'normal' day the population was under surveillance by armed French soldiers, while on an 'extraordinary' day the people of Djibouti saw the use of curfews and identification card checks. The fence surrounded a space that contained multiple regulations enforced on the population, alongside the regular imposition of curfews.

Indeed, the suspension of the right of movement became the norm in the camp created by the encirclement of Djibouti. This curtailment of movement was exemplified in the 1967 referendum that was conducted to determine, as per de Gaulle's promise, the opinion of the public regarding the status of the territory. People were given the choice to vote 'yes' or 'no' on a single question: "Do you want the territory to remain part of the French Republic with the renewed statute of government and administration?"[26] In this framework, the first action the French government took before the election was to annul the right to assemble and the right of participation. The public was reminded that assemblies in public spaces were banned following suspension of the law of June 30, 1881, which had given people the right to assemble.[27] The French authorities, under Order No. 473/AAE, issued on March 16, 1967, ordered the closure of bars and tea houses from ten o'clock at night on March 18, 1967, to eight o'clock on the morning of March 20, 1967.[28]

The election took place on March 19. The majority of the population, officially 60 percent of voters, opted for a continuation of French rule.[29] Despite this, violence and anti-France demonstrations were staged during the election and over the days that followed. In this regard, there were skirmishes on Avenue 13 between the colonial government forces and demonstrators, who were mainly 'Issa Somalis. Similar events took place on Rue des Issa. As in 1966, the French reaction was immediate and involved widespread actions to control people in volatile areas.[30]

Revolutionized Hinterland Spaces: Socialism, the Red Terror, and Mobility

In Ethiopia the downfall of Emperor Haile Selassie and the introduction of the Derg regime triggered a new dynamic that linked Djibouti with Yemenis in Ethiopia when it came to the issue of movement. Djibouti was connected with Ethiopia by the movement of people, even when the latter country was in turmoil. In fact, the French barricade of Djibouti was a response to the threat coming from both Ethiopia and Somalia. Since the 1960s, both countries had made a claim to Djibouti. As part of this claim, the Ethiopian and Somali regimes tried to infiltrate Djibouti with people who would support their respective causes.[31] On some occasions the Ethiopian government even provided Djibouti identification cards to people from the neighboring Wällo region.[32]

In the process of boosting the Djibouti population, Yemenis were not picked up by the Ethiopian state and hence did not become part of the state-driven project of exporting people. Nevertheless, they became part of an involuntary migration pattern because of the turmoil inside Ethiopia shortly after Djibouti's independence. This period was known as the Red Terror, begun by the Derg in 1977. A year after Djibouti's independence was declared, in response to a series of attacks and killings carried out by the opposition Ethiopian People's Revolutionary Party, the Derg began a campaign of repression and extermination of its opponents.[33]

The Red Terror saw the torture, execution, and mass burial of thousands of people. Yemenis were caught up in these events and many were killed. This happened not only because they were living in Ethiopia but also because young people in particular became involved in politics. Although the Derg regime was inclined to criticize Haile Selassie's rule, it surpassed the 'crimes' of the imperial era during its totalitarian rule. The central committee of the new government, which was first led by Teferi Benti and later by Colonel Mengistu Haile Mariam, started to take total control of the country. Media controlled by the regime spread propaganda and an extensive network of surveillance was organized to stamp out any opposition. This surveillance and the general controls that the regime put in place restricted the movement of people in and out of the country. According to official policy, these restrictions were in part because the state needed its people to remain in their country to accomplish the dream of Ethiopian socialism.

As part of the new controls, the government restricted the issuance of passports to Ethiopian nationals. As a diaspora community, Yemenis had a link with their homeland but when it came to documents they were Ethiopian nationals who were under the regime's rule. In these circumstances, Yemenis who happened to be Ethiopians on paper had to obtain new forms of identification to prove that they were of Yemeni origin. As soon as the Red Terror began, there was an urgent need for local Yemenis to drop their Ethiopian identification cards and acquire Yemeni passports. This required Yemenis to go the Käbäles, the local administrative units organized by the Derg, with three witnesses who could testify that the applicant was of Yemeni origin. Once this process was over, they had to go to a Yemeni community leader for further bureaucratic approvals, which consisted of filling in forms to prove that the person was a true Yemeni. Once this was finalized, the paperwork was sent to the embassy for approval.

Of course, the process of getting a Yemeni passport was not as straightforward as it may sound here. Many Yemenis did not have the money needed to go through the process. Paying the airfare was a challenge for many, though some still found ways to complete the bureaucratic procedure. Despite having the necessary money, others were unable to get the required papers from the Käbäles because they did not have tax clearance from Inland Revenue.

Djibouti became an important exit point for Yemenis, especially the young, who urgently needed to leave Ethiopia. As it was relatively calm at that time, Djibouti was considered a safe haven. From there, Yemenis could travel on to Yemen. But getting to Djibouti was not easy. Apart from restricting passports, the military junta also deployed border surveillance units whose task was to prevent people from leaving Ethiopia. Because of this, Yemenis, as well as Ethiopians, had to resort to smugglers, who were often local people with a good knowledge of the area. Most Yemenis reached Djibouti through this process, but a considerable number of Yemenis and other Ethiopians died in the 'Afar desert after being abandoned by smugglers. If an overland route was impossible, there was the option of going by air. But leaving by plane involved a difficult bureaucratic process.

This situation continued into the 1980s. Yemenis took whatever steps they could to leave Ethiopia rather than remain in a nation that had turned into a prison. Djibouti continued to be viewed as a sort of free zone to which people could migrate. For the Yemenis who fled Ethiopia in the 1970s and 1980s, Djibouti was not the ultimate destination. It served as a transit point for an onward journey to Saudi Arabia and other Gulf states. By the 1970s places such as Saudi Arabia and Qatar had strong economies that needed laborers. Previously important ports on the Arabian coast, such as Aden, were replaced by Jeddah and Dubai. These ports became the new destination points for Yemenis who wanted to leave the unstable countries of the Horn of Africa. There they engaged in trade, some becoming quite rich. Others who were less fortunate became laborers.

The homeland of the Yemenis, which was then divided into the Yemen Arab Republic in the north and the People's Democratic Republic of Yemen in the south, was also a destination for Yemenis escaping the troubled Horn. Because southern Yemen was socialist, like the regime in Ethiopia, many chose to go to northern Yemen. Their attempts to travel to the north were greatly assisted by the government of Ibrahim al-Hamdi. Hamdi was a lieutenant colonel in the Yemen army who came to power in 1974 after overthrowing President Abdul Rahman al-Iryani, who formed a government in 1967 at the end of the Yemeni civil war. The war had begun after a coup d'état against Imam Muhammad al-Badr in 1962.[34]

Hamdi wanted Yemenis in the diaspora to come home. As part of this policy his government involved itself in the lives of Yemenis living in the Horn of Africa, particularly after the Red Terror began in Ethiopia. His government organized free passage to Yemen and thousands of Yemenis were able to return to Yemen. Because Hamdi was president of northern Yemen and not the south, however, many southerners were not officially allowed to be part of the rescue mission. Some bribed local officials and acquired false identity cards to get around this barrier.

The Yemeni experience with the space of northern Yemen was complicated. During the time of Hamdi's rule, Yemenis from the Horn of Africa were encouraged to return and reintegrate. The assassination of Hamdi in 1978 changed everything. Hamdi was replaced by Ahmad bin Hussein al-Ghashmi, who was also soon killed. After the murders of Hamdi and his successor, many of the returning Yemenis were viewed as foreigners who had no place in Yemeni society. This hostility was based on racial ideas, that the returnees were somehow not fully Yemeni, but also were due to the period's uncertain political climate.

Royalists considered Yemenis from the Horn of Africa to be pro-republican and saw them as a threat. Yemenis from the Horn of Africa well remembered the identity cards they were forced to carry in 1970s. Unlike all other Yemeni identification cards, those of returnees identified them not as Yemenis but as Ethiopian (Habesha). The place of their birth was written in red so that even an illiterate official or soldier could identify their foreign origin. This was done only to Yemenis from the diaspora.

Saudi Arabia, other Gulf states, and Yemen were not the only destinations for Yemenis in the 1970s and 1980s, however. During this period Yemenis began to travel farther afield, migrating in large numbers to Western Europe, North America, and Australia.[35] One famous example is Abdurahman Al-amoudi, who was born in Ethiopia in the province of Eritrea in 1952 and emigrated to the United States in 1979, becoming an American citizen on May 23, 1996.

Al-amoudi founded the American Muslim Council, which became an important lobby group for Muslims in the United States. For a number of years he selected Muslim chaplains for the United States Army and acted as an advisor to the Pentagon. He was also an advisor to President

Bill Clinton on matters relating to Islam. In 2004, however, he was given a twenty-three-year prison term for his involvement in a Libyan-backed plot to assassinate the Saudi crown prince, Abdullah bin Abdulaziz. Libyan president Muammar Gaddafi was said to have wanted to kill the crown prince after he openly clashed with Gaddafi at an Arab League summit. Al-amoudi was said to have received hundreds of thousands of dollars from Libya, and receipt of the money was an illegal financial transaction as Libya was under US-imposed sanctions.[36]

Neoliberal Space: Mobility in the Post-Cold War Era

The 1990s saw the collapse of socialism, the break-up of the Soviet Union, and the fall of the Berlin Wall. In the Horn of Africa, this led to changes in the way the movement of people was controlled. While Djibouti was not significantly affected, Ethiopia's Derg was overthrown in 1991 by a guerrilla movement, the Ethiopian People's Revolutionary Democratic Front (EPRDF). In the same year, after decades of war, Eritrea's guerrilla army celebrated the country's separation from Ethiopia. In Somalia, where the regime had long been in conflict with both Ethiopia and Djibouti, the government collapsed. This was followed by a fragmentation of the country and the onset of a civil war waged by disparate forces connected to Somalia's many clans and lineages.

With instability spreading throughout the region, the international community launched interventions, both humanitarian and military. The United States became a key actor, sending troops into Somalia in 1992. This intervention, presented as a humanitarian mission, was suspended in 1994 after Somali rebels shot down an American military helicopter, killing all aboard. Film footage showed the rebels dragging the corpses of the dead down the streets of Mogadishu.[37] Following the United States' withdrawal, and despite numerous initiatives, Somalia continued to be immersed in civil war. Over time, however, the civil war took on an international dimension because of the involvement of foreign Islamist military elements.[38] As early as 1991, an Islamist group called Ittihad al-Islamiya, started to operate in Somalia and in the ethnically Somali region of Ethiopia.[39] Following the 9/11 attacks, Somalia was subjected to unprecedented levels of interference, as well as the strengthening of military organizations that followed an Islamist ideology. In 2006, the various Islamist factions in Somalia came under one umbrella to form what has come to be known as the Islamic Court, also known as Ittihad al-Mahakim al-Islamiya.[40] This group then took over Somalia until an Ethiopian military intervention in 2006 drove it out of the main Somali cities. Its ousting, however, did not bring a solution to Somalia. Although a transitional federal government was instituted, the Islamic Court was replaced by al-Shabab (Harakat al-Shabaab al-Mujahidin), which briefly linked itself to al-Qaeda in 2012 (see Hansen, 2013). As the Islamic Court, al-Shabab continued to fight the established government as well as the African Union peacekeepers deployed in the country following Ethiopia's withdrawal in 2009 (see Williams, 2014).

Although these events began with Somalia, the involvement of the West, particularly the United States, has not been confined to Somalia. In 2006 the United States Department of Defense created the United States Africa Command (AFRICOM), which has responsibility for dealing directly with African countries on matters of national security.[41] In a further response to 9/11, the United States created the Combined Joint Task Force–Horn of Africa (CJTF-HOA), which has responsibility for fighting terrorism by boosting the capability of nations in the region without engaging in direct action.[42] Following an agreement with the government of Djibouti, the United States was allowed to establish a base at a former French military camp, Camp Lemonnier (Davis and Othieno, 2007). The camp also serves as the base for CJTF-HOA, which operates under the general umbrella of AFRICOM. The neighboring countries of Ethiopia and Yemen are active partners in the anti-terrorist framework established by the United States. Both Yemeni and Ethiopian forces have been given military aid and training by the United States in order to secure the region more effectively (West, 2005: 11–14, 26–29).

These developments triggered the emergence of a new dynamic in the control of the movement of people. In Ethiopia, the overthrow of the Derg regime by the EPRDF resulted in the deregulation of passports and other travel documents. In addition, a new constitution affirmed people's right to move about freely. Yemenis who left Ethiopia in the 1970s, for places such as Djibouti, returned and established various trades.

Despite this liberalization of movement by Ethiopia and the boosting of the Yemeni population at the regional level, there was considerable tightening of security. One of the major factors in this was the stance of western powers regarding the movement of people in the region and across the Gulf of Aden to places such as Yemen. The United States took the position that the informal circulation of people was a security threat both to the region and to its own national security. While the relative deregulation of borders and the free movement of people was encouraged in the West, in the Horn of Africa the United States sought to tighten borders.[43]

This militaristic policy was reinforced by western security analysts. Jessica Piombo has written,

> Porous borders and migrant groups make it extremely difficult to keep track of people and the flows of people and goods across borders, which can facilitate the transport of goods and commodities such as weapons and people (i.e. slaves) that can be traded for revenue. Along the coast of the Horn and into east and central Africa, small trading boat (*dhouw*) traffic is virtually impossible to monitor, adding a maritime dimension to the difficulties in tracking terrorist activities and financial patterns. (2007: 4)

The age-old migration of people from across the Horn of Africa into Arabia has been reduced to a single concern: western policy aimed at combating terrorism. This securitization process was not only carried out by the United States. The European Union was also concerned with blocking people's movement across territories that do not fall within its jurisdiction. In fact, a number of studies, including those of Boswell (2003), Betts (2009), and Balzacq and Carrera (2006), show that the European Union was concerned with a process of externalizing its own borders. No longer content with defining European borders in terms of the physical borders of Europe, the European Union was actively turning other countries and other places into a security border. Migrants deemed to be illegal would be contained before they could reach actual European borders. In this regard, the European Agency for the Management of Operational Cooperation at the External Borders of the Member

States of the European Union (Frontex) acts as the main European body for gathering information and coordinating measures to block the free movement of people who are not wanted in Europe.

Border areas were redefined and movement along the border was viewed as a security threat to the West. Horn of Africa countries, including Yemen, were encouraged and indeed urged to tighten their borders and border-control mechanisms. Djibouti's response to this pressure was to upgrade its border controls and curb the movement of people. In 2003, Djibouti expelled tens of thousands of immigrants suddenly deemed to be a security risk as part of the new 'war on terrorism.' Of those expelled, ten thousand were Yemeni. The *New York Times* presented the Djibouti government's plan in the following manner:

> Djibouti plans to expel more than 100,000 illegal immigrants, or 15 per cent of the population, because they are considered a threat to security, said Ibrahim Muhammad Kamil, Djibouti's ambassador to Ethiopia. In May, a US-led counterterrorism operation moved its headquarters to Djibouti. The mission, covering Somalia, Kenya, Ethiopia, Sudan, Eritrea, Djibouti and Yemen, is meant to prevent militants operating in a region where large territories are beyond the control of central governments. Mr. Kamil said that of the total to be expelled, 60,000 are Ethiopians, 30,000 Somalis, 10,000 Yemenis and 1,000 Eritreans.[44]

In the following years, Djibouti stepped up its control on behalf of the United States and the European Union by introducing machine-readable travel documents (US Department of State, 2010: 18–19). Djibouti also allowed the International Organization of Migration (IOM) to enter the country. Speaking to a gathering of diplomats, including the United States and French ambassadors to Djibouti, IOM Regional Representative for East and Central Africa Ashraf El Nour said that the aim of the IOM was to reinforce the Djibouti border and immigration policies.[45] He explained, "The main activities will include a capacity-building training in migration and border management for senior government officials; conduct a technical border assessment for appropriate policy and operational response, profiling irregular migrants residing in or transiting through Djibouti as well as strengthening existing task force on migration."[46]

In the same vein, Yemen stepped up its security to control the movement of people. Conceptualized as a "chokepoint" critical to the United States strategy in the region (West, 2005: 26), Yemen's coastguard capabilities were bolstered through military aid, which included in the early years the provision of seven United States–manufactured patrol boats (US Department of State, 2004: 70). Yemen was also encouraged to increase its security along the Yemen–Saudi border, as this area was considered to be a corridor for the entry of illegal migrants and potential terrorists.

The Saudi government engaged in a multibillion-dollar project that included the evacuation of entire villages and the stepping up of border security mechanisms. It deployed M1A2 battle tanks, AH-64D Apache Longbow attack helicopters, and LAV-25 armored vehicles at the border with Yemen. The Saudi border security included a physical barrier constructed with sandbags and concrete-filled pipes as well as electronic equipment that can detect the movement of people.[47] Robert Worth described the Saudi–Yemen border: "Earthen berms now prevent cars from crossing, and layers of concertina wire line the road, some of it strewn with the rags and dried blood of desperate migrants who still try to get through."[48]

In addition, the whole Horn region and Yemen saw the bolstering of what has come to be referred to as 'soft power.' Experts recommended that along with 'hard power,' such as stepping up the defense of border areas, countries should extend their soft powers through the building of schools, health facilities, and the judiciary (Rotberg, 2005; West, 2005: 28). In Djibouti, regarded as a strategic zone, the European Commission funded an awareness campaign to educate potential immigrants about the risks of illegal migration by land and sea.[49]

In the Horn of Africa the net effect of the changes was a marked strengthening of the mechanisms of control. On the one hand, the liberalization of travel in post-communist Ethiopia led to an increase in the migration of Yemenis into and out of the country. On the other hand, the securitization of the area in response to perceived terrorist threats led to the closure of borders and curbing of the movement of people.

Some would-be migrants resorted to illegal routes. One of my informants was Getu, an Ethiopian who paid smugglers to travel to Saudi Arabia, passing through Djibouti and Yemen:

I went to Djibouti a year ago. I was in PK 12. I went from here saying that I was a trader. You take out a fake trade license and people in the embassy will stamp 'visa' on your passport. You can also go if you pay a bribe. You know it is the embassy of the Somalis, so there is no problem. I went from Djibouti to Mukha. But traveling in the small boat was very difficult. It is like facing death. The crew will put on a life vest and they are ready. But they overload the boat. If the boat has a capacity for sixty people they will try to go with two hundred people. As a result, while you are sitting in the boat you can touch the water with your finger.

But of all smugglers, the Yemenis are best. With them you are guaranteed that you will reach the coast. But some of them, especially Somalis, are not good. They will throw you into the sea before you reach the coast. They don't care about death. And there is also a rumor that they sometimes deliberately overturn the boat in the middle of the sea because it is profitable for them to go back and get more people. Personally I have not encountered any problem. They took us to the port. And then they drove us to the warehouse. After that, using other people, they took us to the city. In the city you are free. You eat, you drink, you take a shower, but you cannot escape because the people who are in this business have members who are in the army as well as in the police force. They will catch you and give you to the same people. They have even a well-armed band of people. From the city it is an official who will take you further. You don't pay money in cash but you send him the cash through money transfer.

When he gets the money he will either send you a car or he will come and pick you up himself. Using their connections they will take you to the Saudi border. For example, the car that took us was a brand new Land Cruiser. When you go to Saudi you will face problems. There in the countryside there are armed Ethiopians.

Most of them are Oromo who went from the area of Arsi and Harage. These people live in the small villages. They are either herders or they are working in some other capacity.

But, amazingly, they are well armed and fight each other in a foreign land. In some areas, Oromos from Harar are dominant, and in another area Amharas from Wallo are dominant. So they fight each other. So when you pass, if you are in the wrong place, you will be shot at.

For Yemenis unable to move freely in the wider Horn region but determined to escape the restrictions, there have been two significant consequences. First, the current processes have resulted in the growth of illegal activities. As a result of the contacts that they have in Arabia and elsewhere, Yemenis in both the inland territory and in coastal regions such as Djibouti are engaged in people trafficking. This trafficking involves many levels of society: individual Yemenis take part, as do some Yemeni officials who come to Ethiopia.

Their activities, however, have made them the target of anti-terrorist and regional coastguard units. The securitization of the Horn of Africa means that dhow traffic to Yemen is now controlled by naval forces. But since the onset of piracy on the Somali coast, Yemeni boats and small-scale fishermen have been hard hit by misdirected attacks by foreign naval forces. While I was conducting research in Djibouti in 2009, Yemeni fishermen were attacked by a Russian navy vessel. One of the Yemeni fishermen, 'Awad 'Abdallah Ba Magad, said in a newspaper interview, "They used to mistreat us at sea but would set us free without possession. Now they don't just confiscate fishermen's property, they destroy the boats."[50] The newspaper also recounted an earlier incident that occurred one morning in April 2005:

> Ba Magad and others described one incident that occurred on the morning of April 5 about 112 km from the coastal city of Qusay'ir when a helicopter gunship fired on a number of fishing boats. "We stopped fishing and decided to head back home because we were so terrified and thought it would come again," said Ba Magad.

The helicopter returned and signaled for the fishermen to head west toward a warship. The men described the vessel as bearing the number 543 and flying a white flag with a blue cross—the Russian Navy's ensign. As they approached the ship, they saw 19 other fishermen held on board under armed surveillance. The number and flag description indicates that the warship was the Udaloy-class destroyer RFN Marshal Shaposhnikov. The Russian Federation Navy reported on its website in April that the Marshal Shaposhnikov was "escorting a convoy of 4 vessels through uneasy waters of Gulf of Aden and Horn of Africa where pirate assaults are commonplace." On Wednesday, the BBC reported that the destroyer was still in the area, having been dispatched to assist a Russian oil tanker that had been hijacked by pirates 800 km off the Somali coast. Standing by the remains of his fishing boat destroyed by the Russians, Ba Magad said the crew of the destroyer had robbed them. "They rifled through our boats, taking our money, IDs, GPS units and even asked us to remove our clothes," said Ba Magad. The men were all placed on one of the vessels and ordered to return to Yemen. "We waited for a moment hoping that they might bring back our stolen possessions," said Ba Magad. "Instead, they fired behind the boat to force us to leave." The fishermen managed to recover the burnt remains of one of the boats, which have been put on display in the city of Mukalla to bring people's attention to their ordeal. The fishermen claim that they've suffered about YER30 million ($140,000) worth of damage from these searches and seizures. It is not just the Russian Navy. Other Yemeni fishermen have complained about similar incidents involving the Indian Navy. They say the forces deployed to fight piracy in the Arabian Sea and Gulf of Aden are often as dangerous as the pirates themselves.[51]

Attacks on Yemeni fishermen did not only take place at the hands of an international navy; they were also attacked by pirates. In November 2010, eleven Yemeni fishermen were kidnapped by Somali pirates. The pirates threatened to kill them and sell their organs if their families did not pay a ransom. A year before, in June 2009, twenty Yemeni fishermen were captured by Somali pirates and freed following the intervention of a Dutch naval ship.[52]

Regional wars in relatively distant places have also affected Yemeni movement and welfare. In the first Gulf war Yemenis supported the regime of Saddam Hussein while neighboring Saudi Arabia supported the United States military intervention. Some eight hundred thousand Yemenis living in Saudi Arabia as guest workers, many of whom were from Djibouti and Ethiopia, were expelled en masse from the kingdom.[53] Many of the Ethiopian and Djibouti Yemenis preferred to come to Ethiopia rather than Yemen, as they thought that opportunities in Ethiopia were better. In Ethiopia, however, the Yemenis faced considerable problems. Ethiopia forbids the possession of dual nationality. Even though they may have been born and raised in Ethiopia, Yemenis had to pay an annual residence fee, as on paper they were foreigners. Many of those expelled from Saudi Arabia lost everything and were unable to pay the Ethiopian residence fee. Those unable to pay were forced to remain in the country illegally. Some wealthy Yemenis, such as Sheikh Muhammad Hussein al-ʻAmudi, paid the fees for indigent Yemenis.

In 2003 the Ethiopian nationality law was modified. Although many hoped that the revised law would allow dual nationality, the holding of two passports remained illegal. The Ethiopian government feared that such a change would lead to large numbers of people coming into the country from Eritrea and Somalia.[54] Yemenis turned to buying fake Ethiopian identification cards and passports. This was relatively easy to do as many spoke the local language and had relatives of Ethiopian origin. But there were still risks. Many Yemenis were arrested after they were turned in to the police by local people, sometimes because of a personal grievance. Adding to the regional uncertainty, Yemen has been in upheaval for more than a decade. In 2004 a rebellion broke out in the northern governorate of Saʼda when the Shia cleric Hussein Badreddin al-Houthi revolted against central rule. The governorate was for a century the stronghold of the Imamate of Yemen. Since the creation of modern-day Yemen the government has had little or no control over the territory.[55] The revolt quickly turned into a wider regional issue. The government accused Iran of supporting the

Shia-led revolt, while Houthi's rebels accused Saudi Arabia and the United States of supporting the Yemeni government. In October 2004, the rebels entered and occupied part of Saudi territory.[56] The conflict in the province of Sa'da and surrounding areas came to an end in 2010, when a deal was reached between the rebels and the government.

The turmoil in Yemen, however, was just beginning. A year later, inspired by the Tunisian revolution, thousands of Yemenis demonstrated in the capital Sanaa and across the country against the thirty-three-year rule of Ali 'Abd Allah Saleh.[57] Soon Sanaa was a battleground between pro-Saleh forces and a group of former government soldiers who had joined the opposition. Led by Brigadier General Ali Mohsen al-Ahmar, the rebel troops attacked the presidential palace in June 2011, injuring Saleh.[58]

For Yemenis originally from Ethiopia and Djibouti the instability became a major source of anxiety, revealing the complex relationship they continued to have with global and regional powers that controlled space. Some who were visiting relatives or had settled in Yemen were trapped in the escalating conflict. Others, with connections to Djibouti and Ethiopia, quickly left Yemen. Those who were fortunate enough to be on the other side of the Red Sea attempted to rescue their relatives by sending money and helping in any way they could. Unlike Ethiopia, Djibouti allowed Yemenis to live there without a visa, though they did have to pay for a residence permit.

Oddly enough, however, the Horn of Africa that we are here concerned with was not only open to ordinary Yemenis who fled from the conflict, but also to President Saleh. After he was injured, Saleh flew to Saudi Arabia for treatment, delegating his power to Vice President Abd Rabbuh Mansur Hadi. Contrary to rumors spread through social media, the Yemeni ruler survived his injuries and returned to Yemen, despite calls by the opposition for him to resign. The Gulf Cooperation Council later managed to broker a deal.[59] At one point, people believed that Saleh would go into exile in Ethiopia, the only country willing to accept him.[60] In the end, however, Saleh did not flee to Ethiopia but remained in Sanaa. He later opened a museum where some of his personal belongings are on permanent display.

After that, Yemen further destabilized in a more dangerous manner. In January 2015 the situation escalated when the Houthi militias, backed by forces loyal to Saleh (who sought to return to power or to bring in his son, Ahmed Ali Abd Allah Saleh), took over the presidential compound.[61] This intervention, which led to the resignation of President Hadi and a number of ministers,[62] was followed in February 2015 by the Houthi declaration of the Revolutionary Committee that would lead the country.[63] Shortly afterward, Hadi, who was put under house arrest, managed to escape to the port city of Aden.[64] The situation escalated further when the Houthi/Saleh forces tried to assert even more authority by controlling territories south of Sanaa. Houthi/Saleh forces clashed with pro-government forces, who were losing ground rapidly. They brought under their control key strategic places as well as sensitive military sites such as the al-Anda air base, which the United States was using for counterterrorism purposes.[65] They also moved closer and closer to Aden, causing Hadi to flee the country on March 25, 2015.[66] Hours later, Saudi Arabia involved itself in the war by engaging in an air campaign.[67] The United States and members of the Gulf Cooperation Council and the Arab League then engaged in a military operation that involved aerial bombardment of the Houthi/Saleh forces.

The civil war did not just pit Houthi/Saleh forces against supporters of Hadi. It also involved other groups: al-Qaeda in the Arabian Peninsula (AQAP), which established its presence in southern Yemen and expanded its territorial control after the start of the civil war; the southern separatist groups, who are interested in forming a separate state; the Ansar Allah Islamic military organization, which is pro-Houthi/Saleh; and the Islamic State in Iraq and Syria (ISIS), which took the opportunity to establish itself in the area.[68] Yemen also became a proxy battlefield between Saudi Arabia and Iran. Saudi Arabia had long backed Salafi elements, including those present within the Yemeni Muslim Brotherhood movement (the Islah); Iran was giving increasing amounts of diplomatic and material support to the opponents of the Hadi forces.[69]

From the start of the civil war, Yemen became a zone of entrapment for many refugees who, as described earlier, smuggled themselves into Yemen in order to move on to places such as Saudi Arabia. Numbering over 250,000, the migrants, mainly from the Horn of Africa, became unable to extract themselves from the war situation.[70] Some were unwilling to return to Horn of Africa countries, fearing maltreatment because of their past political involvement.[71]

Migrants from the Horn of Africa are not the only ones stuck in Yemen. Yemenis from the diaspora who happened to be present when the war began have also been stranded. Yemenis from the United States, for example, number in the hundreds. They feel not only trapped, but neglected by the United States government, which has followed a policy of not sending rescue missions.[72] The American-Arab Anti-Discrimination Committee (ADC) and the Council on American-Islamic Relations (CAIR) filed a lawsuit against the United States government in April 2015 on their behalf.[73] Naming Secretary of State John Kerry and Secretary of Defense Ashton Carter as defendants, the lawsuit disputed Washington's decision not to send rescue missions the way other nations did, specifically China, Jordan, India, Russia, Pakistan, and Turkey.[74] It asserted that this decision caused harm to American citizens and infringed on their right to be protected by their government.[75] This led the U.S. House of Representatives to adopt an amendment demanding that President Barack Obama rescue American citizens in Yemen as of May 2015.[76] However, no immediate action was taken.

The war in Yemen not only led to the entrapment of refugees, asylum seekers, and members of the Yemeni diaspora; it also converted ordinary Yemeni citizens into refugees. This instigated a reverse movement in which thousands of Yemenis living in Yemen, along with the migrants, refugees, and diaspora members, crossed over to the Horn of Africa in small traditional vessels. Djibouti became the largest recipient of Yemenis fleeing the country under these conditions. According to the International Organization for Migration, Djibouti hosted 8,896 people who arrived from Yemen in April 2015. Neighboring port spaces also saw the arrival of thousands of people: 1,125 in Berbera, 2,285 in Bossasso.[77] The hinterland territories of Ethiopia and Sudan also saw the arrival of a number of complete flights.[78] In Djibouti, temporary transit centers were established at Obock in the north of the country, where the new arrivals were sheltered in sport centers, orphanages, and a migration center used by the International Organization for Migration, as well as in the Markazi camp.[79]

Although the refugees were safe from the immediate effects of the civil war, their plight seemed to have just begin. Many arrived without papers or any of the identification necessary for relocation, particularly for members of the Yemeni diaspora who had returned to Yemen and become caught in the war. In the absence of these vital documents they faced a suspended existence.[80] For other Yemenis, who were not of the diaspora and therefore did not have passports, the prospect was even bleaker: camp life in the harsh environment of Djibouti until the war ended or they were relocated to a third country.

This latest human tragedy emanating from the civil war in Yemen demonstrates yet again how state/empire structures mobility. These recent events show the ways in which the decisions and actions of the state/empire result in the immobilization of an individual or the entrapment of thousands in a particular space. As Indian Ocean studies routinely demonstrate, there is a strong relationship between places such as southern Arabia and the Horn of Africa. This connection, this movement of people back and forth between the Horn of Africa and Yemen, has not been simply a matter of individual decisions and networking abilities. We cannot speak about the regional mobility of people without looking at issues of power. A number of studies have attempted to acknowledge these issues of power, but often in an abstract way, without closely examining state and imperial power. This failure to examine power dynamics obscures or ignores how the Yemeni diaspora has for centuries adapted to the power of empires and states, an act that is required by all subjects of empires and citizens of states.

Part II:
The Shaping of Yemenis' Opportunities

4. Entrepreneurs, Laborers, and Smugglers: Yemenis in the Economy of States/Empires

On July 16, 1971, near death and far from his homeland, Muhammad Yusuf Ba Naji asked his fellow Muslims to record and witness his last will and testament, which took place at one of his homes in Addis Ababa. Ba Naji's will requested that his countrymen wash and treat his dead body according to the Islamic faith. He also asked them to carry out charitable deeds for the poor.

> When the inevitable judgment of Allah has been passed on me and when the age that is given to me is finished I wish to be turned toward Mecca. I wish my eyes to be closed and my arms and legs to be moved back and forth so that they will be flexible. I wish to be covered in an appropriate cloth. I also wish that my death will be told to my family and my neighbors. Upon my death I wish my body to be washed according to the Islamic faith. Following, I wish to be covered in three large white cloths. I wish that people perform prayers upon me. When all this is terminated I wish to be buried in the Islamic cemetery. In addition, I, Muhammad Yusuf Ba Naji, have the following will. When my dead body comes out from my home I wish that people will distribute three quintals of wheat to the poor. I wish that people will recite the Qur'an for three days.

I wish that the gravediggers will be paid the necessary amount of money. For the above tasks I ask people to spend 4,000 Ethiopian birrs in Addis Ababa. I also wish that people will spend the same amount of money in the country of Wadi Du'an in the village called Rashid so that the same kind of activity will be undertaken.[1]

Beyond these requests, Muhammad Yusuf Ba Naji's will specified that his property in the Horn of Africa and Hadramawt should be divided up. He asked his countrymen to ensure that the palm tree land and other properties bought from Sa'id Ba Harun be donated to Ba Harun's family and divided among his poorer countrymen. Furthermore, he instructed them to distribute what was gained from the sale of the agricultural land to his children and his relatives, and among the poor of Rashid. He asked that the land he inherited from his father, along with his brother's and mother's land, which was under his control, be transferred to the mosque his father had built in Rashid village. He indicated how his property should be divided among his two wives in Ethiopia and his third wife in Hadramawt, and specified the amount of money to be given to each of his children. In total, Ba Naji distributed over forty houses, as well as large tracts of land.

I came to learn about Muhammad Yusuf Ba Naji's will in April 2006. His son Salah Ba Naji was reading it when I came to visit him for an interview. For Salah, his father's will, beyond being an important legal document, was a reminder of his father's love and care and of his sense of moral duty. For me, never having met Muhammad Ba Naji, his three-page will, written in the 1970s, was a document that signified the passing of the first generation of Yemenis who came to the Horn of Africa.

This document also signified a shift in the political climate. Muhammad Ba Naji lived in the first part of the twentieth century, when the British occupied Aden, the French controlled Djibouti, and Ethiopia expanded southward. As we will see later in this book, his death occurred during the process of decolonization in Djibouti and the establishment of communist rule in Ethiopia and South Yemen.

If one follows the story of what happened to Muhammad Ba Naji's property that was divided among the family, the document also shows the relationship that some Yemenis had with the state. Arriving as an ordinary

Yemeni migrant, Ba Naji was initially hired by a French company called Besse, and received assistance from one of the wealthiest Yemeni families in the region. Starting out in this small way, he was eventually able to establish a tannery and distribute his products to a number of foreign companies in Addis Ababa. The wealth he acquired made him an important public figure and brought him close to the Ethiopian royal family. As a wealthy man, Ba Naji was considered to be a notable Arab and was often invited to the palace. This imperial connection helped him to consolidate his wealth. Shortly after he died, however, Ba Naji's property in his home country and in the Horn of Africa was nationalized by the state, which had begun to follow socialist policies. What Salah Ba Naji was holding in 2006 was a document that bore witness to a wealth that had passed into other hands.

This chapter explores the changing economic relationship between Yemenis and state/empire in the region. It explores how the economic activity of the first generation of Yemenis, exemplified by Muhammad Ba Naji, was structured and came to be affected by the establishment of colonial rule in the region, and how this changed over a period of time.

In doing so, this chapter, building on the previous one, assumes that empires/states create enclosures and structure spaces primarily for economic reasons. In the seminal *De l'état: Le mode de production étatique*, the Marxist philosopher Henri Lefebvre (1977) explains how the enclosure of space by sovereign states actually relates to the need of capital to create a smooth ground for its operation. It is only through an effective enclosure that controls space that undesirable categories of people, who might interrupt the economic exploitation of the enclosed spaces, can be regulated. Lefebvre is not alone in making this assertion. David Harvey (2001; 2010), Michael Hardt and Antonio Negri (2000), Giovanni Arrighi (1994; 2007), and, more explicitly, Ellen Meiksins Wood (2003) have shown the intricate relationship between the organization of state and capital. By enclosing space and regulating the movement of people, states/empires present a disciplined workforce for capital to use.

In the previous chapter, we saw how state/empire enclosed and controlled spaces in the Indian Ocean region. I now look at how Yemenis such as Ba Naji were affected and adapted themselves to a situation where state/empire attempted to create a smooth operational ground for capital.

Economic Adaptation in the 'New Economy': Yemenis and European Capital

Immediately before the arrival of the French and the establishment of the colony of Djibouti, Yemenis were active traders in the region. In fact, they were the prime movers of the economy of the western Indian Ocean. Their dominance and importance was aided by the beinning of steamship transport in 1830 and the opening of the Suez Canal in 1869. Yemeni traders dominated the coastal area of Yemen, such as the Tihama. By 1858 a number of Hadrami merchants had established themselves in the port spaces along the coast of the Horn of Africa, including Massawa, Berbera, and Zayla' (Ewald and Clarence-Smith, 1997: 283–89). Yemenis were greatly involved in transporting goods from Arabia to Africa and vice versa. These goods ranged from slaves to spices.[2]

For the first few years following the establishment of colonial-based capital in the late nineteenth century, the economic niche in which Yemenis were able to operate shrank considerably. Traditional vessels had faced little competition from European capital up until this point. Following the establishment of the French colony, however, owners of Yemeni dhows found themselves crowded out of the market by maritime companies that had access to far more capital. By the end of the 1920s the port of Djibouti was served by French-based navigation companies such as Messageries Maritimes, Compagnie Maritime de l'Afrique Orientale, Compagnie des Chargeurs Réunis, and Compagnie Havraise Péninsulaire, as well as by companies from other European countries, including Compagnia Italiana Transatlantica, which ran a service from the Italian port of Genoa to Zanzibar via Djibouti.[3] In addition, foreign companies, especially British-backed Indian companies, became important in the transportation sector. One was the Cowasjee company, which transported goods on small vessels that carried between 200 and 700 tons from Aden, Djibouti, Zayla', and sometimes Berbera.[4] The Italian company Maritima Italiana also ran small vessels among Suez, Port Sudan, Jeddah, Massawa, Djibouti, and Aden.[5]

The most significant challenge came from Compagnie Maritime de l'Afrique Orientale, about which Yemenis complained. The main reason was that such companies took business from small traditional vessels, which were used for offloading goods from the bigger vessels. Despite their dwindling market share, the small vessels were still used for this purpose, but the Compagnie Maritime de l'Afrique Orientale provided a more efficient, mechanized service using the latest machinery, such as trucks. It also provided manpower for offloading goods and charged 15 francs per ton for its services.[6] This service devastated the Yemeni small boat owners' business. They complained of their loss of trade in a lengthy letter to the Chamber of Commerce:

> We are citizens of Djibouti and our only trade is as sailors. We have thirty-six dhows, with which we almost founded the city of Djibouti by transporting rocks for the construction of its houses.
>
> The formation of the new company Compagnie Maritime de l'Afrique Orientale for the loading and unloading of merchandise has quite simply ruined our business entirely. We now have no work, we suffer the poverty of an expensive life, our wives and our children have no bread to eat, and our dhows lie idle on the seashore.
>
> Sir, we are convinced that you are just, we love the clemency of France toward its protectorates and toward the whole world; yes, we are glad of the French occupation of our country; yes, France has civilized us, she has educated us, and she enables us to live. We will never forget our gratitude, and a large number of us served on the French front and spilled their blood for France.
>
> We therefore throw ourselves on your mercy, Sir, to ask you to take action in our case. The dissolution of the Compagnie Maritime de l'Afrique Orientale is the only solution for our livelihood, and we believe that the Compagnie de l'Afrique Orientale is sufficiently strong and rich to be content with its navigation and to leave to us, poor and wretched, the work of loading and unloading merchandise so that we have the work on which our livelihood depends.
>
> We would also ask you to carry out the necessary procedures with the Customs Authority in order to exempt us, if this is possible, from the tax we owe the Authority for our dhows. This is because since the formation of the Compagnie Maritime de l'Afrique Orientale not only has our work come to an end but, believe us, Sir, we also do not even have the means on which to live.

In addition, our dhows, which we have had for thirty years, were made specifically for loading and unloading merchandise and cannot carry out long journeys to other colonies. They can barely travel as far as Celma Harbor.

We proffer you our thanks in advance and hope that our request will have a favorable outcome. Please accept, Sir, our most respectful greetings.[7]

The diminished economic niche in which Yemenis were able to operate in port spaces can also be seen if we look at the share of tonnage transported by larger ships backed by European capital, compared to that carried by the local small boats. In 1929, for example, the port of Djibouti was visited by 476 vessels with a capacity to transport 1,668,502 tons of goods.[8] These vessels loaded and offloaded 102,537 tons of merchandise valued at 822 million francs. In the same year, the traditional vessels made 2,755 port entries. Nevertheless, they were able to carry only 951 tons of goods, which were valued at 18 million francs.[9]

Yemenis faced similar problems in the interior. Before the emergence of colonial capital Yemenis worked as traders in port spaces, which in turn led to the emergence of markets along the coastal region, one of which was the region of Djibouti considered here. European capital was injected into these existing markets, leading to stiff competition that resulted in a decline in Arab regional trade.

This decline, and the competition from European-based capital, can be seen if we compare the number of Arab traders with companies operating with European-backed capital. In the early 1920s, there were twenty-six major companies operating in Djibouti.[10] Of these, only seven were owned by Yemenis. The majority were French- and British-owned, or British-backed Indian companies. There were also a number of Armenian and Greek enterprises. The same kind of change was taking place in the interior. The bulletin prepared for the 1931 Colonial Exhibition held in Paris lists 103 companies in operation in that region. Of these major companies, only nine were Arab-owned; the rest were French or Indo-British.[11]

In both Djibouti and Ethiopia there were more non-Arab companies than there were companies owned by Arabs. However, it was not the numerical superiority of non-Arab companies that was impressive but the monopoly they were able to exercise over the economy. For example, the French company controlled by Antonin Besse was involved in 75 percent of the trade that took place in the interior region.[12] The other major French company, Compagnie du Chemin de Fer Franco-Éthiopien, completely took over the traditional caravan transportation system in which Yemenis had been heavily involved.

Yemeni involvement in the economy dwindled not only because of competition but also as a result of the outlawing of a number of traditional trade activities, particularly slavery and the arms trade. In Djibouti and Ethiopia the sale of slaves was an important part of the local economy. Yemenis took slaves from the interior and transported them to places such as Yemen. Oral histories collected from Ethiopia and Djibouti attest to Yemeni involvement in the slave trade. Monfreid (2002) describes Salim Muti, one of the most notorious slave traders of the period. He dedicates two chapters to the activities of Muti and provides a vivid account of how men working for Muti deliberately drowned a number of Oromo slaves being transported on one of his boats. The British Foreign Office's records on slavery also offer important narratives describing Yemeni involvement in the trade. One such narrative relates to the selling of a young boy by the Ba Zar'a family in Addis Ababa. In a report entitled "An Addendum to Cases of Slavery Previously Reported in Hadramawt" we learn that Nassibu Mubarek was sold from Addis Ababa at the age of two by the Ba Zar'a family to another Yemeni family by the name of Ba Surra, with which he remained until he was freed by his owner.[13]

Another case is the sale of slaves by Sultan Sa'id, from the region of Aden, to the sultan of Lahaj. The men who were sold were working in Dire Dawa in 1906. One among them was named as Demise Khatimir, who came from the region of Togulet in Ethiopia. Sultan Sa'id lured the men into slavery with the promise of a job with the sultan of Lahaj. He told them that British officials in Zayla' had instructed him to recruit soldiers to be paid a salary of 20 dollars a month. In the report that details their case we learn that the promise given by Sultan Sa'id was false and that these individuals had to endure bondage before managing to escape.[14]

The sale of slaves by Yemenis effectively came to an end with the establishment of European colonies. Rather than slave labor, or men held in bondage, the new enterprises needed free labor that was linked to market conditions and, hence, could fluctuate in terms of supply and cost according to the need of capital. The colonial powers sought to suppress and eradicate slavery in the region, although the French were repeatedly accused of not enforcing the agreement because the arid Djibouti terrain did not make it valuable for plantation agriculture like the French-controlled Madagascar, making the territory valueless to France. According to an American diplomat in the region at the time, France would not have minded "if the whole native population were suddenly removed."[15] Ethiopia, the main source of slaves, also came under pressure from the international community to end domestic slavery and to better control the slave trade that was organized from the coast (Miers, 1997: 267–69). This pressure increased after Ethiopia applied to join the League of Nations in the 1920s, leading to a decree to free the country's enslaved people (Allain, 2006; Miers, 1997: 267–69). The suppression of slavery through various agreements and international pressure was considered so successful that by 1936 Harold Ingrams stated that "the importation of fresh slaves in the [Hadramawt] protectorate are probably of utmost rarity."[16] Nevertheless, slavery continued and Yemenis based in Ethiopia still managed to own slaves during the period.[17]

Yemeni arms trafficking was also dealt a blow when the colonial powers imposed restrictions on the trade in arms.[18] The colonial authority saw the movement of arms by Yemenis as a major threat to the territory's stability. The uncontrolled sale of weapons allowed the arming of Abyssinian brigands as well as slave traders.[19] Ethnic groups acquired arms and ammunition from the Yemeni traders, posing a further challenge to colonial efforts to control the region's people.[20] On December 13, 1906, France, Britain, and Italy agreed to regulate the sale of arms, particularly to Ethiopia.[21] This new attempt to regulate arms resulted in the outlawing of Yemeni arms traders and the dhows that had been used to transport weapons. The agreement, signed in London, placed significant emphasis on controlling the use of dhows, now regarded as illegal.[22] Native dhows were to be identified and searched to prevent the smuggling of arms. To enable this, dhows were required to sail under French, British, or Italian flags.[23] In order to prevent any wrongful use of national flags, the colonial powers were required to communicate annually to each other the list of dhows authorized to fly the respective flags.[24]

Economic Competition

In the context of Djibouti and its hinterland, the emergence of colonial capital and the consequent banning of slave labor gave way to paid labor. The access this paid labor had to capital and the spaces controlled by capital was, however, markedly different. Some free laborers in Djibouti were more valued than others. This selection of certain types of labor by capital generated a problem that is outlined below.

In the early days of the colonial economy the French preferred Yemeni workers and recruited them to come to the region. This preferential treatment presented a positive environment for Yemenis engaged in labor recruitment, a sector they came to dominate. Yemeni dominance in this area was further strengthened by the absence of Somali and 'Afar laborers in the newly established cities, who, in the early days, did not migrate to urban areas (Killion, 1985: 204–206).

This pattern of Yemeni dominance began to change as the colony developed. The growth of the colonial economy and increased urban migration of 'Afar and Somali men presented a challenge to Yemenis, especially as the trend accelerated after the First World War. In the interwar period, Djibouti saw the migration of many ethnic Somalis, particularly from Ethiopia and British Somaliland, who wished to be involved in the kinds of jobs controlled by Yemenis. Naturally enough, the growing number of Somali laborers in the port areas was not welcomed by Arab laborers. Arab labor recruiters preferred to employ their kinsmen, and French companies also insisted on employing Arabs rather than Somalis or 'Afar, as they considered them to be more disciplined and hard working. Somalis and 'Afar were effectively blocked from obtaining employment in the port of Djibouti and onboard ships operated by French companies such as Messageries Maritimes (Killion, 1985: 204–10).

The lack of employment opportunities for other ethnic groups drew attention to the Arab monopoly. In early 1902, Somalis organized a system of mutual assistance based on an institution known as Mutuelle des Somalis; in 1934, a new association was formed, Société de Bienfaisance Somalie; and in 1936, Somali workers established the Syndicat des Gens de Mer de Djibouti (Killion, 1985: 211–24). Despite retaining their dominant position, Yemenis also started to formally organize themselves. In August 1938, Yemenis founded the Arab Club, Club de la Jeunesse Arabe, and the Association de Bienfaisance Musulmane, which initially included ethnic Somalis. In 1938, Yemenis in Djibouti established an association for seamen, the Syndicat des Navigateurs Arabes (Killion, 1985: 211–24).

With the help of these organizations, Yemenis and Somalis competed for access to the job market in the port of Djibouti. This competition involved both peaceful actions and more aggressive engagements that created unrest and uncertainty. Somalis tried to infiltrate the economic arena dominated by Arabs by putting pressure on both local colonial officials and the French government in the metropolis. Somalis filed a number of complaints and lobbied for a fairer distribution of jobs. The French government, hoping to maintain a stable workforce in the colony, supported the Somali demands. It initially tried to regulate the identification system that allowed laborers to apply for work in the colonial economy (Killion, 1985: 213).

To be recruited as a laborer or seaman, a worker needed to be a French subject with a passport testifying to this status. Yemenis were in control of the labor market and manipulated the system in favor of their countrymen. They issued passports not only to Yemenis who were French subjects but also to those who were not, creating grievances within the Somali community. Somalis argued that jobs should be distributed only to French subjects and not foreigners who did not belong to the colony.

The French government was keen to maintain order and sought to resolve the dispute between Yemenis and Somalis by putting pressure on the French maritime companies that were only willing to employ Yemeni Arabs. On May 9, 1931, the government issued a decree regarding labor recruitment and immigration, which made it possible for the authorities to force French maritime companies to include Somali workers in their crews and employ inspectors to oversee the new legislation (Killion, 1985: 213).

Despite the new decree, the government encountered difficulties in implementing a more balanced representation of ethnic groups in maritime companies, which continued to resist employing Somali workers. Meanwhile, using all means available to them, Yemenis continued to provide falsified identification cards. These actions, coupled with growing pressure from Somalis, led the situation to a breaking point in 1935. In April of that year, Somalis, through their organizations, demanded that the French government secure work for seven Somalis aboard Messageries Maritimes vessels. When the company agreed to employ only three of them, around five hundred dockworkers staged a demonstration in the city center, leading to a riot that resulted in the imprisonment of eighteen Somalis (Killion, 1985: 214).

The clash can be seen as the beginning of the end of the Arab monopoly of labor and the labor recruitment system. Following the riot, Messageries Maritimes officials were forced to man two of their ships exclusively with Somali seamen, creating a temporary victory for the Somalis (Killion, 1985: 215). Compared to the number of Yemenis involved in the recruitment system, however, Somalis continued to be underrepresented. To remedy this situation, Somalis made further demands and agitated for change. In 1937 the colonial government promised to allocate more ships on which Somalis could work. The promise went unfulfilled, and in April 1937 Messageries Maritimes categorically refused to hire Somalis, which led to further conflict (Killion, 1985: 221–22). On May 1, a heavily armed Somali mob attacked the Arab community of Djibouti, and eight Yemenis were injured.[25]

The conflict that developed in 1937 was only partly resolved the following year through government interventions. After a series of failed attempts, the government brought together leaders from both sides to sign a reconciliation agreement on March 16, 1938 (Killion, 1985: 224). The agreement stipulated the allocation of equal quotas for Yemenis and Somalis. Around this time Yemenis also made a move to join the *Syndicat des Gens de Mer*, which, as mentioned above, had been an all-Somali organization.

The overall situation that emerged as a result of the operation of capital did not lead only to conflict. The preferential treatment also led to the emergence of a class of Yemeni merchants who were not only wealthy but also very close to the colonial administration in Djibouti and to the emperors and royal families in Ethiopia. The Yemeni merchant class was economically positioned above the natives, as well as above fellow Yemenis who had not enjoyed economic success. Among them, however, there were also differences in degrees of wealth and power. Some were more connected to the power holders than others. There was also a particular sort of Yemeni who somehow became important not just in one country but in both Ethiopia and Djibouti and across the region. This is, for example, the case of the Ba Zar'a family and Sheikh Ahmad Salih al-Zahiri.

The first Sheikh Sa'id Ba Zar'a was well known in Djibouti, Ethiopia, and Yemen and had business in Eritrea, Mombasa, and Bombay. In Ethiopia he had good relations with Emperor Menelik and later with Haile Selassie. He also developed a strong relationship with Jimma aba Jiffar, the ruler of Jimma, which was a major commercial trading town.[26] In Djibouti, Sa'id Ba Zar'a was a key figure whose name is found in almost every document signed by Arabs in regard to protests or community affairs. In one report, Alphonse Lippmann, the one-time president of the native court of Djibouti, identified Sa'id Ba Zar'a as a Yemeni merchant who was close to the colonial authorities and who manipulated the political system of colonial Djibouti to his own advantage.[27]

Sheikh Sa'id Ba Zar'a's brother, Sheikh Salim Ba Zar'a, was also well connected. At the time, Sheikh Salim Ba Zar'a worked as a financial manager for Emperor Haile Selassie. In a 1921 letter, the emperor's personal secretary bears witness to Salim Ba Zar'a's involvement in the emperor's financial affairs, and attests that Salim Ba Zar'a has been on many occasions entrusted with the money of Haile Selassie, on each occasion returning the money to the emperor. In view of this, the secretary attests that Salim Ba Zar'a is worthy of the letter of testimony he is writing for him. Salim Ba Zar'a was also given a second letter of reference, from the emperor himself. On December 14, 1926, Salim Ba Zar'a was awarded the Fourth Honorary Medal of Ethiopia by the emperor on the fifth anniversary of his coronation.[28] The certificate that accompanied the medallion reads, "As kings who were richly endowed in wisdom and knowledge as

Figure 3. Salim Ba Zar'a (Photo provided by Ali Ba Zar'a).

well as power had bestowed gifts to their patriots, friends, and servants, we also give to Salim Ba Zar'a the fourth Ethiopian medallion of honor that he will pin on his chest. We have allowed him to bear this medal on his chest, December 14, 1926. Given on the fifth year of our rule at our palace in Addis Ababa."[29]

Figure 4. Ahmad Salih al-Zahiri (right) with his son Hasan (Courtesy of Ahmad Hasan al-Zahiri).

In the first part of the twentieth century, another Yemeni who was well connected and wealthy was Sheikh Ahmad Salih al Zahiri. Zahiri came to Ethiopia from Radaa in northern Yemen and entered into business associated with the railway, becoming well connected to the region's power holders in the process. In Ethiopia, due to his prominence, he served as the representative of the Yemeni government. He was close to Emperor Haile Selassie, acting as his envoy in Saudi Arabia. Zahiri was of particular service when fighting began between Ethiopia and Italy in 1935. During this period, according to a communiqué he wrote to the emperor, he was even engaged in transporting arms and ammunition to Ethiopian patriots. At that time, Ethiopia and Italy were not allowed to buy arms because of sanctions imposed by the League of Nations.

Al-Zahiri's standing is demonstrated by two letters that King Ahmad bin Hamid al Nasir sent to him and Emperor Haile Selassie. In these letters Zahiri is characterized as a faithful and dependable person on whom Haile Selassie can rely.[30] King Ahmad bin Hamid al Nasir also enquires extensively about the health and well-being of Zahiri.[31]

The Yemeni merchant class ran into trouble, however, when the status quo in Djibouti and Ethiopia was challenged in the 1960s by nationalism, anticolonial sentiment, and the Cold War. This era saw the establishment of socialist rule in Africa and particularly in Ethiopia, a subject that is documented at length in the next section.

Winds of Change: Djiboutian Nationalism and Yemeni Economic Adaptation

In the second half of the twentieth Yemenis were affected by rising nationalism and the revolutions engulfing the Arab world and the Horn of Africa. A key factor affecting the economic state of Yemenis in Djibouti was the Suez Canal crisis, which developed following the United States' withdrawal of financial support to Egypt's Gamal Abdel Nasser after he concluded an arms agreement with socialist Czechoslovakia. In retaliation, Nasser nationalized the Suez Canal. Subsequent to this, Israel crossed into Egypt to militarily occupy the canal, leading to its closure until 1957.[32]

For Yemenis in Djibouti, the closure of the Suez Canal and the reduction of shipping was a disaster. The effect was the result not only of external politico-economic factors but also of policies adopted by the French. In response to the economic crisis, French authorities called for the expulsion of all foreigners who did not have French citizenship. A law regulating the presence of foreign workers in the country was passed on March 14, 1960. Referred to as Order No. 60/22, this legislation banned all foreigners from engaging in public- or private-sector work. Employers were asked to submit lists of their employees along with their citizenship status to the relevant authorities.

For Yemenis who earned their living through manual labor, the new law presented a real challenge. In 1960 there were eight thousand Yemenis engaged in various kinds of work in Djibouti. Of these, only around three thousand had French citizenship. The rest now had no legal status and were no longer entitled to work (Dubois, 1997: 284). The new law was also problematic for employers and other businesspeople. Sa'id 'Ali Coubèche aired the general discontent:

> It is time to draw the authorities' attention to the possible consequences, which we deem catastrophic given the current state of the local workforce, of such a decree, which may also lead us to lose the benefits we are reaping from the monetary and economic reforms begun ten years ago. I estimate that application of the decree is contrary to everything we want to do here (the establishment of new companies, investment of capital, installation of a floating dock) and risks the opposite: sowing the seeds of a certain unrest in the minds of those who wish to implement new projects.[33]

In the turbulent years of the 1950s Djiboutian nationalism and anti-Arab sentiment also played a significant role in the problems encountered by Yemenis. Arabs were viewed as collaborators with the French colonizers, as will be demonstrated in the following pages, and there was a push to expel them from the territory. In particular, Somalis, attracted by the pan-Arab ideology of Nasser, menaced both Yemeni Arabs and French traders. Ethiopian small traders and shop owners who were regarded as being opposed to Djiboutian independence were also subject to intimidation, along with Arab traders.

During this period, Yemenis experienced trading problems arising from nationalism not only in Djibouti but also in the hinterland. Historically, labor in the Ethiopian interior had been directed mainly at the domestically oriented agricultural system. When it occurred outside the domestic field, labor was a non-wage undertaking that was regarded as a form of assistance. Agricultural labor was considered to be degrading and was left to occupational minorities, such as potters and tanners, and domestic slaves.[34]

The issue of labor was transformed and radicalized, however, by the time Yemenis migrated to Addis Ababa as a result of a series of reforms. Emperor Menelik II issued a decree in 1906 outlawing the ostracism of labor that occurred outside the field of agriculture (Nogno, 1989). The economy was monetized through the issuance of currencies, which were made the basis for tax payments. One of the direct effects of these reforms was migration from rural areas to Addis Ababa and other cities in the region. Scores of people, particularly ethnic Gurages from southern Ethiopia and people coming from the newly conquered territories of the south, streamed into the capital city in search of work. They needed cash payments in order to pay taxes. Their land had become overpopulated and plots for the growing of cash crops were scarce.[35] Once in the capital, Gurages were most often employed as porters, to the extent that their name became synonymous with the word 'porter.' Gurages also worked as shop assistants for Yemeni-owned businesses in the interior.

In the second half of the twentieth century, the southerners who had been uprooted from their land and drawn to the capital began to compete with Yemenis. This southern group, and especially the Gurages, demonstrated en masse against Yemenis in 1968, using the political events of the 1960s as a pretext to demonstrate against Arabs who were at that time accused of supporting Syria, which was backing the secessionist Eritrean Liberation Front. As we will see in chapter five, these demonstrations led many Yemenis to leave Ethiopia.

Yemeni capital and business investment in the hinterland was also affected by the Derg takeover. The Derg regime, with its socialist ideology, was antagonistic toward the Yemeni merchant class and other traders. Yemeni merchants were considered bourgeois and condemned as oppressors of the proletariat. They were accused of exploiting Ethiopian resources and of sending money home to their country of origin without paying the required taxes. As a result, many merchants were barred from leaving the country until they paid what the government claimed was the correct amount of tax, which in most cases was inflated.

In this changed political climate, members of the Yemeni merchant class were considered supporters of the former imperial regime. In particular, the government accused them of supporting an opposition group, the Ethiopian Democratic Union, which was allegedly fighting for the return of the old regime. Yemeni merchants also started to be widely abused by local officials, who used their positions to seize Yemeni property and money. At their businesses, Yemeni merchants faced labor-related problems due to a government-sponsored union that often used the slightest pretext to create problems.

In addition, the Derg regime moved to nationalize Yemeni property through a series of proclamations. All private land was nationalized in a declaration issued in February 1975. In the same year, property and land in urban areas were nationalized through Proclamation No. 47.[36] Property seized by the state included buildings not occupied by the primary owner. In some cases even unoccupied rooms within a single home were 'nationalized.' A number of Yemeni traders and merchants suffered heavy losses, as most of their wealth was invested in land and houses. Yemenis quickly began to move their capital out of Ethiopia.

While Yemenis were under pressure in both Djibouti and Ethiopia, the effects in each country were different. Despite talk of expelling Arabs, which sent many into exile, Djibouti Arabs were not affected in practical terms. Although there was some hostility, the independent state of Djibouti, which was soon dominated by 'Issa Somalis, refrained from nationalizing the land and property of Yemenis. This meant that Yemenis remained in Djibouti in great numbers.

One key reason for the continued status of Yemenis as traders in post-independence Djibouti was the connections its leaders established with countries in the Middle East. The Djibouti government lacked capital, and soon after independence sought financial assistance from Arab countries.[37] Eventually, Djibouti tried to strengthen its position by becoming a member of the Arab League.[38] These events also led to the adoption of Arabic as one of Djibouti's national languages.[39] Thus, as much as ardent Somali nationalists wished to expel Arabs, it became practically impossible to do so. Expelling Yemeni Arabs would have damaged Djibouti's reputation with the Arab League; it would also have led to the loss of badly needed financial support.

The strength of the Yemeni community and the relations that key Arab traders had with France were further reasons for the continued presence of Yemenis in Djibouti. After independence, Djibouti signed an economic agreement with France on June 27, 1977.[40] Among other things, this agreement was intended to strengthen an accord, signed on the same date, to cooperate militarily with France.[41] The agreements both privileged and secured French interests, including a French military presence, while Djibouti was neither militarily nor economically capable of maintaining itself without French assistance. Over time, this agreement also helped Yemenis in Djibouti.

Yemenis in Djibouti, especially the Coubèche family, were politically and economically linked with France, and within the French system Yemeni families were privileged over others. During the turbulent period of decolonization it was Yemenis who acted as intermediaries between the 'Issa and the French. In view of the strong political and economic links that Yemenis had with France, it was difficult if not impossible to eject them from Djibouti, as had happened in Ethiopia. Despite this, throughout the post-independence period and until relatively recently, Yemenis in both Djibouti and Ethiopia were viewed as second-class citizens. This trend started to change in the post–Cold War era, when investment in a liberal economic framework became the order of the day.

The Post–Cold War Period: Investment and Clientage in Postcolonial Djibouti

Since the 1970s, the relationship between capital and state throughout the world has been profoundly transformed. In the pre-1970 period capital grew within the confines of the state, as the state was based on a Fordist model of production.[42] This situation changed because of the transfer of liquid capital outside the state framework and by the formation of capital outside the control of any particular state. This benefited the transnational class, which is not linked to any nation-state. Labor has also been globalized and national labor pools have merged into a single labor pool.[43]

The effects of these changes were initially felt in the Horn of Africa through the policies of the International Monetary Fund (IMF) and the World Bank. The IMF and the World Bank pushed for emerging nations to privatize, including by selling state-owned property to private interests. This opened up the economies of the region. Seeing these new opportunities, Yemeni and other businesspeople increased their investments in Djibouti and Ethiopia. Some were Yemeni families who had long been resident but had not earlier invested in the local economy because of their uncertain status.

One of the best examples of this is Sheikh Muhammad Hussein al-'Amudi. He was born in Ethiopia, the son of an Ethiopian mother and a Yemeni father. His family migrated from Ethiopia to Saudi Arabia in the 1970s. The family made a fortune in Saudi Arabia through its connection to the Saudi royal family. Ranked as the world's sixty-fifth wealthiest billionaire, 'Amudi returned to the Horn of Africa in the post–Cold War era and invested heavily in Ethiopia and Djibouti. 'Amudi has major financial interests in many countries, including construction projects in Saudi Arabia, an oil refinery in Morocco, oilfields in West Africa, and oil refining in Sweden (where he is the country's single largest foreign investor). Sweden's King Carl XVI presented 'Amudi with the Order of the Polar Star, the highest honor that can be given to a foreigner.

In Ethiopia, 'Amudi established MIDROC Ethiopia and, in the post-socialist era, now owns an astounding 64 percent of formerly state-owned companies (Abegaz, 2001: 193). 'Amudi has invested in Ethiopian gold mines, a hotel, construction, and agriculture, including a 10,000-hectare farm. He has also built a number of factories, including a 640 million dollar cement factory and a steel factory with a capacity of 1.6 million tons.[44] In Djibouti, 'Amudi invested 40 million dollars to build the first fully automated grain and fertilizer terminal at the port of Djibouti.

Another Yemeni who came to the region after the collapse of the Soviet Union is Tarek bin Laden. Tarek bin Laden's father migrated from Hadramawt to the port town of Jeddah at the beginning of the twentieth century and worked in the port. He later invested in construction, eventually working for the Saudi king. Today the bin Laden family has investments all over the world, including the United States.[45]

The bin Laden family has been contracted by the Djiboutian government to build a new city, Nur, the first of ten cities planned for construction around the world.[46] Tentative plans are to link the city with Yemen, on the other side of the Gulf of Aden, with a 29-kilometer bridge.[47] The bin Ladens would be working with two American companies, Allied Defense Group and Lockheed Martin.[48]

The bin Laden and 'Amudi families are not the only Yemeni families who have invested in the region. They are the best known because of their massive wealth and because their business interests are symbolic of the dramatic shift seen since the end of the Cold War. Unlike the pre-1970s Yemenis, bin Laden and 'Amudi are not Yemenis who are attached to a particular state or who operate within the confines of a state. They operate everywhere in the world, and serve as the best examples of the importance of transnational capital. Tarek bin Laden and Muhammad Hussein al-'Amudi are part of a transnational class in its own right and are qualitatively different from the Yemenis of earlier eras.

Despite this, however, even in the post–Cold War period Yemenis maintain a high degree of collaboration and interaction with those in power. They are deeply enmeshed in a patron–client relationship with the state. The need to accommodate and work with these power holders is real. Just as in the past, noncompliance with the state can lead to repercussions, even the expulsion of businesspeople who are otherwise powerful on the world stage. This was the case with Abdourahman Boreh, a Somali businessman who was one of the wealthiest people in Djibouti. He was expelled from the country because of a dispute over an investment with Kadra Mahamoud Haid, the wife of President Ismail Omer Guelle. Yemenis, even the wealthiest, have always been vulnerable to sudden reversals in power and influence.

In conclusion, the economic interactions of Yemenis with states/empires demonstrate how Yemenis have lived with sovereign space. The sovereign space that was enclosed by imperial powers and fashioned into nation-states was an economic microcosm where capital operated. In the colonial period the operation of capital in these spaces entailed a decline of Yemeni business. But it also meant a situation where some of the economic activities that were of no use to capital, or hindered the performance of capital, were banned, including slave trading and arms trafficking.

In the region, the operation of European capital meant differential access to space that was enclosed by capital. Some Yemenis obtained more access to employment opportunities, as well as to the space of Djibouti, because they were favored by capital such as that represented by the French company Messageries Maritimes. This differential access to space and linkage to capital, however, created tensions and conflict between Yemenis and other natives. We see this in the case of the Gurages and Yemenis in Ethiopia, as well as in Djibouti in terms of the relationship between 'Issa Somalis and Yemenis.

The relationship that Yemenis have had with states, however, was not always one of being dominated. This is also apparent in Yemenis' more recent interactions with the state, where the relation between capital and state has been reversed. Even under these conditions, however, Yemenis need to be mindful of the power of the state actor and the politics of the postcolonial state.

Given the stories of this chapter, there is a clear need in Indian Ocean studies to appreciate the importance of power, the working of capital, and the dynamics that are created by this working of capital, be they conflict or the creation of new types of relationships with the state. The discipline rightly views port spaces as economic microcosms, but fails to appreciate the constraints of capital and fully interrogate issues raised in this chapter. Using a state/empire model, rather than a network model of port spaces, shows that the region was not only a cosmopolitan space or contact zone where the trading capacity of the diaspora community created economic and cultural exchange.

5. Colonial Intermediaries, Emperors, Abettors, and Enemies of the People

On January 19, 1974, President Ali Aref laid the foundation stone for an Arab community building in Djibouti. Ali Aref had come to power in 1967 and assumed a pro-France, anti-independence stance. Indeed, he actively opposed the calls of the Organization of the African Union (OAU) for the decolonization of Djibouti. Such demands, he contended, interfered with the sovereignty of the territory of Djibouti.[1] In a 1974 public appearance, however, Aref changed the subject. For once, he did not give one of his anti-independence speeches that so irritated a number of Djiboutian politicians. Rather, he spoke about the place of the Arab community in Djibouti, and the role the community building should play in the affairs of the nation:

> The Qur'an says: "The Good God has created people and tribes so that they can know each other." . . . We are fortunate here to be 'Afars, 'Issas, Arabs and other ethnic groups, but we have the great chance to have here in Djibouti a common denominator: we are all French. I hope this house, which will be the house of the Arab community, will be a house that promotes unity and not division. I hope that this community, which has the disposition to do so, will make a house that will be the house for all people in

[Djibouti] . . . . The real force that represents the Arab community in this city attests to its presence here since its origin. So they are not considered as strangers who came from abroad. They are part of an ethnic group that is French and they are an integral part of this territory. And I ask the Arabs not to consider themselves as foreigners but as people who are an integral part of the territory.[2]

What Aref pointed out was not so much the possibility of a rosy future but the reality of the territory's political situation, and especially the position of Yemenis. In mentioning the fact that Yemenis were not strangers, Aref was in fact drawing attention to the ways in which Yemenis were viewed in terms of Djiboutian politics. As is discussed in the following pages, contrary to Aref's speech, Yemenis were seen as strangers—and as strangers who should be expelled from the country. In this chapter, I turn my attention to the political position of Yemenis. As in the previous chapter, I discuss the means by which Yemenis adapted to changing times, the forces that affected their political existence, and the overall political framework in which they found themselves.

Established in the early 1890s, the political system of Djibouti in its initial phase was typical of that found in other colonies. In the politics and ideology of the colony, and unlike the situation during the precolonial period, Yemenis and other colonial subjects were systematically denied any involvement as citizens with rights. In terms of political status and citizenship rights, the French empire regarded natives as having no legal rights, either to vote or to be represented in the French political system. Natives were regarded as *sujets français*, as subjects of the French empire, while the white French population was referred to as *citoyens français* (Girault, 1904: 648–67).

Like the white French population, Yemenis and other natives in Djibouti were French nationals. They were not, however, citizens, which was the crucial status when it came to political involvement. By being nationals but not citizens, Yemenis and other French subjects were regarded as beings outside the political realm. They were deprived of political rights, including the right to vote and be represented by French administrative bodies. Despite being French nationals, then, they were regarded as racially and culturally inferior to the white French population. They were also characterized as having customs that were incompatible with the notions of political freedom that existed in Europe (see Girault, 1904: 655).

In Djibouti the initial system established for indigenous people was the Service de Sécurité et des Affaires Indigènes, which was created in 1914. Placed under the direct authority of the governor of the territory, the Affaires Indigènes was responsible for connecting the governor to important authorities in the local area, such as the sultan of Tajura. The institution was also responsible for the police force (le Pointe, 1914: 15–16).

In the early days of the colony, Yemenis and other indigenous people were regarded as a special case in terms of the judicial system. Because there were few white settlers in Obock, the French did not consider it necessary to create a fully fledged judicial system composed of different bodies.[3] Instead, based on a decree on September 2, 1887, they relied on *justice de paix*, a rapid justice system which focused on resolving the small day-to-day problem of natives through conciliation and through a simple procedure that takes into account local social reality. In Djibouti the function of the judge was fulfilled by a commissariat in charge of administrative service (Commissariat Chargé du Service Administratif), or, in case of his absence, by an officer appointed by the commandant.[4] Within this initial judicial model, the indigenous population had a separate juridical status. Civil transgressions were regarded as internal matters that should be dealt with by the local or indigenous system.[5]

In December 1900 a decree was passed that related to the judicial system. In May 1901 and February 1904 the judicial system was reorganized. Under this decree, the unequal treatment of Yemenis and other indigenous people continued.[6] For example, under the terms of the decree of February 4, 1904, a first-degree tribunal *(tribunal du premier degré)* and a court of appeal *(tribunal d'appel)* were established.[7] As before, Yemenis and other indigenous people were put under a justice system established just for them when it came to matters that did not involve a white French person.[8]

Being political outcasts yet allowed a separate existence, Yemenis, when compared to other members of the indigenous population, actively participated in the bureaucratic and political machinery established by the French. Yemeni involvement in the French colonial framework began when France started to control Djibouti and its associated territory. Initially, Yemenis were involved as translators and negotiators. Yemeni families of Hadrami origin, such as the Ba Nabila family, became especially important as translators because the colonizers did not have any knowledge of the local people, and the colonized had not yet mastered the language of the empire. Traders in particular faced problems as a result of the use of French as the official language of the colonial bureaucracy. In view of this language problem, Yemenis such as the Ba Nabila family, who were fluent in Arabic and French, became an integral part of the colonial administration.

In the early years of the colony, the government spent a considerable amount of money on Affaires Indigènes. A large part of the funding was allocated to maintaining native intermediaries. This can be seen in the 1913 budget of the Affaires Indigènes, where 30,300 francs were allocated for use by local chiefs, such as the sultan and the vizier.[9]

In addition to directly funding intermediaries, the French created a form of dependence through the provision of aid to indigenous people. This extra funding was used as a means of creating loyalty among people who in real terms were not integrated as citizens in the French political system.

The process of creating Yemeni intermediaries was also achieved through the education system. Yemenis were able to attend Qur'anic schools, a number of which were established throughout Djibouti. For further education, Yemenis traveled to a religious school established in Aden by the Ba Zar'a family. In the later colonial period, Yemenis were able to attend the École Franco-Islamique, which was administered by Hadramis but funded by the Coubèche family. There was also the possibility, albeit to a limited extent, of Yemenis obtaining a modern education by going to schools established by the state or French missionaries. At these schools, however, Yemenis were only allowed to complete a primary level of education, at the end of which they received a primary education certificate, which was referred to as Certificat d'Études Primaires Elémentaires Françaises. With this certificate, Yemenis were considered to be an 'evolved' native (*évolué*), and were used as mediators between natives and French colonizers.

To gain more political space, Yemenis attempted to move out of the category of native. That category would make them eligible for the status of *évolué*, but this would still not lead to citizenship that included full political rights. Well aware of this, Yemenis attempted to obtain citizenship status. Under the French system, this was not possible, but an opportunity arose when northern Yemen, after the First World War, achieved a form of independent sovereignty under the leadership of Imam Yahya. Before the war, northern Yemen was dominated by Ottoman Turks. Their defeat in the First World War led to the weakening of their position in Yemen and their replacement by Imam Yahya, who had long challenged their presence.

Within this postwar context, Yemenis made a move to claim the right of citizenship in Djibouti. On December 8, 1927, members of the community wrote a letter to the colony's procurer, referring to the independence of Yemen as proof that it was inappropriate to classify them as 'native' *(indigene)*.[10]

> The Arabs who reside in Djibouti form a distinct group and they are citizens of a state that has a national government which is not administered by an imperial power.
>
> This state is the state of Yemen.
>
> Since the war, Yemen has an independent state that is not placed under any power. The country's territorial integrity is guaranteed by international treaties.
>
> Its situation is the same as Abyssinia [Ethiopia] and no power can proclaim the annexation of its territory.
>
> This shows that we actually enjoy a status that does not have any analogy with those who are indigenous to the French Somaliland [Djibouti] because the status of the latter is subordinate to the will of the French government.[11]

The political aspirations of Yemenis in Djibouti were not only expressed in the above terms. Yemenis also sought a more active political engagement by reviving the 'morals' of the Muslim community of Djibouti. Some of the more politically active members of the community were particularly attracted to the ideas of pan-Arabism and pan-Islamism, then current in the region. In the 1920s, places like Cairo and Aden saw the emergence of a reform movement that aimed to strengthen the political position of Muslims by reforming their moral conduct and establishing a region-wide pan-Arabic and pan-Islamic unity. In Cairo, the Young Muslim Association and the Muslim Brotherhood were formed during this period (Botman, 1991: 116–19). The influence of both organizations quickly spread throughout the Muslim world. Aden also saw the formation of the Arab Club, begun by a group of Yemenis following a Salafist perspective on Islam (Reese, 2012: 71–75). They wanted to encourage Muslims to adopt a much stricter form of Islam.

In Djibouti, the revivalist movement challenged the imperial power. There was growing support among local Arab Muslims for pan-Islamic and pan-Arabic unity that crossed colonial borders. One of the earliest signs of the spread of a revivalist Islam was the 1920 arrival of a blind Salafi sheikh in Djibouti. According to a French source, the blind sheikh came from Aden to the port of Djibouti and began calling for a Wahhabi form of Islam.[12] The French authorities asserted that this Yemeni sheikh was the first in the territory to advocate Wahhabism.[13] Whether this is true or not, the career of the sheikh, from what we read in French documents, appears to have been short-lived. The sheikh was sponsored by a fellow Yemeni, 'Abd al Karim Dorani, who the French suspected was a supporter of Salafist Islam. The visiting sheikh was able to preach only for a short while before local sheikhs, opposed to his teachings, pushed for his expulsion.[14]

In Aden the supposed moral decadence of Muslims was a concern to people like Ahmad Muhammad al Asnaj and Muhammad 'Ali Luqman, leaders of the Arab Club. In Djibouti, the theme of moral decadence among Muslims was picked up by Hassan Ba Nabila, a Hadrami and a member of one of the most prominent families in the Djibouti Arab community. Ba Nabila complained about poor morals in the Muslim community in a letter that he wrote from Saigon.[15] He stated that he had earlier written about the problem of alcoholism, and that now his objective was to speak about the evils associated with prostitution. For Ba Nabila, the only thing that separates man from animal is man's ability to control his sexual desires. He wrote at length about sexually transmitted diseases contracted when having sex with prostitutes. He argued that prostitution spreads disease and, hence, is the root of all problems among Muslims of the territory. He particularly questioned if the role of a colonial state such as France, which justified its presence on grounds of moral superiority, should be to introduce alcoholism and prostitution in the colonies.[16]

Attempts to rejuvenate morals in Djibouti went beyond the interventions of individuals like Ba Nabila. The Association Islamique de Bienfaisance was founded on February 10, 1930 by seven prominent Arab merchants and three other natives.[17] It was headed by an Arab merchant, Ahmad bin Ahmad. The organization's official purpose was to support fellow Muslims during deaths and funeral ceremonies,[18] but the group was actually engaged in a moralistic endeavor aimed at eradicating social evils. One theme that preoccupied the organization was that taken up by Ba Nabila: prostitution. Shortly after it was founded, the organization constructed houses for the prostitutes on the outskirts of Djibouti.[19] The cost of the houses was 5,583.75 francs. The society wanted to create a closed zone for prostitution, restricting prostitutes to the houses.[20] In doing so, it hoped to give Muslim society peace and also discourage its members from engaging in the evils of promiscuity.[21]

In short, the status of Yemenis within the French system in the early colonial period was marked by both presence and absence. Taken as a whole, Yemenis were regarded as French nationals but not as French citizens with the right to be involved in the political life of the country. Despite the restrictions, Yemenis made a move to change their situation by taking part in a kind of soft politics, reviving the matter of morals and unity among the Muslims of the territory. As we will see in the following section, Yemenis were in a similar subordinate position in the hinterland region of Ethiopia. There, as well, they tried actively to change the lot of their community, as well as that of other Muslims living in the hinterland.

Yemeni Political Space under Monarchic Rule: Stories from the Hinterland

Throughout the history of Ethiopia, Muslims had a problematic relationship with the Ethiopian emperors, who were intent on suppressing the country's Muslim population. In the medieval period, Ethiopian emperors campaigned against Muslim principalities in what is now eastern Ethiopia, and managed to dominate them (Trimingham, 1952: 76–77; Cuoq, 1981: 130–39; Braukämpar, 2004: 12–90). In the sixteenth century the Christian kingdom fought with the 'Ādalə sultanate, led by Ahmad ibn Ibrahim al-Ghazi (popularly known as Gragñ, meaning 'the left-handed'). The war, from 1529 to 1543, saw Gragñ defeated through the aid of the Portuguese army, fighting in support of the Christian kingdom at the request of the emperor (Trimingham, 1952: 84–95; Cuoq, 1981: 139–45; Aregay, 1974).

Although there was never a major war between the ruler of the Christian kingdom and the Muslims, in later periods the country's Muslim population became pawns in the hands of the state's Christian rulers. Traveler James Bruce (1790) testified to the political impotency and barebones existence of Muslim groups in the Ethiopian empire. In Gondar, the then capital of Ethiopia, Bruce reported on the segregation of Muslims and described atrocities committed against them. He noted that Emperor Yohannes I, who reigned between 1665 and 1680, forced Muslims of the capital to eat Christian food, which was against local custom: "Yohannes I seems to have had the seeds of bigotry in his temper; from the beginning of his reign he commanded that the Mohametans eat no other flesh but what has been killed by Christians" (1790: 423–24).

After Bruce's visit, Muslim groups were discriminated against in a similar manner. Emperor Tewodros II, for example, regarded Muslims as the enemy and engaged in extensive repression. According to Walter Plowden (1868), Muslims during this period were the country's main traders and controlled almost all the customs offices of the empire. He explains, "A Negadeh Ras, or chief Merchant, is appointed in six towns of Abyssinia—Ayjubay, Derrita, Gondar, Sokota, Doobaruk, and Adowah. In five of these the officer is a Muhammadan; at Doobaruk, somewhat inferior in importance, he is a Christian" (1868: 130). Despite their economic importance, Muslims were few in number because of Emperor Tewodros' repression.

Guillaume Lejean (1865) visited Ethiopia during Tewodros' reign. He observed that the *islambiet* (Muslim merchant houses), which were the center of Abyssinian commerce, were almost destroyed. Tewodros issued a decree that all Muslims should be converted.to Christianity, so they fled from Gondar (1865: 174–75).

The persecution of Muslims continued after Tewodros' reign. His successor, Emperor Yohannes IV, affirmed that "from the time of Mahomet (Gran) until this day the Ethiopian kings have become weaker and weaker, and they are not content with the country that they already possess but now they want to take all Ethiopia" (Ullendorff, 1969: 137). To contain the perceived problem, Yohannes IV set out to forcibly baptize Muslims in the Muslim-dominated regions of the empire, such as Wallo. He also oversaw the burning of the Qur'an in this region (Ahmed, 2001). Yohannes IV was later killed during a battle against Mahdist Sudan, which added to the perception of Muslims as a threat to the Ethiopian empire.[22]

Yemenis traveling to Ethiopia in the twentieth century were confronted with these long-standing harsh conditions. They nevertheless tried to alleviate their political disenfranchisement by drawing on Wilsonian sovereignty, the 1919 initiative, after the end of the First World War, to establish a new world order. In that year, the Versailles Peace Conference began in France and United States president Woodrow Wilson pushed for a worldwide reconfiguration of the logic of sovereignty. In this new approach, the political order was to be based on popular sovereignty and the accountability of government to the people, alongside the establishment of the League of Nations. According to the Wilsonian logic of sovereignty, ethnic groups occupying a minority position within an empire were to be accorded the right to self-determination.[23]

For Yemenis residing in Ethiopia, Wilsonian sovereignty was seen as an opportunity to overthrow the long-standing repression of imperial Ethiopia. A Hadrami, Hajj Abd al-Qadir 'Umar Ba Wazir, wrote to the consular office of the United States in Aden on April 23, 1919, appealing to President Wilson to acknowledge the injustices Yemenis faced:

> We, the Muslims of Abyssinia, would like to take the opportunity provided by your presence in Addis Ababa to submit to you this summary of the situation and the main claims of the Muslim community of Ethiopia. We would like to ask that you bring it to the kind attention of the president of your country, to whose charity the eyes of all oppressed people are currently turned:

The Muslims of Ethiopia account for approximately three-quarters of Ethiopia's total population, and the territory occupied by them also accounts for approximately three-quarters of Ethiopia's total area. We are also the hardest-working segment of the national population. We are almost the only farmers, the only industrial workers, and the only tradesmen in the country.

Despite our great superiority in numbers and quality, we live under the oppressive regime of a small minority (Shoa) that has oppressed us for only forty years, and that is driving us to decline and complete annihilation. A little investigation will demonstrate to you that the world has never seen a regime so cruel in any country or in any century. We have freely welcomed happy, peaceful Oromo people in our countries for centuries. Forty years ago we numbered around thirty million, and today there are barely eight million of us. Never mind political rights; we do not even have human rights. Our life, liberty, religion, honor, our property, fields, wives, children, and our work are at the mercy of our Shoa oppressors. In another half-century we will have disappeared completely.

Because of this intolerable situation we entreat President Wilson to guarantee to us too (the unhappiest of all oppressed people) the following rights when world affairs are debated:

- Proportional representation of Muslims in the overall administration of the country
- Full administrative autonomy for all parts of the country in which Muslims are the majority: equality of civil and political rights
- Total freedom of religion, education, assembly, association, and work
- Abolition of the confiscation system *(varas)*
- The return to its former owners of our land that was confiscated by the government or by Amhara chiefs
- The establishment of independent Muslim courts in Muslim regions, with executive power and answering only to Muslim courts of appeal and ultimately to a Muslim religious chief who resides in the capital and is elected by the Muslim community with no involvement by the central government

- The formation of a Muslim militia for each Muslim region and a withdrawal of destructive "Amharic" troops from our countries
- Free implementation of the reforms deemed useful by each Muslim region, by its elected bodies (communal councils) within their own boundaries
- General establishment of the inviolability of the person, home, and property throughout the country and for citizens
- Promulgation of a free political constitution for all of Ethiopia, decided upon by a proportional general assembly, which establishes the fundamental basis of communal interests and mutual relations in all components of the country
- Special guarantees for the rights of Muslim minorities.

These are approximately the main wishes of all the Muslim and even non-Muslim population. If President Wilson or the conference so wish, we can bring together for you all the Muslim chiefs of the country, who will confirm to you these same demands. However, before this we would require the conference's protection from any hatred or revenge by the Amharas.[24]

The Yemenis here claimed to represent the Muslim population of Ethiopia; they were expressing their grievances within the new logic of international sovereignty. Their problem was age-old oppression and the solution, for them, was nothing less than a Wilsonian-style self-determination that would lead to the expulsion of the oppressor Amharas from the area that prior to the formation of the modern state was occupied by Muslim sultanates. The new international sovereign logic was thus used as a means to attack the old imperial sovereign logic under which Yemenis, along with all other Muslims, faced repression.

Seen over the longer term, Wilsonian sovereignty does not seem to have helped change the lot of Yemenis and other Muslims in Ethiopia. Yemenis continued to exist in a state of vulnerability, at the mercy of the ruler. One particular incident that illustrates this vulnerability was a conflict between the Yemeni community and the Armenian residents of Addis Ababa on October 14, 1928. This period was marked by the coronation of King Täfari Mäkonənə as emperor of Ethiopia. Prior to his coronation as Haile

Selassie I, King Täfari Mäkonənə served as regent of the empire, following the overthrow of Lij Iyasu. The latter was the grandson of Emperor Menelik II, who came to power as crown prince after Menelik II was incapacitated as a result of illness (Sohier, 2011). Lij Iyasu's eccentric behavior, coupled with his association with Muslims, Germans, and Turks, led to his having a bad reputation among the Ethiopian nobility and foreign diplomats stationed in Addis Ababa (Erlich, 2014). This led to his overthrow and the coronation of the daughter of Menelik, Zäwuditu, with Rasə Täfari as regent (Abebe, 2001).

The deposition of Lij Iyasu was not totally successful, however. He managed to escape capture and sought refuge among Muslims to whom he was related by marriage (Soulé, 2014). His escape led to conflict and animosity between Muslims, who largely backed Lij Iyasu, and Christians, who tended to support Rasə Täfari.

It was within this context that the conflict between Yemenis and Armenians occurred. But the incident that set the fighting off was the refusal of an Armenian to pay his debt to an Arab merchant. This seemingly apolitical affair was interpreted in terms of the power struggle taking place between the Muslim-backed Iyasu and the new emperor, who had the support of the Christians. As the Arabs were Muslims and the Armenians were Christians, the conflict between the two was interpreted as an attempt by the Muslims to cause problems for the emperor. The Arabs were accused of instigating trouble in order to destabilize the unconsolidated rule of Haile Selassie and strengthen their alliance with the pro-Muslim Iyasu.

The Arab community in Addis Ababa wrote a six-page letter to Emperor Haile Selassie, which was copied to the various consulates in the city. The letter read, in part:

> Armenians, though the sole promoters of the aggression, have hoped to use such incidents, provoked and incited by themselves, to spread disorder in the quiet population of the country (not a new thing for them). History is the impartial witness of the ruination of states where the Armenian has received shelter. There is not one of the people who have welcomed and received them with hospitality that has not bitterly regretted having extended them kindness. As to us, Sire, our history in all the countries where Arabs have lived attests to

our love of peace and our gentleness. We seek nothing but to work for the economic development of the states that welcome us, in an atmosphere of tranquility and quietude. At no moment have we participated in a conspiracy aimed against the existence of states, or tried to create animosity among people. And in this country, long before the Armenians, and from the time of the late illustrious Emperor Menelik II and of your august father, the late Rasə Mäkonənə, we have settled in Hara and in Addis Ababa. We have from the first hour been devoted with honor and peace to all the trades and we have been considered as brothers of the natives of Ethiopia.[25]

While the Yemenis presented themselves as apolitical people who had never attempted to dismantle a state structure, this was, of course, far from the truth. Yemenis on various occasions, including during the medieval conflict between the Christian kingdom and Gragñ, had attempted to throw off the rule of Christian Ethiopia (Martin, 1975). For our purposes, however, the relevance of the letter above does not lie in its degree of truthfulness but in what it tells us about the Yemeni political position. Contrary to their dream of having an autonomous Muslim domain, Yemenis continued to lead a tenuous existence—their very lives depended on the goodwill of the sovereign.

With their plan to gain rights under the new Wilsonian logic in disarray, Yemenis would have to wait to gain some level of constitutional rights. When this finally came about, it was in the form of bribery on the part of the Italian colonial regime that occupied the country for five years. Before the Italian occupation in 1936, the country had seen the adoption of its first constitution. Supported by Emperor Haile Selassie, it did not lift Yemenis and other Muslims from their subordinate position. Rather, it unequivocally established the power of the sovereign: "The person of the Emperor is sacred. His dignity inviolate and his power incontestable."[26] The constitution did include articles enabling the formation of a senate and chamber of deputies, but the emperor remained in complete control of the government, as he was given the power to both form and dissolve parliament.[27] The senate and chamber of deputies were not, in any case, entities that would have satisfied Yemeni aspirations, as the members were not elected by the people but designated by the emperor from the ranks of the nobility.[28] The people were not considered to be in a position to elect their own representatives.

The sovereignty of the emperor was finally truly challenged with the Italian invasion. Following a brief war the emperor left the country to appeal unsuccessfully to the world's nations. The occupying fascist force was faced with a country in revolt.[29] As part of their attempt at pacification, the Italians engaged in a process that was tantamount to bribing the country's Muslims. In the rhetoric the Italian government used, the fascist regime both before and after the invasion was portrayed as a champion of Muslims. Having gained a foothold in Libya, it tried to appeal to the wider Arab population in the Middle East (Erlich, 2007). On the eve of the invasion, the fascist regime attempted to portray itself as destroying the illegitimate Christian nation that had resisted Islam and repeatedly wounded Arab pride (Erlich, 2007).

Once they occupied Ethiopia, the Italians continued to act as champions of the Muslims. In fact, they tried to divide and rule the country by portraying Muslims as the oppressed and Orthodox Christians as the oppressors. They started to favor Muslims in the building of mosques and the establishment of sharia courts (Sbacchi, 1985: 163). Some Yemenis, especially those living in Addis Ababa, became, out of fear or by free will, active supporters of the colonial regime. In August 1936, seven Yemenis wrote a letter to the Italian periodical *Giornale di Addis Abeba* expressing their support for the Italian government and the favorable conditions established for Muslims in the region.[30] They declared their "unity and cordial participation with other Ethiopian Muhammadans in thanking the Italian Government for its interest in the affairs of the Arabs and Native Moslems, and hope that this epoch is the beginning for the good and advancement of Muslims and the Islamic faith."[31]

Subsequently, some Yemenis formed a committee to represent the hundred Adenese, four hundred Hadrami, and more than a thousand Yemenis residing in the city.[32] Sayyid Muhammad al Mihdar was initially chosen as the committee representative, but when he declined, Sayyid Ahmad bin 'Abdallah Idris, from the Sanaa region, became the committee's leader.[33]

Following this selection the Arab community held a demonstration in Addis Ababa in support of the Italian administration. Toward the end of the demonstration they went to the palace to show their support for Marshal Rodolfo Graziani, the viceroy of Ethiopia.[34] Here, the Yemenis were well received and their representatives were personally greeted by Graziani, who "shook each one by the hand and engaged him in several minutes of conversation, asking after him and his family's health, his occupation and his particular line of activity in Addis Ababa."[35] During the occasion, Graziani "prolonged his talk particularly with the noble chief Idris, with Qadis and the 'Ulama', with the teacher of the local Arab school, with the caravan proprietors, each of whom owns from three to four hundred camels employed in the age-old traffic with Kaffa and Jimma."[36]

Following this cordial reception an Arab representative gave a lengthy speech on Italy's occupation of the country. The speech, written by a certain Marconi and read by Sayyid Muhammad al Mihdar, congratulated the Italians and went on to endorse Italian colonialism, noting how it would benefit Muslims and Arabs residing in the country:

> Your high government willed the conquest of this country in order to civilize, educate, and instruct. You have actually conquered it and have taken possession of it, and you have won a clear, great, and brilliant victory in its conquest. It has become the duty of every wise man to present to your government, the warmest congratulation for this attainment and abundant thanks for its intentions.
>
> Here you are beginning the fulfilment of your true intentions, founding a visible palace for civilization that we shall shortly see completed.
>
> You have lighted the city by night with electricity, arranged to run buses through the streets, and at the same time begun to organize the commerce of the country and its economic affairs. Periodicals are issued in three languages, and by this you have brought to life our Arabic language, and thus it has become easy for every resident to follow the general and local state of affairs from your elegant journal.
>
> We, the Arab communities, are pleased with the kindness and benevolence displayed toward the Muslims and the interest taken by you in our language as well as in our affairs.

> We have become united by the grace of your care under one leader, the respected son Sayid Ahmed Ibn Idriss, whom we have accepted as our link with you, and you have been so generous as to agree.
>
> We hope that by your good policy we, as well as all the Muslims in this country, shall reach the highest success, both worldly and godly.[37]

The Yemenis' actions at the Italian palace put them in a strange position with regard to the other colonial powers, especially the British, who were formally their protectors, as most came from either Hadramawt or Aden. Mihdar felt it necessary to convince the British legation in Addis Ababa that the Yemenis had acted because of pressure from the Italians. In this, he seems to have succeeded: writing to the Aden office, a British staff member at the British legation in Addis Ababa informed his superior about Mihdar's actions in a positive and reassuring way:

> The great majority of the British protectorate Arabs attended, in spite of themselves, so I am assured by Sayid Muhammad, who apologized further for not telling me about it first, saying that he was afraid he might be put in an impossible position by being told not to take part. Although he is a rugged old man, he nearly broke down, explaining how difficult their position was, loyal to Great Britain as they were, with spies everywhere ready to denounce them to Italian authorities for disloyalty to Italy. "When I leave you now," he ended, "I shall be stopped at the legation gates and cross-questioned about my business here with you. But rather than neglect, in future, my duty to the British government, I will gladly go to prison, and deem it an honour."[38]

The Yemenis did not only face problems with the British. The Orthodox community was particularly agitated by the Arab demonstration described above. Graziani explained to them the reasons for the Yemeni demonstration. The British reported these circumstances, and the explanation given by Graziani:

that the policy of pronounced favor to the Muslim element . . . has caused some alarm in the local Coptic church, which official circles are now anxious to still. On the feast of the trinity here celebrated on the 14th July, following an address by 'Äbunä Kirillos appealing for pacification and submission to Italian rule, Marshal Graziani received the heads of the clergy and favored them with an address.

He had heard, he said, that murmurs were being raised against the Italians on the ground that they intended to abase the Coptic church in Ethiopia in favor of Islam, but nothing could be more false. All religions were equal before the Italian authorities. He begged for confidence in the sincerity of their intentions, despite the false report disseminated by interested foreign quarters. Let not those responsible for these reports flatter themselves, for the Italian authorities would find a way to round them up and take the necessary measures against them.[39]

Yemenis, because of the Italian presence, seem to have indeed been put in a difficult situation. There is no denying that the Italian policy of favoring Arabs satisfied to a certain extent Arabs' aspirations, as it set up dynamics that would be hard to reverse in the subsequent period. The institution of the sharia court and the building of new mosques were especially important: educated Yemenis could become qadis at the newly formed court and imams at the new mosques.

In the Ethiopian context, Yemenis were often notable religious figures who led the Muslim umma. For example, 'Abdullah al Qaiti was a leading religious figure in Dire Dawa and the founder of a Muslim seminary. The al-Bar family, particularly Sayyid 'Abdallah Mahajus al Bar, were also religious figures who were important in the affairs of the Muslim community. Sayyid 'Abdallah Mahajus al Bar was the first imam of Awel Mesqid, later named Benin Mesqid, which was the second mosque to be established in the city of Addis Ababa.

What the Italian initiative did was to increase the formal religious participation of Yemenis at the national level. Amid these new opportunities, Salim Ubad 'Aqil, who originally came from the city of Shibam in

Hadramawt, participated in the Sharia court established by the Italians in the regions of Harar and Dire Dawa. In Dire Dawa, Ahmad Seif al Kabrie, Sheikh 'Abd al Rahman Ba Makhrama, and Hajj 'Umar Ahmad Seif al Kabrie all acted as imams at the mosque.

Although Yemenis benefited from the new opportunities provided by the Italians, not all of them worked with the Italians and not all were in favor of their presence. Indeed, numerous Yemenis took part in the antifascist movement, such as the previously mentioned Sheikh Ahmad Salih al Zahiri, who campaigned relentlessly in Arab countries on behalf of the Ethiopian emperor. When the Italians occupied Addis Ababa they tried to find Zahiri; his backing for the Christian empire was regarded as being against the ideological strategy of the fascist regime. At one point the Italian government even tried to bribe Zahiri in an attempt to stop his actions.[40]

Indeed, during the return of the emperor to the city following the defeat of the fascist regime a number of Yemenis went out to greet the emperor in the streets of Addis Ababa. The national Arabic-language newspaper *al-'Alam* noted that Yemeni communities were among those present during a celebration marking the emperor's return from exile. The issue of May 6, 1942, listed those in attendance as including Sheikh Sa'id Ahmad Ba Zar'a, Ahmad al Mihdar, Ba Harun, and Ba Hubaysh. From northern Yemen, it listed 'Ali Mahmūd al Nusayri, 'Abd al-Hadi, and 'Abdal-Qawiyy al Khurbash.

Despite this show of allegiance, Yemenis and Muslims were more generally regarded as a threat and as plotting against the Ethiopian empire, the Ethiopian nobility, and the Ethiopian Orthodox community.

Political Games in a Reformed Environment: Election, Citizenship, and Political Action in Djibouti

In the first half of the twentieth century the political situation for Yemenis in Djibouti and its hinterland underwent a significant change. This occurred as the imperial powers began to reform their policies across the world. In the territory of Djibouti, the change in the rules of political engagement occurred through a number of decrees that gave the right of citizenship to French subjects. One such legal reform was Order No. 45–1.87, issued on August 22, 1945. The first article of the decree allowed all overseas territories to be represented in the National Constituent Assembly (Assemblée Nationale Constituante). The other articles detailed how this was to be achieved.[41] Under the new legislation all French colonies (excluding the colonies of Madagascar, the Côte Française des Somalis, and Archipel de Madagascar) were to have two distinct electoral colleges, one belonging to an electorate of citizens and the other to members of the electorate who were not citizens.[42]

In the three colonies not included in Order No. 45–1.87, the formation of a single electoral college was prescribed, to be composed of both citizens and noncitizens. In the case of the noncitizen electorate, in the Côte Française des Somalis, the legislation stipulated that the list would constitute French subjects of both genders who were older than twenty-one and would include, among others, evolved natives *(notable évolué)*.[43] In addition, the Fourth French Republic Constitution of October 27, 1946 transformed French subjects into French citizens.[44]

Under the new framework established by the French, Yemenis became actively involved in the political system. In the first election under the new rules, held in March 1946, 228 Somalis, 250 Arabs, and 146 'Afars were registered to vote. Two Yemenis were elected for the *territoires conseil representative*, the representative council of the colony: Sa'id 'Ali Coubèche (from the powerful Coubèche family, which, as we have seen, had ties with the French) and Ahmad bin Ahmad, along with 'Afars, 'Issa Somalis, non-'Issa Somalis, and Europeans.[45]

November 1946 saw an election of deputies to represent the territory in the French Assemblée Nationale (National Assembly), which led to the selection of Jean Martine (backed by non-'Issa Somalis and Arabs) over an 'Issa candidate.[46] A month later there was another election, this time for the French Conseil de la République (Council of the Republic), which was won by a Somali with a Gadabursi background. In 1947, the Yemeni Sa'id 'Ali Coubèche was elected to the Assemblée de l'Union Française (French Union Assembly). In 1948, Djama Ali obtained a considerable amount of financial support from the Yemeni population and was elected to the Conseil de la République.

Yemeni involvement in the new political system, either as candidates or as financial backers of candidates upholding Arab interests in Djibouti, was met with fierce resistance from other ethnic groups, especially 'Issa

Somalis who claimed that they were unfairly represented. In addition, 'Issa Somalis resented the potentially disastrous political plan initiated by the newly elected Sa'id 'Ali Coubèche. In a move to increase the benefits of the Arab population, Coubèche, through Jean Martine, the representative of the territory at the French National Assembly attempted to push through a bill to enfranchise the territory on the basis of literacy in Arabic and French (Thompson and Adloff, 1968: 63–64). Compared to the territory's other populations, this step clearly favored Yemenis, partly because they were more familiar with the French language as a result of their integration into the colonial bureaucracy and partly because Arabic was their native language.

Thus the 'Issa characterized Yemenis (such as Sa'id 'Ali Coubèche, who was increasingly active in politics) as foreigners who did not deserve to participate in the political life of the community. In 1949, for example, 'Issa Somalis of the district of Ali Sabih summoned the governor-general of the territory, Paul Siriex, to inform him that he should not allow Arabs and their associates to manipulate the Djiboutian political system.[47] Invoking the treaties signed between France and the local chiefs, the assembled 'Issa Somalis reminded the governor-general that France had originally made an agreement with local chiefs, not with Arabs. They warned that they would declare independence or sell off their territory to Ethiopia or the United States if the situation continued.[48] A report on the matter follows, written to the Addis Ababa branch of the Chemin de Fer Franco-Éthiopien:

> The 'Issa have first asked the governor if the stones and the land they held in their hands belonged to 'Issa, the Arabs, or the people coming from Somaliland. When the governor stated that these stones and the earth were the property of the 'Issa, they replied to him saying: "Why, then, have you sold our land to the Arabs? Are you French or German—if you were French, you would not have sold our country to foreigners."

The 'Issas finished by declaring that they would make a decision after having received an answer to the following three questions:

1. Does France still want Djibouti and the rest of the territory? If they don't want it, the 'Issa would take back their country. On the other hand, if France wants to maintain its position France should exclude from its administration Arabs and people whose origin is Somaliland.
2. Will France continue with its policy of allowing foreigners to represent the territory in the National Assembly? The 'Issa are not opposed to the fact that they are represented in the Assembly. But, if France requested the 'Issa to be represented, only the Ougaz, the traditional leader assisted by members of the twelve lineages of 'Issa, should appoint the person who is going to represent the 'Issa. The 'Issa do not want a candidate, even with an 'Issa background, to represent them in any election without the consent of their tribal association.
3. France should oblige Jean Martine (the representative of the territory in the French National Assembly) to resign because he is injurious to the interests of the 'Issa and Danakil ('Afar), as he has lied to them through false promises. Martine promotes Arab aspirations without taking into consideration the interests of indigenous people. The Arab Sa'id 'Ali Coubèche, adviser of the French Union, and the Gadabursi from Somaliland, Djama Ali, should be warned and they should not take a role in politics or the administration of the country. If they refuse the government has to forcibly evict them.[49]

Beyond these complaints, a serious physical threat arose against Yemeni politicians and their associates. On January 18, 1949, Djama Ali, who was backed by Arabs, was attacked while walking in the street. Subsequently, an intense ethnic conflict broke out in the streets of Djibouti between the 'Issa and the Gadabursi (Thompson and Adloff, 1968: 63). A few months later, the Arab community was targeted. On the evening of October 19, 1949, four Arabs were shot in front of the house belonging to the father of Sa'id 'Ali Coubèche, leading to the deaths of Coubèche's uncle and the president of the Arab Club.[50]

Even though the Yemeni community was attacked, its members continued to participate in the political affairs of the territory through direct

Political Games in a Reformed Environment | 125

and indirect means, the latter including the formation of social clubs, such as the Club du Communauté Arabe, which had a political agenda. Despite their political involvement, Yemenis remained foreigners in the eyes of nationalists, and especially to Somali 'Issa. Although Yemenis were French citizens legitimately residing in Djibouti, there were repeated calls for the Yemenis to be expelled from the territory. After the Second World War this call was made by Hassan Gouled Aptidon, who would become the first president of an independent Djibouti. At the time, he was leader of the main 'Issa-based political party.[51] In an inflammatory speech at the French parliament, Aptidon claimed that the solution to Djibouti's political problems was the expulsion of all foreigners from the territory, starting with Arabs.[52] The net consequence of such politics was a general perspective that Yemeni Arabs were lesser or illegitimate citizens who, despite having the necessary papers, lacked legitimate political rights.

After the Second World War, however, the confrontation Yemenis faced was shaped by more than domestic events particular to Djibouti. And it did not relate only to the problematic relations they had with 'Issa Somalis. Internal political divisions besieged the Yemenis, which were greatly influenced by political developments in Yemen. The 1940s saw increased opposition to the rule of Imam Yahya in Yemen and the eventual formation of the Free Yemeni Movement, a political group that aimed to put an end to Imam Yahya's rule and bring reform to the country.[53] This group naturally extended itself and sought to gain the support of Yemeni communities in Djibouti.[54] The activists particularly sought to obtain financial support for funding the periodical *La Voix du Yémen*, and to this end the group sent a demand to Djibouti Arabs through Muhammad Ahmed Chelan, who was a French subject, and Hassan Abdallah Garadi, a merchant in Djibouti.[55]

Some of the Djibouti Arabs become supporters of this organization, and a document written by the colonial authorities tells us that Abdallah Ibrahim Fadil and Al Fagih Abdul Alim were the chief contacts of the movement in Djibouti, while Abdul Qawi Qurbashi was the man who represented the organization in Addis Ababa.[56] Some Yemeni Arabs, however, refrained from taking part in the movement. This created considerable internal divisions, particularly during the 1947 election of the Arab Club of Djibouti, which was called to select a new president. On May 15, 1947, the privacy of those who did not support the movement was violated.[57] On that day those who were in opposition found tracts denouncing them and Imam Yahya in their beds, as well as in their personal belongings.[58]

The tracts included such phrases as "May God curse those who glorify Imam Yahya," "May God curse those who injure Yemenis," and "May God curse those who love Imam Yahya."[59] The report of the French colonial authorities tells us that among the notables engaged in anti-Imam Yahya propaganda were Ibrahim Mobin, Sa'id 'Ali Coubèche, Muhammad al-Bedhani, a merchant stationed near the Hamaoudi mosque, and al-Khamis, another Djibouti merchant.[60]

Shortly afterward, the involvement of some Yemenis in the Free Yemeni Movement made them more visible and hence a target of empire/state. In 1948 the Free Yemeni Movement assassinated Imam Yahya. He was replaced by Al-Sayyid Abdallah bin Ahmad al-Wazir. This takeover by the Free Yemeni Movement was of great concern to Djiboutian authorities. Dorani, one of the territory's most prominent Yemenis, wrote to Al Sayed Abdallah bin Ahmed al Wizir, congratulating him in the name of the six thousand Arabs of Djibouti. But the assumption of power by the Free Yemeni Movement lasted for only a short period of time. Imam Yahya loyalists soon regained control. As part of their crackdown, they focused on Yemenis in Djibouti and Ethiopia. They accused some of having direct involvement in the assassination and sought to expel them from the region.

Yemenis in the Politics of Nationalism and Decolonization in the 1950s: Pan-Arabism, Decolonization, and the Decline of Arab Politics

In the first half of the twentieth century Yemenis participated in the political affairs of Djibouti. As a result of their engagement in these matters, Yemenis experienced the intense reaction of local ethnic groups who felt that Yemenis should not be involved in the colony's politics because they were foreigners—despite having citizenship. The campaign against Yemeni participation in political affairs continued into the 1960s and 1970s. The demand to expel Arabs was particularly strong among the youth of Djibouti, especially in student and other youth associations that brought the territory's political situation to the forefront of debate.

Although the threat to expel Arabs from Djibouti did not materialize during the decolonization process of the 1970s, it could be said that Yemenis lost their importance in politics. As a result of the turbulence of the 1970s, including violent anticolonial protests, France did not have any option but to allow the territory to decolonize. The decolonization process entailed, among other processes, a negotiation among the country's ethnic groups for parliamentary seats. Although Yemenis were involved, the main negotiations occurred between the majority ethnic groups—the 'Afar and the 'Issa—who were also considered by France to be the proprietors of the country, as they were thought to be its founders. For Yemenis, the outcome of this negotiation marked the beginning of political isolation. In the final settlement of the parliamentary seats, thirty-four were allocated to the 'Issa, thirty-three to the 'Afar, and one to the Yemenis.[61]

In the post-1950s era Yemeni political isolation was sealed by the stance taken by France. As the power holder in the country, France favored Yemenis, including Sa'id 'Ali Coubèche, over other ethnic groups.[62] In the second half of the century, however, France abandoned the Yemenis in reaction to the spread of pan-Arabism.[63] During this period many young Yemenis started to oppose France and follow Nasserite agendas, which were influencing political events emerging in Yemen.[64] The French started to doubt the benefits of continuing a politics that relied on the Arabs of Djibouti. In the circumstances of the time, what France did not need was domination on the two sides of the Gulf of Aden by pro-Nasserite, anti-French, anticolonial Yemenis.[65] A French official expressed his concerns regarding the Yemenis of Djibouti:

> In an estimated population of eighty-one thousand, forty-one thousand live in the capital, eight thousand have no Arab component, three thousand are French citizens, and five thousand foreigners, including three thousand Yemenis and the remainder coming from the Hadramawt. They practice a wide range of professions: agriculture, they supply the capital, they maintain small and medium enterprises. A large proportion of them are employed

as dockers; this is a robust, stable workforce. This minority has never caused any problems and remains aware that our presence is of use to them. Only the young are susceptible to Nasser's propaganda. Some French citizens, such as the president of the Chamber of Commerce and the chief of the Arab community, have firmly sided with us, while others are more cautious. If Yemen moves toward Nasser's line, that Arab colony might interfere in the life of the territory.[66]

Such worries, coupled with the assaults on Yemenis, meant that the Arab community lived in a politically inferior position, which soon started to be reflected in the way Yemenis engaged in the political life of the territory. Yemenis started to adopt a mediating position rather than take a stance that would clearly label them as political actors. A useful example of their declining position, marked by such mediation, is the reaction of Yemenis during the 'Afar–'Issa conflict that led to the signing of the Arta agreement in 1963. In the 1940s, as outlined above, the Arab community, with all its wealth, pushed for an electoral law that was clearly in favor of Arabs. However, this determination and zeal was lost in the 1960s. In the Arta agreement, for example, rather than taking a position, Yemenis acted as friends of both camps. Led by Ali Tahir Salih, the community made a declaration in support of the two groups.[67] This declaration was followed on the same day by a statement by another group of Arabs led by Sa'id 'Ali Coubèche, which expressed similar sentiments toward the Arta declaration.[68]

This mediating role was not confined to the Arta agreement. It became characteristic of the political elite of the Yemeni community, especially during the struggle for independence.[69] Given Yemenis' proximity to French power holders, and the favoritism shown in this relationship, Yemeni political leaders were used extensively to mediate between ardent nationalist elements, such as 'Issa Somalis, and representatives of the French government.[70] In this regard, Coubèche played a pivotal role. During the negotiations between France and Djibouti regarding the future of the Djiboutian franc, Coubèche was used by the nationalists to broker a deal with France and managed to convince the French authorities

Figure 5. The Djibouti delegation at the Arab league. (Courtesy of 'Abdallah Mohamed Kamil).

to continue to guarantee Djiboutian money.[71] It was also Arabs who once again supported the new rulers of the country when Djibouti, after independence, managed to gain membership in the Arab League.[72]

The Expulsion of Yemenis: Eritrean Arabism and Anti-Arab Sentiments

In the hinterland region beyond Djibouti, Yemeni political adaptation was also affected by the events of the 1950s. Here, decolonization was not an issue, as Ethiopia had not been colonized, but pan-Arabism threatened the very existence of Yemenis.

For Yemenis, the problems relating to pan-Arabism started with the bombing of an Ethiopian airliner in Frankfurt in March 1968 by the Eritrean Liberation Front (ELF), which had launched a guerrilla war against the central government. The ELF sought independence for Eritrea, then the northernmost region of Ethiopia.[73] It was supported by Arab nations that hoped to form a unified Arab homeland that would include Eritrea. From 1960 to 1963, Egypt, under President Gamal Abdel Nasser, hosted the organization and allowed it to make broadcasts from Cairo (Erlich, 1995: 130–52). Following this, the ELF obtained support from the Syrian Baath Party government, which also wanted to form an Arab homeland composed of "that area which extends beyond the Taurus mountain, the Gulf of Basra, the Arabian sea, the Ethiopian mountains ... the Atlantic Ocean and the Mediterranean Sea, and constituting one single complete unity in which no part therefore may be alienated" (Erlich, 1995: 152). The ELF was given Syrian military training at an Aleppo military base in 1952. Later, it received support from the Palestine Liberation Organization (PLO) and the Iraqi Baath Party (Erlich, 1995: 130–52).

Arabs backed the separatist groups in order to further estrange Eritrea from Ethiopia, considering it a future Arab nation. They hoped that this would give them control over the Red Sea region and, hence, allow them to confront the state of Israel, which transported its imports and exports through this area.[74] The ELF was more than willing to enter these alliances because of its opposition to the government of Ethiopia, Haile Selassie's regime, following its annexation of Eritrea.

Not surprisingly, this strategy and the actions of the ELF antagonized the Ethiopian Orthodox population and their sovereign. Encouraged by the government, a number of demonstrations were held throughout the country against Syria (which was correctly identified as the backer of the group), and against Yemenis living in the country, who were accused of sympathizing with the ELF and its Arab backers.

The first demonstration occurred in Asmara, the capital city of Eritrea. It was attended by over ten thousand people.[75] The demonstrators started out from the city's main Queen of Sheba Stadium and marched to the compound of the governor-general. They denounced the actions of the Syrian government and the ELF's bombing of the plane.[76] They shouted slogans that emphasized Ethiopian state integrity, used anti-Syrian and anti-Arab expressions, and called for the expulsion of Arabs residing in the country.[77] Toward the end of the demonstration, the marchers made speeches through their representatives and asked Eritrea's governor, Prince Asrate Kassa, to speak to the emperor about their concerns and demands,[78] including for the expulsion of Arab residents from the country.[79]

This demonstration was symbolically held in Eritrea; later, similar events took place throughout Ethiopia. Anti-Arab demonstrations that concerned the theme of territorial integrity were held in the cities of

Däše, Jimma, Assab, Harar, Dire Dawa, and Addis Ababa. People also marched to oppose the actions of the ELF in many rural areas.[80] As in the Asmara demonstration, anti-Arab and anti-Syrian slogans were used.[81] Representatives made statements to various local officials who were asked to transmit their messages to the emperor.[82] As in Asmara, one of the major themes in the speeches delivered around the country was the call for Arabs to be expelled from Ethiopia.[83]

The state-owned newspaper that reported the countrywide demonstrations echoed the demonstrators' demands, questioning the loyalty of Yemenis living in Ethiopia. The editorial section of *Addis Zemen*, the Amharic daily newspaper, was particularly vocal:

> We have not brought them [Yemenis/Arabs] because we wanted their skills. We have not invited them because of their capital. Many of them have faced problems in their country and have asked to be a guest. When measures have been taken on several occasions to transfer the skills that were held by expatriates the generosity that the government has shown to Arabs living in Ethiopia is not comparable. . . . Indeed some Arabs living in Ethiopia may not be the supporters of the mischief created by some Arab countries and Syria. However, so far we were not able to distinguish the wheat from the chaff. The Arab descendants living in Ethiopia have not shown their opposition to Arab countries who have been creating mischief against Ethiopia. The fact that they have not shown their loyalty to the people of Ethiopia and the government is saddening and, beyond that, it is a cause of suspicion.[84]

To counter such accusations, Yemenis held their own demonstrations. Anti-ELF and anti-Syrian protests were organized by Yemenis in the towns of Däse, Dire Dawa, Addis Ababa, Təgərayə, Assala, Agaro, and Bahir Dar.[85] They made statements through their representatives to local officials. Yemenis also went to the emperor's palace to meet Haile Selassie in order to express their support for the territorial integrity of Ethiopia.[86] The representatives of the Yemenis expressed their absolute loyalty and friendship to the government and the hospitable Ethiopian people, affirmed with great respect that they would keep their loyalty to the great Ethiopian people, and further asserted that meddling in Ethiopian affairs was shameful and blameworthy.[87]

The emperor responded to this speech with reassuring words. After mentioning the long relationship between Ethiopia and the Arab people, and the unexpectedness of the Syrian action, and after explaining that Ethiopia would defend itself, the emperor continued to stress the positive role of Yemenis in Ethiopia.[88] Despite these positive remarks, many Yemenis were forced to leave the country.

Within the Nation-State: Yemenis in the Politics of 'Independent' Djibouti

In the post-independence period the position of Djibouti Arabs in the political system did not improve. In fact, it seems fair to conclude that it worsened. Djibouti politics ended up in the hands of 'Issa Somalis, who, as discussed above, came to have a small majority in parliament. Headed by Hassan Gouled Aptidon, an 'Issa from the Mamassan clan, the new power holders posed as a political entity that would work for Djibouti rather than for a particular ethnic group. President Aptidon, who had earlier called for the removal of all foreigners, including Arabs, made a speech that was eventually printed in a pamphlet and distributed throughout Djibouti.[89] Published on May 8, 1977, the pamphlet was a bitter statement against tribalism, which Aptidon declared the enemy of the new independent nation, as running contrary to the spirit of independence, and a tactic that was only employed by those opposed to the nation's sovereignty. Rather, Aptidon stated, national unity was the phenomenon that could withstand all manner of menace.[90]

For the president, a key reason for this rejection of tribalism was what he saw as the threat it posed to the nation-state. Because tribalism relies on family networks rather than competence, besides due to the clientelism and the consequent rivalry it tends to engender, Aptidon argued that tribalism threatened the efficiency of the nation's bureaucracy and would hamper the country's economic development.[91]

The pamphlet described the issue of tribalism in terms of economic processes rather than electoral politics. Noting the concentration of

French capital in the southern part of Djibouti during the colonial period, the pamphlet claimed that the consequent loss of the traditional caravan trade in the north had had a negative effect on development in the northern region.[92] In the new politics, Aptidon claimed, through equitable distribution and investment tribalism would disappear as a result of the disappearance of the regional economic inbalance.[93]

The president also envisioned a new way forward for the young nation of Djibouti: rather than tribalism, he said the population should rely on hard work and the creation of communities of workers.[94] It was his conviction that Djibouti's sense of nationalism should be based on national service and respect for different cultural heritages, particularly the nation's linguistic legacy.[95] Through these processes, the new national leaders hoped that the postcolonial state of Djibouti would surpass what Aptidon referred to as *l'élitisme tribal* (tribal elitism), which had come about as a result of the imposition of a colonial structure that, he claimed, forced each clan and tribe to give its members to the colonial administrators for the purpose of representing native people.[96]

Some Yemenis, at least publicly, seem to have bought into the argument outlined by Aptidon. Haydar 'Abdallah 'Awad, the grandson of one of the first Yemeni families to have come to Djibouti, whose father managed to gain a seat in Aptidon's parliament, wrote nostalgically about June 27, the day the country gained its independence:

> 27th June, memorable unity, an unforgettable day,
> Let us sing aloud and dance in our joy!
> 27th June, you, my nation, my beloved,
> You will be my destiny,
> In unity, equality, and peace,
> We have founded our home.
> 27th June, date of our independence,
> Decline is over.
> That day, for all the people of Djibouti,
> Is the time for unending pride.
> 27th June, I well understand,
> I must fight for my country (Awad, 2000: 8; author's translation).

Post-independence politics failed to create equal citizens. But it certainly determined the destiny of the country and that of Djiboutian Yemenis, as Haydar 'Abdallah 'Awad prophesied. From the beginning of President Aptidon's regime, all ethnic groups, excluding the 'Issa Somalis, were isolated.[97] Even among 'Issa Somalis, the Mamassan clan—the president's clan—was given more access to key political positions. As a result of this marginalization Ahmed Dini, the 'Afar politician who held the prime minister position, resigned.[98] Although Dini was subsequently replaced by Abdallah Kamil, the 'Afar politician who was president of the government council during the transitition period to independence, the latter was also sacked for not showing sufficient allegiance to the Somali population.[99]

Eventually, Hassan Gouled Aptidon's government reneged on the agreement reached between the political groups, and all political parties, except the one that he himself had formed, were banned. This led to a complete breakdown in formal political engagement for Yemeni Arabs and other ethnic groups.[100] Despite this ban, elections were held in 1981 and 1987, each of which resulted in the unopposed reelection of Aptidon.[101] In 1992, the government allowed the establishment of a multiparty system following a referendum.[102] In the same year, the ruling party, the People's Rally for Progress (PRP), and two other parties, the Democratic Renewal Party (DRP) and the National Democratic Party (NDP), registered for national elections. Claiming irregularities, the NDP withdrew and the ruling party competed with the DRP. The elections were tainted by irregularities, however, and the 1993 presidential vote saw Hassen Gouled Aptidon reelected president once more.[103]

In the subsequent years, the new multiparty system failed to produce real change in Djiboutian politics. In 1999, a nephew of Aptidon, Ismail Omar Guelleh, who had headed up Djiboutian security and been an advisor to the president for more than twenty years, was elected president. The controversial vote reaffirmed the continuing domination of the 'Issa Mamassan clan.[104]

'Issa domination of the political system was one of the factors that led to the 1991 civil war between government forces and an 'Afar-backed rebel group, the Front for the Restoration of Unity and Democracy (FRUD).[105] In 1994 the government signed a peace agreement with members of FRUD. The agreement led to the absorption of the moderate wing of the rebel group into key government positions.[106] Since the incorporation of FRUD, Djibouti has had a number of elections, all of which have resulted in the unopposed election of Guelleh.[107]

Through the political arrangement established in Djibouti, Yemenis have become marginalized and their political role has stagnated. In the division of ministerial positions, only one is always assigned to the Yemenis. Although Yemenis have been included in various bureaucratic positions, their involvement remains fairly minimal as a result of an ethnic preference for giving jobs and positions to majority 'Issa and 'Afar groups.

Because of their marginalization, key political actors in the Yemeni community have opted to remain in the shadows rather than confront the system and fight for their rights. Paralyzed by the fear of repression, and particularly of expulsion and the loss of their commercial interests, Yemenis continue to support whoever is in power. They also act as mediators and power brokers in cases of political conflict. Recalling the role that Arabs played in the Arta agreement, for example, the former minister of commerce Rifki Abdulkader Ba Makhrama acted with others as a broker between the government and FRUD during the civil war.

In the various 'democratic elections,' Yemeni political leaders continued to hold an intermediary position. For example, this was the case for Sa'id 'Ali Coubèche, the chief Arab activist who led Arab politics in Djibouti. When Aptidon transferred political power to his nephew, Ismail Omar Guelleh, in the controversial election of April 1999, Coubèche, who had pushed a pro-Arab agenda in the 1940s, declared that he was "globally in favor of the new president of the Republic."[108]

These good relations with the new leader are a continuation of the kind of politics the Coubèche family has long excelled at in Djibouti: namely, the politics of working in the shadows and assuming a subservient position to those in power. The role played by the Coubèche family, the wealthiest and most influential in Djibouti, continued even after Coubèche's death. At the age of ninety-two, Coubèche fell ill and died in Cannes, France, on January 16, 2009.[109] Soon after his death, a registry was opened at the Djibouti Chamber of Commerce, and a number of politicians came to sign.[110] This important Arab politician had a state funeral attended by President Ismail Omar Guelleh, Prime Minister Dileita Mohamed Dileita, and other high officials.[111]

Shortly after his death, his daughter, Magda Sa'id 'Ali Coubèche, was presented with a medal on his behalf, the Haute Dignitaire de la Grande Étoile de Djibouti, which is the highest distinction a person can obtain in the state of Djibouti. She gave her thanks to the assembled people, including the prime minister:

> For this great honor that you have conferred upon my father and that honors his memory, I would like to ask you, Prime Minister, to pass on the thanks of the whole family to the Head of State, His Excellency Mr. Ismail Omar Guelleh, and to tell him how touched we have been by all the tributes that have been paid to my father by the whole nation between Friday the 16th and today. We know that he is the driving force behind this whole movement and we thank him from the bottom of our hearts.[112]

Despite these pleasant words and the cordial ceremony, the Coubèche family remained conscious of the potential danger surrounding them, which was made clear when Sa'id 'Ali Coubèche's biography was published. It was co-written by Colette Dubois, a well-respected historian at the Centre d'Étude des Mondes Africains at the University of Aix-en-Provence, and Jean-Dominique Penel. The biography details the political history of Coubèche with information drawn from a series of interviews. When it was published, Coubèche was no longer active, as he was in the last year of his life. His daughter Magda presented the book to the president in a ceremony organized for that purpose at the presidential palace. Later, however, it was discovered that the biography Magda had presented to the president was not the original edition of the book.

Colette Dubois had written an earlier version of Coubèche's biography, which detailed the political conflict the family had been involved in since the 1940s. Here, Dubois mentioned the conflict between Sa'id 'Ali Coubèche and the presidential family. She also mentioned the first president's comments about chasing away Arabs. In the book that Magda presented to the president these sections and other sensitive material were completely removed. Interestingly, this removal occurred with the full knowledge of the author. After submitting the earlier version to the French library, upon the insistence of Magda Coubèche, Dubois, together with the Coubèche family, stopped the distribution of that version and wrote a second one in which all the sensitive material was deleted.[113] In the second version, Coubèche is presented as a great friend of the Guelleh family, and as especially close to Hassan Gouled Aptidon (Morin, 2008).

The important point to be taken from this strange affair, in which a reputable academic is involved, is not so much to do with the scholar's ethics but with the constraints faced by Yemeni families in this region. What seems clear from these events is the general political position of Yemenis in Djibouti, which since the 1940s has been marked by uncertainty, fear, and a reliance on the politics of survival rather than active engagement.

The possible danger Yemenis face and the need on their part to balance their relationship with state power holders is further demonstrated by the case of Muhammad Saleh Alhoumekani, a Yemeni who formerly worked as a bodyguard for Ismail Omar Guelleh. On October 19, 1995, the French magistrate Bernard Borrel, who came to Djibouti to help in the reorganization of the justice system, was found dead in mysterious circumstances. Soon after his death an inquiry was opened to determine the cause of his death, and France's relations with Djibouti were strained. It was in the middle of this affair that Alhoumekani went to Belgium and asked for political asylum. As part of his application for asylum, Alhoumekani implicated the president of Djibouti in the death of the French magistrate. This led to severe repression of his family back in Djibouti. Despite their full citizenship, some of his relatives were rounded up and deported to Yemen. Their expulsion was effected within twenty-four hours, and the courts were not involved.

In August 2013, Alhoumekani faced further problems. Traveling on a Belgian passport, he went to Yemen to visit his family. Because of the strong relations between Djibouti and Yemen, Alhoumekani was arrested and held in a Yemeni prison. Djibouti made a formal request for his extradition, claiming that it was not in revenge for the allegations against the president but in connection with another crime. The alleged crime involved allegations that Alhoumekani had tortured a Djiboutian citizen while he was resident in Djibouti.

The case of Alhoumekani clearly demonstrates the need for Yemenis to use caution when dealing with postcolonial powers. A balancing act is necessary in order to bypass the arbitrary power exercised by the power holders of the postcolonial nation-state. Conflict and confrontation may lead to repression and illegal actions by the state, such as the extradition of a citizen without any court procedures.

On the other hand, having close relations and being enmeshed in the patron–client relationship is something that can bring rewards for Yemenis. An example of such a case, and one that stands in sharp contrast with that of Alhoumekani, is Djibouti's ambassador to Paris, Rachad Farah. Farah, who is close to the presidential family, is one of the few Yemenis to hold a senior diplomatic position since the country's independence. As a close and devoted ally to the Guelleh family, Farah has held a number of diplomatic posts abroad. He has even run for leadership of the United Nations Educational, Scientific, and Cultural Organization, with the support of the president of Djibouti. This is an example of how Yemenis continue to exploit patron–client relationships.

Yemeni Political Activity in EPRDF-dominated Ethiopia

Within the Ethiopian context, the EPRDF period saw the proliferation of ethnic alliances (Aalen, 2002). Under the EPRDF, regions that previously were organized on the basis of geography were reorganized along ethnic lines (Aalen, 2011). The EPRDF encouraged the expression of ethnic affiliation. Such expressions were seen as liberating the various ethnic groups within Ethiopia from the domination of a single ethnic group. In line with this, the EPRDF regime demonized the old Amhara-led regime. Amharas were derogatorily referred to as *neftegna*, or 'holder of the gun.' Orthodox Christianity, which for centuries was connected with the Ethiopian state, has also been identified as a bastion of Amhara power.

The EPRDF reorganized administrative and regional divisions within Ethiopia along ethnic lines (Turton, 2006). In the pre-EPRDF period, Ethiopia was internally divided into *kəfələhägərə*. The basis of delineating a *kəfələhägərə* corresponded more or less to the geography of an area, and different ethnic groups found themselves delineated within the same *kəfələhägərə*. In the EPRDF period these geography-based regions were dismantled and reorganized on the basis of ethnicity as federal states with their own administrations. Each of the nine federal ethnic states also had its own official language, following the single ethnicity linked to each state. They were entitled to distribute identification cards showing an individual's ethnic identification. Not all regions were able to be included in a specific federal state, however. Addis Ababa, which is claimed by the Oromia region, was turned into a federal city under the direct control of the federal government, as was Dire Dawa, which was contested by the regional states of Somalia and Oromia.

A number of political groups active in the formal political scene in Ethiopia shared the EPRDF's ideology in relation to ethnicity and encouraged people to celebrate their particular ethnic culture. Thus, in the early 1990s, Ethiopia had several ethnicity-based political parties with an agenda similar to that of the EPRDF. Among them were the Oromia Liberation Front (OLF), the Sidama Liberation Front (SLF), and the Islamic Front for the Liberation of Oromia (IFLO), which sought the liberation of Muslim-dominated areas of Oromia.

For Yemenis, the spread of ethnicity-based federalism and the fact that the government openly encouraged ethnic groups to celebrate their cultures was consistent with the political agenda some of their leaders had been advocating for a number of years. After all, what Yemenis had requested from United States President Woodrow Wilson was a separate state where they would be able to exercise their rights, free of Amhara domination. When a politics based on ethnicity and anti-Amhara rhetoric proliferated in the 1990s, some Yemenis saw it as an opportunity.

This participation of Yemenis in the new political environment can be seen in the politics of Dire Dawa. Shortly after the EPRDF overthrew Mengistu, the city of Dire Dawa was enmeshed in bitter ethnic conflict between Amhara and Oromo. The city was divided into two, each ethnic group dominating one sphere while the youth from both sides fought with each other. The Yemenis of Dire Dawa largely supported the Oromo and took part in attacks on Amhara youth. A rich Yemeni family living in a multistory building in the Oromo-controlled area went so far are to install a submachine gun on the roof. The sons of this rich family, along with other Oromo youth, used the machine gun to fire on Amhara youth advancing to attack the Oromo-controlled area. Although the number of people killed and injured is not known, many Oromos were grateful for the Yemeni family's support. Amharas, of course, are bitter over what the Arabs' support for Oromos has done to them.

The ethnic federalism and politics of ethnicity introduced by the EPRDF did not provide a lasting solution to the problems of the Ethiopian state. The rivalries of the different ethnic groups have continued. Yemenis have had to learn how to balance themselves in this new environment, where ethnicity has become an important element of political life. Yemenis now identify with ethnic groups designated as oppressed in the new political system, including the Oromos. Many Yemenis intermarried with those who are classified as oppressed, such as the Oromos. Identifying with these minority groups was initially seen as a means of political security. Some Yemenis joined ethnicity-based political parties, including the Argoba People Democratic Movement (APDM), and took identification cards distributed by the regional states.

Violence was directed at people from the Amhara ethnic group and, later on, those affiliated with the Tigre ethnic group, from which the majority of EPRDF leaders and soldiers come. Tigrayans are now seen by other ethnic groups as the new oppressor. In areas inhabited by formerly oppressed ethnic groups, including the Oromia region, people of Amhara descent were asked to leave the region. Those who did not leave willingly were targeted for violence (Markakis, 2011: 283). Moving around Ethiopia also became a problem, as a number of people were killed by militant groups who attacked them on the basis of their ethnicity, as shown on their identification cards. In this climate, having the right identification card was therefore of prime importance. Yemenis sought to get the cards as a way of protecting themselves.

Ethnic categories and affiliation, however, are never rigid and the ethnic categories that were celebrated or demonized in the EPRDF period were in many ways a bad fit to people's actual ethnic affiliations. Throughout history, Ethiopians intermarried. Families were often a mix of oppressed and favored ethnicities.

This was also the case among Yemenis. After 1990, those who had intermarried and had children with Amharas had to find a way to hide their hybrid identity. For many the only solution was to acquire identification cards that listed them as members of formerly oppressed ethnic groups. But even that was no guarantee of safety. Some of the ethnic groups included in the oppressed category are still engaged in bitter conflict with the EPRDF regime. This is the case of the Oromo, where the Oromo Liberation Front has been waging a small insurgency war against the Addis Ababa government. Needless to say, most Oromos are not part of the liberation movement. But the fact of being Oromo could cause problems. Ethnic groups linked with insurgencies have suffered widespread imprisonment. Yemenis who identify with these ethnic groups also face heightened risk as compared to other Yemenis.

The uncertainties of Ethiopian politics have further distanced Yemenis from taking part in national politics, the clashes in Dire Dawa being an exception. In this regard, they resemble their Djiboutian counterparts, who must perform a constant balancing act. As in the case of Djibouti, leading members of the community are attached to Ethiopia's rulers. This attachment involves a sort of patron–client relationship, the balance of which can quickly change.

In Ethiopia, one of the best examples of the politics in which Yemenis were involved is the case of one of the richest Yemenis living in Ethiopia, Muhammad Hussein al-'Amudi. 'Amudi's involvement with the ruling party had been rumored for a number of years. During the national elections in 2005, 'Amudi went public with his support for the EPRDF. In the run-up to the election, over a period of several months, the government and civil society groups sponsored televised political debates between the opposition party and the EPRDF. Both the EPRDF and the opposition called huge rallies and hundreds of thousands of people came into the streets of Addis Ababa.

It was during this period that 'Amudi actively supported the EPRDF regime, to the dismay and anger of the opposition party. In the pre-election period 'Amudi was seen wearing a T-shirt bearing an EPRDF campaign image. He also made a speech that called on people to support the EPRDF. In doing so, 'Amudi was publicly reaffirming his alliance with those in power. This calculation seems to have worked, further ingratiating 'Amudi with the regime: he was soon showered with a number of state honors. Shortly after the election, 'Amudi received an honorary doctorate from the state-run Addis Ababa University. In 2006, when Ethiopia celebrated its millennium, 'Amudi was given a Man of the Millennium award at the national palace, in a nationally televised ceremony. But this success appears to have been short-lived.

In the years since, 'Amudi's public profile has somehow lessened, and his face is no longer seen on Ethiopian television. He seems to have fallen out of favor with those in power. The National Bank of Ethiopia has asked 'Amudi to pay back an outstanding loan. The municipality of Addis Ababa has asked him to return some plots of land that were leased to him, claiming that he has kept the land for years without undertaking the investment he had promised. While the demands appear legitimate, the fact that they are only being raised now, when 'Amudi's public profile has fallen, is taken by most citizens as a strong sign of the precarious position 'Amudi currently holds. There is also increased criticism of 'Amudi's business activities. *The Reporter*, an influential newspaper run by Amare Aregawi, a former member of the EPRDF, has published a series of damaging articles about 'Amudi and his activities in Ethiopia. This campaign is in marked contrast to the earlier public acclamation that 'Amudi received.

In conclusion, in their interaction with state/empire Yemenis were excluded from the political field in both the colonial and the postcolonial period. In Djibouti, from the colonial era until the Second World War a distinction was made between citizens and nationals. When this distinction was adjusted through reform, Yemenis continued to be discriminated against because of their foreign origin. Autochthonous groups considered them to be lesser citizens who should not be involved in politics. This kind of view continued into the postcolonial period, which came to be dominated by the 'Issa ethnic group.

In Ethiopia, Yemenis also faced exclusion. Because they were Muslim, they were left out of the political community, which was dominated by Ethiopian Orthodox Christians. Here, Yemenis found themselves in a relationship of conflict, and in the 1960s a substantial number were expelled from the country.

Although they were politically excluded, Yemenis were active agents who tried to adapt to the specific state/empire context in which they found themselves. They took the opportunities created by key events—such as United States President Woodrow Wilson's new agenda—to advance their interests. We have also seen that they benefited from Italian colonialism and from various developments in the postcolonial period. Yemenis throughout their history and in the present have worked to integrate themselves into states and empires. In Djibouti, for example, the Coubèche family actively engaged with colonial power holders. In Ethiopia, the Ba Zar'a family, the Zahiris, and the 'Amudis managed to integrate with the political elite.

In the next chapter I extend this analysis to look at the religious sphere. At the beginning of the twentieth century, Yemenis were not only political but also religious. This calls for an analysis of the religious dimension in the interface between Yemenis and empire/state. The need to look at this aspect of their lives does not come only from the religiosity of Yemenis; the empires and states operating in the region had specific perspectives and strategies regarding religion, particularly Islam. It is therefore necessary to explore Yemeni lives not only from economic and political angles but from a religious perspective as well.

6. State Vision, Imperial Hierarchies: Being a Muslim Yemeni

In the French imperial mind, Islam, the religion followed by Yemenis, held a peculiar position. At the time of Napoleon Bonaparte's expedition to Egypt, Islam was considered a challenge to the French colonial mission (Ferry, 1905: 3). This was certainly the case for France's earliest colonies, including Algeria. The French considered Islam to be a threat (Soares, 2005: 52). They particularly regarded the activities of religious sects with suspicion and categorized their leaders as dangerous elements who needed to be watched and controlled.

The French not only viewed Islam as a threat but also placed it on an evolutionary ladder, below Christianity (Triaud, 2000: 169–87). Although considered inferior to Christianity, Islam was seen as a more evolved religion than the traditional or animist beliefs followed by many African people. The French made a distinction between the Islam of Arabs and the Islam of black people, referred to as "black Islam" (Harrison, 1988: 2–4; Brenner, 2001: 154–55). The latter was considered to have been diluted with animist beliefs, and its followers were considered prone to evolutionary regression. The Islam of Arabs was considered the 'true' Islam, but also more radical. African Muslims were seen as vulnerable to becoming radicalized by Arab Muslims, whom the French considered to be fanatical in their beliefs (Triaud, 2000). The Yemenis living in Djibouti were subsumed under this French colonial mentality, the origins of which had predated the establishment of the colony.

The French generally considered Somalis and 'Afars to be unintelligent, and to be following a form of "black Islam" in which fetishism was part of the religion. Even if Africans converted to Islam or Christianity, it was widely believed that the black inhabitants of Djibouti would return or degenerate to their fetishistic beliefs. The French missionary M. Cadars, for example, traveled from France to Korea in the early years of the twentieth century, passing through Djibouti. He wrote about what he believed to be the nature of the Muslims he encountered there: "'They are big, sly children,' the Capuchin priest said to us, 'Obviously capable of improvement but always prone to unsettling regression.'"[1] Being at such a 'savage' stage of evolutionary development, Somalis were said to be in need of protection from Arabs and from the influence of Islamism.[2] To support this aim, aid and the missionary work of the Catholic Church were seen as crucial.[3] Being placed under the protection of the Catholic Church, it was thought, would prevent Somalis from succumbing to the dangerous passions of Islamism.[4]

Within Djibouti's Muslim community, however, a hierarchy between the more evolved but nevertheless fanatical Arabs and the corruptible Somalis or 'Afar savages who practiced 'black Islam' did not exist; thus, Yemenis were cordially accepted. Muslims from Yemen were regarded as holy men, the descendants of the Prophet Muhammad. This perspective arose because the Prophet Muhammad himself was Arab. Consequently, Yemenis were given land, and local Muslims offered their daughters in marriage to resident Yemenis. Giving one's daughter to a Yemeni was considered to be an act that would bring a blessing *(baraka)* to the family and the community. It was also a practical strategy that enabled the local community to retain Yemenis in the area, as they tended to be regarded as having more knowledge of Islam than Muslim peasants or pastoralists, who most often could not read or write Arabic.

While most Yemenis were respected by other Muslims, some were accorded a higher status because they were believed to be direct descendants of the Prophet Muhammad. The Yemeni community itself was divided into four hierarchical groups: the Sada, Masha'ikh, Qabili, and Nakis.[5] Of the four groups, the Sada were considered the proper descendants of the Prophet, as they were able to prove their lineage. The Sada were followed by the Masha'ikh, who were mostly religious scholars. Some in this group claimed descent from the Prophet but were unable to prove their lineage. Next came the Qabili, who were mainly tribesmen whose families were engaged in agro-pastoral work. Last were the Nakis, men and women engaged in menial occupations, including leather and metal work and hair cutting.

In the late nineteenth century and the early twentieth century, the Sada were highly respected by Muslims in Djibouti and in the region in general; they had followers and were worshiped and venerated when they died. Their burial sites often became the focus of annual pilgrimages that drew large numbers of people. Among them is the tomb of 'Abdallah al Qaiti in Dire Dawa. Originally from Aden, al-Qaiti traveled through Djibouti before settling in Dire Dawa. Informants affirm that he was venerated for what were seen as miraculous abilities, including the taming and commanding of wild animals such as lions and leopards. When he died, his burial site became a pilgrimage destination.

For French colonial officials, who already viewed Arabs as fanatics, the Sada were a source of anxiety. From their early days in Algiers, French leaders viewed sheikhs and sufi orders as secret societies, and often compared them with Europe's medieval secret societies.[6] The Sada and their Sufi orders were considered a source of pan-Islamism, seen by colonial powers as an obstacle to civilization, and so were viewed as enemies of the French empire (see, for example, Vignon, 1919: 69). They were also demonized as idolaters and practitioners of sorcery. Although in Djibouti itself the Sada created no significant problems for the French, reactions to Sayyid Muhammad 'Abdullah al-Hasan's opposition to British rule in Somaliland made apparent the underlying French perception of the Sada. Referred to as the "Mad Mullah" by the British, Sayyid Muhammad 'Abdallah al-Hasan campaigned against colonial rule (Hess, 1964; Gray, 1980). For the French, his political activities showed the potential threat posed by the Sufi orders and their leaders:

> For the last three years a false prophet created dissolution in the country. Muhammad 'Abdallah was born from poor parents who lived in the southern part of Somaliland.... During his adolescence,

he went, they say, to be with the Danakils to study the science of the occult and learn from them the practice of witchcraft. This tribe, who have some lineage with other Somalis, is known for its great number of witches and sorcerers. He was educated at the school of the Wadad (Sada), who taught him the prayer of the Qur'an and the Arabic language. . . . People who are unaware, and those who are dominated by superstition and fear inspired by men whose power is said to include an ability to talk with gods or demons, loaded him with gifts: camels, herds of cattle, sheep.[7]

To counter the influence of religious leaders, the French employed various strategies. In Djibouti, Christianity, and particularly Catholicism, was used to mitigate pan-Islamism and Islam.[8] Djibouti was characterized as a country full of thorns,[9] where one could see "a negro, so dark, who actually creates pain for the eyes."[10] People were called on to raise their hearts to God in order to nourish the small white flower of Catholicism that was growing in the desert country of the black people.[11] The Catholic agents of the empire were confident about the power of Catholicism among the Muslims of Djibouti:

In town, a coach drawn by two lean nags took us to the Capuchin missionaries. On our way we have come across appropriately dressed children, holding a knapsack full of books. They greeted us, made the sign of the cross, and jumping on the steps came to sit on our knees. They have learned quite a bit of French and we were able to have small talk with them. They are Catholics, go to the school of the priest, and like French people.

"Why do you like the French?"

"Because without the Capuchin fathers I would be pagan and I could not go to heaven."

Oh! This small Negro! How well he has answered. It is not because the French have brought money and are making business (something that he does not know yet) that he likes the French. It is because the Capuchin fathers have taught him that he has a soul created in the image of God and destined to eternal happiness. Later,

148 | State Vision, Imperial Hierarchies: Being a Muslim Yemeni

when he grows up, when he understands that merchants, traders, and French officials care little for his soul, and that they are here for their interests, this Somali will nevertheless love France because a French Capuchin priest has revealed to him his true destiny.[12]

In addition to promoting Catholicism, the French colonists engaged in the task of managing Muslims by drawing on their experience with Muslim communities in places such as Algeria.[13] In Algeria, the French dedicated themselves to detailed studies of the Sufi orders. A French expert on Islam recommended the establishment of a government-sponsored ulama, which was eventually done. Alfred le Chatelier boasted about the success of French policies in Algeria:

> It was in Algeria that we first came in contact with Muslims in Africa. In eighty years we have produced a unique Islam, without Boubous, with a government-sponsored mosque, qadi who are affiliated with the colony, an authorized pilgrimage, and now a newly modeled code, which is a mix of Muslim law and French jurisprudence.[14]

The French policies conceived and developed in North Africa were used in Djibouti to rule the local Muslim community, including Yemenis, who were regarded as the source of all fanaticism. In Djibouti, as in North Africa, le Chatelier recommended that they should study the hagiographies of leaders. "In Djibouti," le Chatelier explained, "where the development of Mahdism led by the Mad Mullah of British Somaliland has made a distant echo it would not be without interest to know the traditional hagiology of the Muslim population."[15] As Djibouti is strategically placed in terms of the Gulf of Aden region, it was also thought that it could become a center of information where the French could learn what was happening in the hinterland region of Ethiopia (where Muslims were settled), as well as in Hejaz and Yemen.[16]

In the quest to create a passive Muslim, French experts such as René Basset supported the strategies followed in Algeria. Concerning the Sada and their Sufi orders, Basset urged the French to use them as an instrument of penetration:

The current organization of Muslim cults should be maintained and improved, as it is for us a tool for action that it is unwise to relinquish. For us it is a means of inculcating, through formal education, in a class of native officials, the element of science, and to some extent, critical reason and European method. From this point of view the Medressa [Islamic schools] could be of great utility.[17]

The French were interested in the development of compliant Muslim officials, and Yemenis, given their already high status among the Muslim inhabitants of the country, were their primary choice. For example, Ba Nabila, a Yemeni, became the chief qadi of Djibouti.[18] On the eve of Djibouti's independence from French rule, Yemenis continued to play an important role. One of those who were prominent during this period was Sayyid Abu Bakr al Saqqaf, a member of the Sada family. His position as a qadi lasted until the French left the territory. His deputy was another Yemeni, Ba Makhrama. Both men were employed by the colonial administration.

Despite the creation of this docile Muslim elite, among whom Yemenis were clearly favored, French colonial authorities remained deeply concerned about the activities of Yemenis resident in the territory. They continued to view them as fanatical and more prone to agitation than the natives. Yemeni contacts with Arabia particularly fueled French fears, given that the Arabs were also considered extreme in their religious beliefs. One of the early connections that led to a confrontation between Yemenis and the French authorities was the arrival in the territories of a blind sheikh who was inclined to what the French called Wahhabi thinking.[19] The blind sheikh, the French claimed, had been sponsored and encouraged to come by 'Abd al-Karim Dorani, from one of the richest families of Djibouti. The family had become wealthy through its connection to the Banque d'Indochine.[20] The sheikh became of particular concern to the French after a number of young Arabs started to follow his teachings.[21] They were relieved after local sheikhs expelled the blind preacher back to Arabia.[22]

The other incident that brought Yemenis into conflict with the French authorities was the 1936 Arab revolt in what was then referred to as Mandatory Palestine. In that year the country was engulfed in revolt when Palestinians rose up in opposition to British policy that encouraged the mass migration of Jews to Palestine.²³ Yemenis, as Arabs and Muslims, were sympathetic to the Palestinian cause and signed a petition in support of the revolt.²⁴ Led by ʿAli Coubèche, the Yemeni community of Djibouti sought to support Palestinians abroad.²⁵ They set about collecting money to send to a Palestinian organization.²⁶ The French colonial authorities, alarmed by the unity this act signified, prohibited all fundraising, which included, among others things, selling posters and flyers.²⁷ Yemenis found selling flyers in the streets of Djibouti were arrested and jailed.²⁸

Later, a political connection that prominent Yemenis had established created another issue between them and the colonial authorities. The controversy started in January 1936, when Dorani went aboard the vessel *Le Chenonceau* to greet and welcome Dr. Abdel Hamid Said Bey, who was then the head of the Egyptian Red Cross.²⁹ Abdel Hamid Said Bey was not only received by Dorani; Muslims and other Arabs were invited to a formal dinner at Dorani's home, which was followed by a conference attended by men from the Arab elite.³⁰ For the French authorities, this event was clear evidence that the Yemenis were working toward creating a political movement based on Islamic unity. The *commandant de circle de Djibouti* now considered Dorani to be involved with an underground Islamic organization, the members of which included three Yemeni notables: Salim Muti, Ba Zarʾa, and Seif Saʿid Muhammad.³¹

French fears grew when Dorani organized yet another conference later that same month. The participants of this meeting included prominent Yemenis, among them ʿAli Coubèche, Salim Muti, Ba Zarʾa, Farah Samatar, and Saʿid Ahmed.³² The key speaker was Saʿid al-Asnag, a Hadrami who was the head of the Aden-based Arab Reform Club.³³ Asnag gave a strongly worded speech that called for Islamic unity. He argued that Islamic unity would give hope and inspiration to youth living under foreign rule.³⁴ As an example of what steps Djibouti activists could take, he told them that his organization in Aden had forced the British colonial administration to include Qurʾanic studies in the school curriculum, a subject the British were reluctant to offer.³⁵ The French authorities were alarmed by this development and were prepared to take serious action against the Yemenis, including deporting Dorani from the territory.³⁶

Being Yemeni Muslim in the Hinterland

In the hinterland region of Ethiopia, Yemenis faced a similar negative process of inclusion. In this instance, the ideological basis of the discrimination was not a Darwinian theory of social evolution that regarded Arabs as somehow better than black people, but still as 'lesser beings' next to the French. In Ethiopia, discrimination based on concepts of 'race' was a long-standing practice or norm. Within the Ethiopian community, especially among people of the Ethiopian highlands, darker-skinned people from the south, who had historically been used as slaves, were discriminated against.

Referred to as Barəyas ('negro'), people from Ethiopia's southern region, as well as those from the rest of 'dark' Africa, were seen as inferior. As in Europe, there were a number of phenotypical markers, such as the curliness of the hair and the flatness of the nose, that were believed to provide evidence of inferiority. Semitic people were seen as having a more refined facial appearance and were regarded as superior. The assumed inferiority of darker-skinned people was linked to a perceived racial inferiority.

Kinship was defined in part as being a relation of bones, and the bones of the Barəyas were considered to be inferior. Sayings such as ባርያ ከአጥንቱ ነው መገማው. (a Barəya stinks from his bone) attest to the general attitude toward Barəyas. Signifying this non-socialness, Barəyas were not referred to by their proper names. It was also commonplace for people to liken Barəyas to monkeys and refer to them as *totəyə* (Amharic for 'monkey').

Within this logic, Yemenis, with their lighter skin color and narrow noses, avoided discrimination because of their phenotypical features. They were nevertheless subject to social hierarchies and discriminated against because of their religion. Arabness, a term used interchangeably with 'Muslim,' was also subject to negative stereotypes. A key reason for this was the Christian history of the Ethiopian state and the cosmology that it developed.

For much of its history, what is now known as the Ethiopian region has been dominated by the highland Christian kingdom in the north. This area was ruled by Ethiopian Orthodox Christians who claimed lineage to the House of Solomon in Israel. According to the legend of the state, which was recorded in a medieval text, *Kebra Nagast*,[37] the association of the Ethiopian kingdom with the House of Israel came about as a result of the journeying of the legendary Queen Makeda.[38] According to the legend, Makeda ruled over Ethiopia and traveled to Israel upon hearing about the wisdom of King Solomon of Israel from a merchant called Tamarin. The journey resulted in a romantic affair between Solomon and Makeda, which led to the birth of a son, Menelik I. According to *Kebra Nagast*, Menelik I was the founder of what came to be known as the Solomonic dynasty, which only ended in 1974, after the socialist-inspired military coup.

Historically, this state cosmology has played a key role in the interaction of the kingdom and its Orthodox Christian subjects with the neighboring Muslim population. It has also affected the interaction between host communities and migrant groups. By associating themselves with Israel, the kingdom's rulers believed they could assert that Ethiopians were 'God's chosen people.' They also believed that this claim was strengthened by the *Kebra Nagast* account of Israel's loss of the Ark of the Covenant during King Solomon's rule. According to *Kebra Nagast*, the Ark of the Covenant was stolen and brought to Ethiopia by Menelik I, following a dream. In the dream, the sun is seen moving beyond Israel. This vision, coupled with the alleged presence of the Ark of the Covenant in Ethiopia, was claimed to be a clear sign of God's preference for Ethiopia over Israel. Ethiopia was declared the new Zion and Christian Orthodox Ethiopians were said to be the new Israelites, God's chosen people. In the state cosmology, Ethiopia's uniqueness has been further affirmed by the fact that the Ethiopian king 'Izana accepted Christianity as far back as the fourth century. In much of highland Ethiopian history, Ethiopian rulers have conceptualized their territory as a Christian island under constant attack from pagan and Muslim communities.

This state cosmology was another factor in the development of society along hierarchical lines. In Ethiopian society, Yemeni Muslims were ranked lower than Christians, as they were outside the category of 'chosen people.' To enforce this distinction and this hierarchy, an actual boundary mechanism existed between Ethiopian Christians and Yemeni Muslims. Although there were exceptions, generally, Ethiopian Orthodox

Christians refrained from marrying Yemenis, and Yemenis were not allowed to marry into the Orthodox community. Social attitudes suggested that Yemeni Muslims were impure, or pollutants, and at best they were considered shabby and unclean. These assumptions fed on Islamic rituals that require members of the faith to perform a cleansing ritual that involves washing the genitalia five times a day. This ritual, from the perspective of the Orthodox Christian community, presented Yemenis and other Muslims as unclean beings unworthy of association.

The social attitudes of the traditionally dominant Orthodox community also considered Yemeni food to be unclean. This was particularly true of food made from animals slaughtered by Yemenis. When a Muslim kills an animal, Allah is called upon, rather than the Christian God, and hence the food was considered unclean (see Ficquet, 2006; Zellelew, 2015). The container holding the food was also considered to be polluted. In extreme cases, even a container from which a Yemeni had been drinking was considered unclean. Among traditional Ethiopian Orthodox communities the impurity created by the presence of Yemeni Muslims required a ritual that usually involved the sprinkling of holy water by an Orthodox priest who was familiar with specific rituals used to cleanse the pollution. If someone ate Yemeni food, especially meat slaughtered by a Yemeni, they would also need to perform a cleansing ritual. A person who ate meat slaughtered by Yemenis was even, in many instances, required to be rebaptized in the Ethiopian Orthodox Church because they were considered to have become Muslim.

In administrative terms, this cosmology meant that Yemenis lived in a hegemonic Christian system. The Christian state attempted to curb the proliferation of mosques, for example. Yemenis were not allowed to own land or hold key formal positions in the Ethiopian imperial administration. Sometimes they found themselves trapped in Muslim–Christian conflicts that became violent. This, for example, is what happened when Lij Iyasu was deposed in 1916. As we saw in chapter five, Lij Iyasu was at the time based in Harar. Upon learning of the order for his arrest he fled to the Afar lowland, where he had alliances. Harar city, where a number of Yemenis were resident, was, however, engulfed in a Muslim–Christian conflict in which Christians killed Muslims, as they were considered sympathizers of Lij Iyasu. It is not clear how many of these Muslims were Yemeni, but the severity of the situation and the bloodbath in which the Yemenis found themselves can be discerned from the first report that came out of Harar. Sent by a representative of the Muhammad 'Ali Company, the report said that the killing of Muslims by Christians on October 9 lasted the whole day and was only stopped by the order of the British consul in Harar.[39]

Despite these problems, the Ethiopian emperor actively sought out and associated with important Muslims, particularly Yemenis. During the main Muslim festivals it was traditional to invite to the palace important Yemenis along with other important Ethiopian Muslims: indeed, wealthy Yemenis were frequently invited to the palace. In recruiting Muslims to the imperial court the government tried to control the Muslim population of Ethiopia, which was substantial in terms of numbers.

In the Ethiopian region, the landscape of Islam changed with the Italian invasion. The Italians adopted a divide and rule policy, and because of their Libya colony tried to favor Muslims. As with the French in Djibouti, the Italians fantasized about being custodians of Islam. As Napoleon had declared himself the friend of Muslims on his visit to Egypt, the Italian fascist leader Benito Mussolini solemnly swore his benevolent intentions toward Muslims on his visit to Tripoli in March 1937. Waving the sword of Islam that had been presented to him by Libyans, he declared, "Fascist Italy intends to guarantee the Muslim population of Libya and Ethiopia peace, justice and welfare, the respect of the law of the Prophet, and wishes to show its sympathy to Islam and the Muslims of the entire world" (Allievi, 1996: 183).

For Yemenis in Ethiopia, particularly those settled in Addis Ababa, this declaration, although made for strategic and ideological reasons, had a positive impact. For the majority it meant a peaceful existence during the difficult period of Italian rule, although some worked against the Italians, including Sheikh al Zahiri. As we saw in the previous chapter, Yemenis living in the capital were favored by the Italian regime for propaganda purposes. As in the imperial period, the Italians continued to invite Yemenis to the palace and to adopt a favorable disposition toward Arabs and Muslims.

Despite this favoritism, as in the case of Djibouti, Yemeni Muslims in Ethiopia remained subject to racist classification based on evolutionary thinking. In Italy, the fascist government made a distinction between northern and southern Italians, for example. The northerners were said to be of Germanic and Aryan origin, compared to the southern Italians who were regarded as touched by the Arab race.[40] This early division was further developed and extended outside Italy once the state acquired colonies in Africa. Here, classification based on race was at the core of the fascist strategy. A key element was the manifesto of Fascist intellectuals, *Manifesto degli scienziati razzisti* (Manifesto of Racial Scientists), which was published in 1938. Much of this manifesto became law shortly after its publication, affirming the purity and superiority of the Italian race. Considering Italians to be a pure Aryan race, the manifesto asserted the notion of hierarchy among people: "It is not enough to admit only that there exist major groups that are commonly called races that are differentiated only by a few characteristics, but one must admit that there exist minor groups . . . differentiated by a large number of common characteristics."[41] Encouraging the people of Italy to call themselves "openly racist," the manifesto further asserted that it was "necessary to make a clear distinction between the Mediterranean people on one side, and the Orientals and the Africans on the other side."[42]

In the Ethiopian context, this manifesto became an important guideline. Yemeni Arabs and Ethiopians were regarded as racially inferior to Italians. To ensure the purity and superiority of Aryan blood, Italians were urged both in Ethiopia and in the wider Italian colony not to intermarry with the natives, who were believed to be a degenerate race (Milkias, 2006: 330). However, within this racist hierarchy, as in the case of Djibouti, Yemenis were considered superior to the general Ethiopian population. Beyond the racial justification, anthropology was employed to justify the racial superiority of Arabs over black Ethiopians.

Before the Italians colonized the region it was widely believed throughout Europe that Africans, including Ethiopians, were descended from the biblical character of Ham. Based on the Bible, people were divided into Caucasian, Semitic, and Hamitic—these groups being the descendants of Japheth, Shem, and Ham. In the Bible, Ham was cursed and ordained by God to become a slave. Colonialists often used this biblical narrative to justify the enslavement of black people.[43]

When the Italians occupied Ethiopia, this racist/mythical hierarchy was more difficult to maintain because of the existence of archaeological and historical sites. It was the presence of such sites in areas of the Hamite Ethiopians that led to the classification and eventual conceptualization of Arabs as superior to Ethiopians. The Italians made this shift by employing anthropology. Aldobrandino Mochi wrote an article entitled "Gli oggetti etnografici delle popolazioni Ethiopiche," which stated that during the Paleolithic era the areas of Ethiopia and Egypt were inhabited by a pure black race such as that still found in Senegal. This black race, he claimed, was subsequently fertilized by the Hamitic–Cushite mixture, leading to the development of civilization during the Nilotic period. In the framework developed by Mochi, Ethiopians were said to be a hybrid of the Semites who had moved to the region after the earlier migration of the Hamites.[44]

Another prominent Italian anthropologist, Giuffrida Ruggeri, from the University of Naples, wrote a book that claimed to explain the origins of Ethiopians. He wrote that Ethiopians had migrated from Asia long ago, and their physical features, which were not 'negroid,' were the result of their intermarriage with pre-Islamic Semites from Arabia (Caponetto, 2008: 49–50). Later, Enrico Cerulli advanced a similar argument regarding the foreignness of Ethiopians, asserting that Ethiopian civilization originated with the migration of Sabeans from the present-day southern Yemen region.[45] The Sabeans, he claimed, colonized the indigenous black areas, resulting in a 'higher' form of civilization.

This externalization of Ethiopia seems to have raised Ethiopians up the evolutionary hierarchy followed by the fascist regime, but these theories also put them in an inferior position compared to Yemeni Arabs, from whom all Ethiopian civilization was believed to have derived.

The Italian fascist era came to an end with the restoration of the Ethiopian monarchy in May 1941. However, the monarchy and the local population saw the Muslim community as a threat, and actions were taken to prevent the spread of Islam. In Islamic centers such as Harar, the government proceeded to close the sharia court, which the Italians had earlier allowed, and Muslims were encouraged to use Amharic rather than Arabic in their schools (Erlich, 2007). Significantly, a new constitution adopted in 1955 made it clear that Ethiopia was a Christian country in which Muslims had no say in official matters. Articles 16, 21, and 126 of the constitution affirmed the status of the Ethiopian Orthodox Church as the state church, and stated that all monarchs should be adherents of this faith.

During this period, Yemenis were under suspicion, as were many Muslim groups, but they were not in any way harassed. In Addis Ababa, the Yemeni school used Arabic as the medium of instruction. Some of the Yemeni merchants who were closely associated with the emperor were retained in their capacity as advisors or as part of the wider entourage. As before, Muslim festivals were not viewed as official holidays, and Yemenis, along with other important Muslims, visited the imperial court during these holidays.

Being Muslim: The Second Half of the Twentieth Century
The case of Djibouti

In Djibouti, the early part of the second half of the twentieth century witnessed further attempts to reduce the influence of Islam. The French empire had been under pressure from nationalists who wanted to remove French soldiers. In this period the Yemeni qadi of Djibouti was important in providing a moralistic interpretation of the world in the hope of maintaining the status quo. A remarkable text demonstrating the domestication of Islam in Djibouti and the role of the Sada in this process is a series of public speeches given by the Yemeni qadi of Djibouti, Sayyid 'Ali Abu Bakr al Saqqaf, and various governors of the territory.

The general tone of these speeches, given during various Islamic festivals, including Arafa and Eid al Adha, is not one that reflects the stereotype of Islam outlined above. This is a carefully phrased discourse that constantly emphasizes the unity of Muslims and Christians. The speeches focused on the peaceful nature of their mutual existence in the territory of Djibouti, which is characterized as a peaceful country despite occasional problems:

On the occasion of such a meeting that brings Muslims and Christians side by side, it is always a great pleasure for us to note the climate of cordiality, understanding, and tolerance that reigns in this city, even though various different races and religions are in constant contact here. In our world, so troubled and now so much smaller, where the problem of men's mixing and coexisting will become more and more relevant, it is no trivial matter, in fact it is of the greatest importance, that areas of peace and tolerance such as ours continue to exist.[46]

France is portrayed here as a bastion of tolerance where Muslims could live in comfort. The governor-general of the territory, in his 1966 speech, given on the occasion of Eid al Fitr, observed that Muslims and Christians have affection and respect for each other. He claimed that no other country better demonstrated the fraternity and respect that Christians felt toward Muslims: "Among the Christian communities they have never been better understood or better put into practice than by the French nation, and it is not by chance that today no city in Europe holds as many Muslim students as Paris."[47]

It was to such an ideology that Yemeni religious leaders subscribed. They tried to justify it to people calling for revolution, especially in the 1960s and 1970s. Sayyid Abu Bakr al Saqqaf often characterized the French colonialists as tolerant and concerned with the development of the territory. He made a number of remarks that endorsed French rule. For instance, while the territory's Muslim population was generally opposed to the French presence, which was demonstrated during the visit of Charles de Gaulle in August 1966, Saqqaf endorsed the election of de Gaulle and eventually publicly lamented his death. During the 1966 Eid al Fitr celebration, he noted that the festival "is one of the good occasions that have arrived after his Excellency General de Gaulle has been reelected gloriously as the president of the Republic of France, which has resulted in great satisfaction in Muslim circles, who are happy and pleased by this successful election."[48]

Although the majority of the population was dissatisfied with French rule and ready to overthrow it through violent means, Saqqaf preached tolerance and the rejection of violence. He wrote about the general brotherhood between Muslims and Christians, which the French administration also emphasized. In a speech in January 1960, after the governor of the territory asked the population of Djibouti to reject all forms of enmity, Saqqaf put forward a similar position to his fellow Muslims.[49] After thanking the governor for his wise counsel and guidance, Saqqaf endorsed Muslim and Christian friendship, which he said was necessary for the benefit of the country. He called for the rejection of all dissension and discord among the population.[50]

Saqqaf's speeches would not be worthy of attention if it were not for their ideology. His call for peace between the two religions becomes an ideology when one realizes that those referred to as Christians are actually the French colonial power holders and their families in Djibouti, where the native inhabitants are Muslims. What was being asked by the French administrators, and what those such as Saqqaf were seeking, was the maintenance of the status quo in favor of the French empire.

At the time, Saqqaf was explicit in officiating in his role as the administrator of the ulama. For example, in 1965 he instructed young people, saying:

> Muslims are celebrating the blessed festival. . . . Yet their hearts and minds are with the pilgrims who went to the holy place of Mecca—who were yesterday at Arafa—a remarkable reunion that cannot be compared to anything else, which animates all the faithful, in the obligation and fear which erase any difference between kings, nations, presidents, rich, poor, all are equal in the sight of God.
>
> On this occasion, I ask each to forgive—to cleanse the soul—and I ask the youth to learn the Muslim belief, and in addition French and the good education it provides because it is a language that is generally important. They must be obliged to learn it and it would be important to teach it to young people who want to improve their lives.
>
> In conclusion, I warmly thank the governor for participating in our celebration. We wish great success in their undertakings to the vice president and all the personalities in the government. And we extend our wish for happiness and prosperity for Great France and her president (His Excellency General de Gaulle).[51]

Figure 6. The Yemeni Vice Qadi of Djibouti during an official ceremony before the independence of Djibouti (Courtesy of 'Abdallah Mohamed Kamil).

In the Djiboutian context, this association of religious figures with colonial power holders had a devastating effect on Yemeni communities when the country finally achieved its independence in the 1970s, especially in terms of the high-profile Sada. Among Somali and 'Afar Muslims there was a high degree of mistrust toward Arab and Yemeni religious figures. At an official level, this meant giving key religious positions, including Saqqaf's position, to non-Yemenis, particularly Somalis of 'Issa origin. During this period, disrespect toward Arab religious figures increased because of the change in ideas. The catalyst among the local community was exposure to a more puritanical interpretation of Islam that originated in Saudi Arabia. This interpretation of Islam, which had been established in Arabia since the eighteenth century, started to make itself felt in the emergence of the Saudi state in the 1930s (Østebø, 2012: 130–31). By the middle of the 1950s, the Saudi state began to export their puritanical version of Islam as a way of countering the Egyptian-based Nasserite ideology, which was anti-Saudi and antimonarchy (Østebø, 2011: 638).

In the new interpretation of Islam, local sheikhs and religious figures, including the Sada, came to be considered 'just another set of Muslims' rather than a special category of people that should be venerated. The new interpretation actively discouraged the worship of Muslim saints, including the Sada. Given the misgivings of local Somalis and the 'Afar population in relation to Arabs, this idea was actively welcomed by some segments of Djiboutian society. By the middle of the twentieth century the pressures on the Sada came not only from Somali and 'Afar Muslims but also from within Yemeni society more widely. This was not only the case for Yemenis in Djibouti; these changes reverberated across the Indian Ocean region.

In the Horn of Africa, the first part of the twentieth century witnessed a widening of the Yemeni diaspora. By the second half of the twentieth century, Yemenis in the diaspora were able to gain money and influence. But the fortunes Yemenis subsequently earned in overseas territories were not distributed according to the principles of hierarchy, as noted earlier. Like the Sada, by working abroad and engaging in trade and labor, traditionally inferior groups were able to gain wealth. This newfound economic strength was translated into action and influence in a number of ways. At one point Yemenis were involved in the reconstruction of their homeland; at other times they sponsored insurgency groups to topple unwanted regimes in southern and northern Yemen. For example, in the Horn of Africa, some northern Yemenis gave financial contributions to try to secure the overthrow of Imam Yahya; others raised contributions to overthrow the British colony established in southern Yemen.

These economic gains had another effect: reforming and challenging age-old social attitudes. Traditionally low-ranking social groups that were now wealthy started to challenge the position of the Sada. In places such as Indonesia, Yemeni associations became divided between the Sada, who tried to maintain the old social attitudes and their hierarchy, and those low-ranking social groups that tried to invert the old social attitudes by forming their own associations and educational facilities.[52] In the new processes formed by the economic gains of lower social groups, debate and contestation were framed in terms of religious discourse. The Sada, quoting the Qur'an and Islamic traditions, affirmed that they should be respected by virtue of being the descendants of the Prophet Muhammad. Those who had been in lower social positions also referred to the Qur'an, in this instance to affirm equality among men, thereby challenging Sada dominance. In day-to-day activities, their discontent was expressed in terms of deliberately omitting to follow the traditional way of greeting a Sada man, wherein those in lower social positions were required to stand when a male Sada entered a room and to kiss a Sada's hand in greeting, and then his forehead.

The case of Ethiopia

The situation for Yemenis in Ethiopia took a different turn compared to events in Djibouti. Until the 1960s, being a Yemeni Muslim in Ethiopia meant being subject to the Ethiopian state, which, as has been described above, was organized around the supremacy of the Ethiopian Orthodox Church. This trend changed in the 1960s when the Ethiopian monarchy faced challenges from students and other sectors of society. Inspired in part by the Nasserite aim of uniting all Arabs, the Yemeni of Ethiopia and their co-religionists began to affirm their Arab identity and Islamic religious affiliation. In this regard, Nasser's official visit to Ethiopia in the early 1960s was a precursor of this revivalism in the region when, to the surprise of non-Muslim Ethiopians, many Muslims (including Yemeni Arabs) flocked to the airport to greet him (Ahmed, 1994).

This event was viewed with some surprise by the Orthodox population because of the non-assertiveness of Muslims and Yemenis in the Ethiopian imperial context. It was followed a few years later by another demonstration calling for respect for Islam and rights for Muslims. Among other things, the demonstrators demanded recognition of Islamic festivals as national occasions, and for the separation of state and religion (Ahmed, 1994). This demonstration, in which many Yemenis resident in Addis Ababa participated, was opposed by the Orthodox Church, which presented a report to state officials concerning the threat that the recognition of Islam presented to the ancient Ethiopian state, which had always been Christian.[53]

For the Yemeni community in Addis Ababa, however, the struggle for recognition that occurred immediately before the downfall of the monarchy was not only a matter of asserting Muslim identity. It was also a reaffirmation of Arab identity, which they felt had been trampled by imperial powers and the Orthodox Christian state. Nasser's appeal, which, as we have seen, reverberated across Ethiopia and Djibouti, was the main source of inspiration in these events: his ideal of Arab unity was enthusiastically welcomed. Until recently, for example, the Yemeni school in Addis Ababa still displayed Nasser's picture on its walls.

With the Derg takeover, Yemeni interactions with the state took another turn. The Derg came to power opposing the old regime and viewed Muslims, including Yemenis, as an oppressed class (Ahmed, 1994). Some Yemenis were considered to be bourgeois but, insofar as they were also Muslim, the Derg viewed them as oppressed. As one countermeasure, the Derg declared Islamic festivals to be national occasions. In the spirit of equality, the Derg also asked the Muslim community leader to refrain from coming to the palace during the festival. A Derg official proclaimed such practices to be part of the ancient regime of feudalistic customs. In view of the regime's favorable disposition toward them, the Muslim authorities became favorably disposed toward the Derg. Muslim officials instructed the wider Muslim public to follow the Derg's directives. They also sought to demonstrate similarities between socialism and Islam—for example, by referring to Muslim economic practices (Ahmed, 1994).

These early developments under the Derg government were received with mixed feelings by Yemenis. Among the young people, who were part of the revolutionary demonstrations that toppled Haile Selassie's regime, the socialist vision of the world adopted by the Derg was a source of inspiration. Given their vision of a society where people could be treated equally, young revolutionary Yemenis, like other Ethiopian youth, used these new ideas to challenge the old social attitudes that had structured their lives. They also used them to challenge state cosmology and colonial ideology. Among the older generation, however, the Derg's Leninist and Marxist perspectives, which viewed religion as the opium of the people, were regarded with considerable mistrust and dislike.

As in the context of Djibouti, the reimagination of the social stratification and the presence of a new state vision did not enable Yemenis to escape the grip of the enduring structure of social memory.

In Ethiopia, despite the new political developments, Orthodox Christians continued to regard Yemenis as the historical enemies of the state. Such labels were activated during the Derg government era when they were faced with an insurgency sponsored by Arabs. Yemenis who returned to Yemen as a result of the rhetoric of nationalism in the Horn of Africa encountered the power of the old structures there as well. Whatever their origin, whether they were from Djibouti or Ethiopia, returning Yemenis, who were often of mixed-race origin, were considered to be Ethiopians, or Habesha, as Ethiopians are referred to in Arabic.

This creation of similarity was made possible by similarity in skin color. The label 'Habesha' indicates that Yemenis were viewed as the old enemy who had once tried to destroy the Ka'ba, Islam's holiest site. Thus, in the middle of the twentieth century, old social memories were reactivated and used to categorize newly arriving Yemenis. The return of the diasporic community to its origins also generated a distinction between those who were full or pure Yemenis, Asli, and those who were of mixed-race origin from the Horn, Muwalladin. Based on these distinctions a new hierarchy was created. The Muwalladin were considered to be unworthy in marriage terms, as they were seen as morally inferior to mainland-born Yemenis.

The Post–Cold War Era: Hierarchies and Enduring Attitudes

In the Horn of Africa, Arabs and Muslims witnessed both new trends and the repetition of old social attitudes. Within the Djiboutian context, being Arab was taken to mean being superior to Somalis. Yemenis working in various capacities in Djibouti considered the rest of the population, particularly Somalis, as Muslims but not as complete Muslims and, hence, they regarded them as morally inferior. Somalis, particularly Somali women, were regarded as promiscuous and less strict in the observance of Islamic seclusion. Yemenis take pride in following a strict segregation of men and women. Although marriage between Somalis and Yemenis does take place, the majority of Yemenis prefer to marry other Yemenis. In terms of marriage, Somalis are regarded as immoral and are thus considered as far from ideal partners. This ranking of people in a moral hierarchy is exercised not only by Yemenis but also by Somalis: Somalis consider Arabs to be lesser Muslims and view them as womanizers.

However, both groups view Ethiopian Orthodox Christians as lower in the moral hierarchy. The main reason for this is the involvement of many Orthodox women in prostitution in Djibouti. This is regarded as immoral, and thus Ethiopians are considered by both Yemenis and Somalis as effectively degrading Yemeni morality. Yemenis might associate with Orthodox women, including prostitutes, but they rarely want to be seen with them, much less to marry them.

This sense of moral superiority and the lower ranking of others, particularly Ethiopians, is not something new, however. It has been present throughout history. Muslim Ethiopians were respected by Yemenis by virtue of being from Ethiopia, one of the earliest nations to give refuge to early Muslim converts. It is also a land where famed Muslim figures lived. For example, Bilal, the first muezzin of the Prophet, was an Ethiopian slave. Nevertheless, Ethiopians in Arabia have appeared as concubines; in fact, Ethiopian women were the most sought-after concubines in Arabia.[54] As a result of this, Ethiopians are viewed as promiscuous and seen as a factor in the moral degeneration of Muslims and Yemenis in particular. Of course, in such a system not all Ethiopians are ranked equally. Both Yemenis and Somalis are favorably disposed toward the Hararis, whose homeland has historical links with the coast. After the Hararis, Yemenis and Somalis are more favorably disposed toward people from the Wallo area, who are present in Djibouti in great numbers. Unlike the Hararis, however, Wallos are referred to derogatively as *argo*. This term not only signifies their designated inferiority: Wallos are popularly categorized as being very short-tempered people, quick to use knives in a fight. In the social attitudes of Yemenis, the next group down the ladder is the Oromos, who are viewed as inferior, being illogical and uncivilized people. The lowest position is taken by the Amhara, particularly Amhara women, who are viewed as immoral and promiscuous, and often assumed to be prostitutes. Because the Amhara were state holders in Ethiopia, they are also considered to be cunning, and unfavorably disposed toward Muslims.

There was an attempt to create a hierarchy among Yemenis, using past state and imperial encounters. In this regard, a broad division operates between northern and southern Yemenis. As southern Yemen was part of the British Empire, paradoxically this oppression is seen as a mark of civilization. By virtue of being colonized, southern Yemenis regard themselves as more civilized than northerners, who were under Imam Yahya's rule. Referred to as *jebeli*s, northerners are viewed as rude, uncivilized, and morally below the more civilized southern Yemenis.

Among the Yemeni community, the reenactment of colonial discourse is not confined to Djibouti. In Ethiopia there is a similar sort of hierarchy based on morality, as well as a sense of moral superiority that is perceived to have come from being colonized. As in Djibouti, southern Yemenis view northerners as less civilized because of their noncolonial history. The utilization of colonial experience as a tool of hierarchy is employed not only among Yemenis, however, but also in their relations with Ethiopians. In this regard, the Italian fascist theory of the superiority of Arabs is frequently deployed to explain the civilization and moral superiority of Yemenis over Ethiopians. Although Yemenis do not in any particular instance refer to the fascists, and do not seem to be aware of the origin of their discourse, they nevertheless employ the same kind of language employed by the Italians to lay claim to their superiority. Ethiopian civilizations, they argue, are derived from Yemen. In this discourse, the Queen of Sheba, whom both Ethiopians and Yemenis regard as their queen, is a bone of contention. Yemenis use a reading of the Qur'an to refer to the moral superiority of Yemenis over Ethiopians.

Managing Muslims in the Age of Terror

The post–Cold War period saw the introduction of new hierarchies and classifications that originated with state and imperial power, particularly the United States. The more recent context has been a redefinition of 'the enemy' away from former Soviet areas. Internationally, in the relative absence of a communist threat, Islam (which has always been regarded, historically, as the enemy) has become the new threat to the global supremacy of the United States and its allies. For example, one observer notes that Islam came to be described and characterized as a cancer spreading across the world:

> Now that the Cold War is becoming a memory, America's foreign policy establishment has begun searching for new enemies.

Possible new villains include "instability" in Europe—ranging from German resurgence to new Russian imperialism—the "vanishing" ozone layer, nuclear proliferation, and narcoterrorism. Topping the list of potential new global bogeymen, however, are the Yellow Peril, the alleged threat to American economic security emanating from East Asia, and the so-called Green Peril (green is the colour of Islam). That peril is symbolized by the Middle Eastern Moslem fundamentalist—the "Fundie," to use a term coined by *The Economist* . . . a Khomeini-like creature, armed with a radical ideology, equipped with nuclear weapons, and intent on launching a violent jihad against Western civilization.[55]

The post–Cold War context presented a challenge to Yemenis and their Muslim compatriots: on the whole, it resulted in a restructuring and reinforcement of state/empire control over Muslims and Islam. The post–Cold War period also resulted in a return to the old ways of dealing with Muslims.

The characterization of Islam as the new post–Cold War enemy of the West resulted in the creation of a division of between 'good' and 'bad' Muslims.[56] Similar in a way to the colonial discourse on Islam, the local indigenous population was regarded as being moderately oriented, good Muslims who practiced Sufi Islam. Their version of Islam and their moderate natures, however, were believed to be in the process of being corrupted and radicalized by Arabs from the Middle East who practice a radical version of Islam—Wahhabism. In both Ethiopia and Djibouti, United States embassy experts have even gone to the extent of claiming the presence of Wahhabi imperialism. For example, the following is an extract from US embassy correspondence entitled "Wahhabi in Ethiopia as Cultural Imperialism":

> Arab Wahhabi Missionaries, mainly from Saudi Arabia, continue to make inroads in to the Ethiopian Muslim community, but are meeting increased resistance in doing so. Islam has existed in Ethiopia since the time of the Prophet Muhammad and the mainly Sufi community has enjoyed traditional custom and cultural practices that have endured for centuries. Yet this indigenous Muslim

culture has come under attack since 9/11 by Wahhabi missionaries engaging in what amounts to cultural imperialism against Ethiopian Islam. . . . Indigenous Ethiopian Muslim culture is under assault and the Ethiopian Muslim community need US support to counter extremist influence.[57]

To curb this Arab-backed radical Islam, western governments (particularly the United States, but including Djibouti and Ethiopia, both allies of the West) sought to implement a number of strategies. The key strategy has been the creation of docile Muslim leaders or councils of *ulama*, similar to French colonial actions during their presence in Djibouti. For example, the Djibouti government formed the High Islamic Council (HIC) in 2004. Directly controlled by the Ministry of Muslim Affairs, which was formed following independence, the HIC was given the task of looking into the management of mosques and the preaching of sermons there. The HIC also examines and monitors the issuance of fatwas as well as the orientation of the *dawa* service. In short, the HIC was established to create passive Muslims and prevent the radicalization believed to be threatening the local community.

A similar strategy is being followed in Ethiopia. Since the downfall of the Derg regime, one of the major tasks of the EPRDF government has been the creation of ulama, including the Islamic Affairs Supreme Council, through which it controls the appointment of imams as well as the content of sermons preached in mosques. The government-appointed imams are required to report unapproved sermons. Arab Islamic preachers are particularly targeted and followed. Recently, the government's attempt to manage 'bad' Muslims has gone to the extent of encouraging the introduction of an Islamic sect, the al-Ahbash (known formally as the Jamiya al-Mashari al-Khayriya al-Islamiya), from Lebanon. It was founded by Sheikh Abdallah Muhammad al-Harari, an Ethiopian who was born in the Harar region of Ethiopia but lived for many years in Lebanon as an exile. Al-Ahbash is regarded as a Sufi sect, inclined toward tolerance and more or less indigenous to the country. Its introduction was considered a positive action that would act as an antidote to Salafism.

Taking this view of the sect, the government organized conferences on its behalf, as well as numerous training sessions, by inviting al-Ahbash figures from Lebanon. By directing such training particularly at the sheikhs and ulama of Ethiopia, the government sought to instill the beliefs of this sect, and thus to counter extremism. However, this action on the part of the government caused a backlash, leading to confrontation between the Muslim community and the government, as the former accused the latter of interfering with their religion. The disagreement eventually led to many demonstrations, and to a government crackdown in which not only ordinary demonstrators, but also a number of key Muslim intellectuals who were organizing the demonstrations, were arrested. The arrests led to continued confrontations and further violence.[58]

As part of the local Muslim community, Yemenis in Ethiopia have been affected by this tense situation. Yemenis view the theological orientation of al-Ahbash as deviating from Islamic teachings, and debate among themselves the sect's teachings concerning the whereabouts of Allah or how Allah should or should not be described. They also question the peacefulness of al-Ahbash; they believe that its leaders may have been involved in past violence in Lebanon, such as the assassination of Lebanon's prime minister Rafic Harriri in 2005. They also participated in the demonstrations against the government's introduction of the al-Ahbash sect.

In addition to the actions of Ethiopian and Djiboutian state authorities, United States embassies have become involved in the task of managing affairs in relation to Muslims in both countries. Embassy staff encourage 'good' Muslims by inviting them to the embassy during the main religious festival. Aid is also used as a way of preventing the encroachment of 'bad'/extremist Muslim ideas into areas that are thought to have a moderate orientation.[59]

The United States has also engaged in a systematic attempt to control and regulate Muslims in both countries. In Ethiopia, for instance, the diplomatic mission is involved in 'cultural programming':

> Every culture that has adopted Islam has its own unique traditions and practices for expressing their Faith. This is manifested

through shrines, literature, faith rituals, and objects that include manuscripts, art, and even clothing and other accoutrements. In countries with mixed faith traditions, tolerance and mutual respect are usually enshrined in theological teachings, but foreign missionaries and other external influences can undermine that balance and force change on teachings. This cultural imperialism can be contoured through cultural programming that focuses on places, objects, and traditions as they relate to indigenous Muslim communities. Similarly, it is important to help local Muslim leaders resist the external forces intellectually by providing materials written by Muslim authors that support a more Orthodox interpretation of Islam in local languages. Doing so supports US foreign policy objectives and may contribute to countering Islamic extremists.[60]

In Ethiopia, a number of projects have been implemented as part of the United States cultural program. A US-funded project has renovated Muslim sites such as the Täfari Mekone house in Harar and the Muhammad Ali house in Addis Ababa.[61] The United States has also supported a project that focuses on Islamic manuscripts,[62] funding the Institute of Ethiopian Studies to establish an Islamic manuscript preservation center and sponsoring a scholar to assess Islamic manuscripts in Harar.[63] In terms of the tradition component, the United States government sent three experts from the Harar region to study how to develop oral history programs for high school students.[64]

Seen from a broader perspective, the US cultural program is underlined by three assumptions. First, it assumes that Wahhabis are against shrines and Islamic sites. Second, it assumes that 'Ethiopian Islam' has a textual tradition that is being eroded. Third, it assumes that Ethiopian Muslims pass along information orally. Strengthening these cultural aspects is thus seen as way of combating Wahhabi Islam and its attempts to alter Ethiopian Muslims by challenging Islamic sites and trying to integrate Ethiopian Muslims into the wider umma.

Donald Yamamoto, who was the United States ambassador to Ethiopia from 2006 to 2009, upon completion of a report entitled "Countering Wahhabi Influence in Ethiopia through Cultural Programming," asserted:

Any culture is usually proud of its contributions to the world's religious heritage and efforts to protect those contributions are widely appreciated within that culture. Such cultural programming does not have to be expensive, especially when considered within the larger context of US assistance, but it can have a significant public diplomacy payoff for the United States and contribute measurably to foreign diplomacy success. When all is considered and executed creatively, cultural programming can make a real difference in turning back Islamic extremism and turning public opinion against activists who seek to overturn the existing order and import a brand of Islam that breeds conflict through its corrosive teaching that runs counter to more orthodox interpretations of the Koran.[65]

In Djibouti, the cultural program described here by the ambassador was introduced through the implementation of United States values, including use of the English language. Djibouti was perceived as a country under assault by Wahhabi imperialism and possible anti-US sentiment. Because of this, the United States embassy in Djibouti urged the formation of a drama club, an English club, and an American library as a way of influencing local Muslims, especially young Muslims, who are regarded as the focus of any cultural program.[66] Embassy officials reported that "winning hearts and minds is less a function of clever advertising than of maximizing the positive role the US plays here on a daily basis through US aid programs."[67]

For the Yemeni community in Djibouti and Ethiopia, living under the shadow of the governments' explicit control of Muslim affairs and United States–led cultural programs has resulted in both constraints and opportunities. In relation to the former, the presence of social attitudes based on 'bad' and 'good' Muslims has meant living in a constrained situation. This is particularly true for Yemenis, as they are Arabs considered to be terrorists working for the establishment of an Islamic state in the Horn of Africa, as well as building mosques. Such allegations are particularly made against wealthy Yemeni businessmen, who started to invest in Ethiopia in the post-Derg period. These kinds of social attitudes, however, are entertained not only by state or imperial powers but also by the local non-Muslim population. The situation of Yemenis in the Horn is exemplified by the story of Sheikh Muhammad 'Amudi.

Among Orthodox Christians, 'Amudi is considered a key actor intent on changing Ethiopia into a Muslim land through the building of mosques and by encouraging the conversion of Christians through money. Although it is not uncommon for Christians to express such views in public, comments on Ethiopian websites are especially explicit about the resentment felt toward Arabs:

> It is rather sad to see my country changed to this. The whole of the street of Addis occupied by Muslims who weren't there a few years back. Have all Muslims from everywhere transferred to Addis? In the old days there were only two mosques in Addis and now they have taken over the whole city. What next? Should we all be Muslims? This religion advocates the killing of all non-Muslims but I read the most hypocritical postings as if this religion of hate is normal. They are only 23 percent but they behave as if they are the majority of the country. Ethiopia is a Christian country, an island among nonbelievers and it should stay as such. No place for beheadings and stoning of women. Thank God, I am a proud Christian. Nonetheless, have a good time with your "holiday."[68]
>
> Does the Ethiopian Orthodox Church leader, Abuna Paulos, know al-'Amudi's hidden agenda. . . . Al-'Amudi would ask Meles to build a second Mecca somewhere in Ethiopia so that the Ethiopian Muslims don't have to make a Hajj every year to Saudi Arabia and spend their money there; instead they would spend it here in Ethiopia. This is a noble idea, I think; King Lalibela did it; why not al-'Amudi?[69]
>
> Ethiopia was closed for Arab Wahhabis for a long time. I heard the golden Emperor Haile Selassie . . . deported every single Arab out of Ethiopia for spreading sexually transmitted diseases and encouraging prostitution and homosexuality. He also closed many corrupt Indian shops and deported a lot of Indians out of

Ethiopia for manipulating and mistreating Ethiopians, just like what they are currently doing in Kenya, Zambia, Zanzibar, etc. Ethiopians owned businesses in Ethiopia and ruled their own destiny. Now, the two parasites (Indians and Arabs) along with other foreigners are back in action, in full force in the name of leasing land and investment. As long as they throw dollars and grains at [President] Meles, he will gladly lick their hairy behinds. He evidently doesn't give a damn about Təgərayə Christians or any other Ethiopians for that matter.... Ethiopia before Arab and Indian investment was much better off. At least people ate food, could afford basic items, and were dignified and respectable. We all know what Ethiopia has become over the past two decades. Now, they are trying their very best to create tension between Muslim and Christians by importing radical Wahhabis.[70]

The United States, which noted the increasingMuslims population and the proliferation of mosques identified 'Amudi as one of the individuals who funded the building of mosques.[71] Shortly after 9/11, 'Amudi was accused on an international level of funding Osama bin Laden and his organization al-Qaeda. It was reported in the western media that 'Amudi, Khalid bin Mahfuz (another Yemeni), and Salah Idris (a Sudanese businessman from one of the wealthiest Saudi-based families) were transferring money to al-Qaeda.[72] 'Amudi was also mentioned in a report allegedly submitted to the United Nations Security Council. The report, written by Jean-Charles Brisard, a French investigator who led the JCB Consulting Group, claimed that 'Amudi was one of seven people who were funding Bin Laden (Brisard, 2002: 7).

In 1999, the United States authorities investigated 'Amudi's bank, the Capital Trust Bank.[73] After the 9/11 attacks, the victims' families demanded that 'Amudi and Bin Mahfuz, whom they considered to be the funders of Osama bin Laden, pay $3 trillion in compensation.[74] 'Amudi was also listed as Osama bin Laden's financier in Paul Thompson's *The Terror Timeline* (2004) and "The Complete 9/11 Timeline" website.[75] At the time, 'Amudi, Mahfuz, and Idris hired the law firm Akin, Gump, Strauss, Hauer, and Feld, established by two former Federal Bureau of Investigation agents and considered well connected with the White House.[76] Despite these changes in fortune, 'Amudi later cleared his name, and Paul Thompson made a formal apology.[77]

Despite the explicit targeting and challenges that some Yemenis are facing, others see an opportunity in the current situation. This is particularly true in Djibouti, where there are large numbers of United States military personnel. Many Yemenis see the US presence as a factor that will integrate the country into the wider world. American influence and presence is regarded as being better than that of France, which is widely considered to have contributed nothing to the country's development. Many Yemenis are enthusiastic to learn about and engage in US-financed projects. Despite this, other Yemenis (and this is also true of other Muslims) do not subscribe to the American classification of 'good' Sufis and 'bad' Wahhabis. Such classifications are regarded as ignorant and at best as a strategy employed to create division among Muslims.

In Ethiopia, the majority of Yemenis feel the same way as those in Djibouti. However, some accept the US vision and have integrated with the structures established by the local government and maintained by the United States. For instance, Sheikh Elias Radman, whose family is originally from northern Yemen, became an active player in the public affairs of the Muslim community following the formation of the Ethiopian Islamic Affairs Council. Siding with the government, he was offered the position of vice president of the council. He was unpopular among many Muslims in Ethiopia because he holds views similar to the United States and Ethiopian governments.[78]

Yemenis between Jihad and Counterterrorism

In the post–Cold War period, the classification of Islam as a security threat that is internally divided into 'bad' and 'good' Muslims has not only been received passively through the expression and affirmation of the unity of Muslims. In the wider Muslim world the demonization of Muslims has led to the emergence of a number of Muslim intellectuals committed to defending Islam and the umma (Soares and Otayek, 2007: 12), often using the media as a means of communication. This has had an impact on Yemenis in the Horn of Africa.

As African countries have been engaged in processes of liberalization, including in terms of the media, the work of these intellectuals came to be seen by a great number of people. Newly introduced satellite channels, such as those owned by the Arab Satellite Communication Organization, brought Islamic sermons into people's homes. They often presented a narrative that vilifies the West and the Christian community. As most of these sermons were in English, they were translated into local dialects and distributed by newly formed Muslim-owned studios. In many African countries the distribution of these materials led to the development of polemical religious discourse between Muslims and the followers of other religions.[79]

Yemenis living in Djibouti and Ethiopia were affected by these worldwide developments, although the effects in the two countries were different. In Djibouti, the proliferation of Islamic sermons was openly accepted. As the majority of people follow Islam, there was no serious conflict or tension as a result of the introduction of these sermons. In the hinterland region of Ethiopia, however, post-1990s developments led to a different scenario. In this traditionally Orthodox Christian state, the spread of sermons in defense of Islam within the context of the war on terrorism and the increased demonization of Muslims since the collapse of the Soviet bloc has been imagined as an accurate indication of increased Muslim radicalization.[80] The Orthodox community in particular considered the sermons to be a direct attack against the Orthodox Church.

In retaliation, many in the Ethiopian Orthodox community, especially through its Sunday school department, Mahebere Kedusan, wrote articles that opposed and sought to delegitimize Islam. The early articles portrayed Islam as a false religion that had evolved from ancient pagan beliefs in Arabia.[81] In 2009, at an Epiphany ceremony, the Orthodox community reactivated the old social attitudes that represented Ethiopia as a Christian nation. The community printed T-shirts with slogans claiming that Ethiopia was a "Christian island." The wide distribution of the T-shirts created tension, and the Muslim community responded by entering Church property in groups of several dozen, where they proclaimed, "Allah is great."

The situation that developed as a result of the spread of Islamist media meant an increase in tensions between the Muslim and Orthodox communities. As part of the wider Muslim umma, Yemenis were offended by the Orthodox reaction, and especially by more recent developments such as the Epiphany ceremony discussed above. Muhammad, an informant, explained the tensions to me this way:

> It is something that activates the jihad that is within you. You know the small shops near the post office? You can find the T-shirts there if you go. However, they are not the only T-shirts. There are T-shirts that say "Ethiopia" and then put the pictures of Christian emperors such as Haile Selassie, Emperor Yohannes, and Menelik. This does not represent the Muslims. Do you know what the Muslims said when the Orthodox claimed that Ethiopia is a Christian island? They said, "If Ethiopia is an island, we are its creators." An island cannot be an island without the surrounding water, can it?

Muhammad's question does not lead to any specific answers, but it does illustrate the tension that Yemenis face while living as subjects of empires and citizens of states.

The tension that developed in this age of 'war on terror' was not confined to the realm of media. Some young Yemenis also engaged themselves in the path of jihad, further contributing to the construction of 'bad' versus 'good' Muslim. During the fieldwork period for this book, a member of one of the prestigious Yemeni families in Ethiopia traveled to Yemen. According to his relatives he started attending mosques frequently and associated himself with youth who have jihadist inclinations. Eventually he, along with others, was killed when they attacked a petrol station in the south of Yemen. Another Yemeni family also related what happened to their son. In their case the son traveled to Iraq in the aftermath of the 2003 United States invasion of that country. The last time they heard from their son was on his way to the battlefield. After six months they learned that he had died fighting.

At the level of state/empire, the post–Cold War period has been about more than the distinction between 'bad' and 'good' Muslim for Yemenis in the Horn. War has become a reality, particularly as a result of the rise of al-Qaeda in southern Yemen, in which many Yemenis participate as jihadists. In addition to ground combat, drone attacks have proliferated and

Djibouti and Ethiopia act as key Horn of Africa states that facilitate the war in south Yemen by providing, for example, secret drone bases.[82] Their deep involvement has made them a target of threat or attack. In the past, Ethiopia has been threatened by Dr. Ayman al-Zawahari, the number two man in Al Qaeda, right after the country's intervention in Somalia in 2007.[83] As the recent release of Osama bin Laden's correspondence by the United States Government Office of the Director of National Intelligence (ODNI) shows, Ethiopia was also characterized as comiting an act of immorality that should not be forgiven.[84] Djibouti suffered a grenade attack in a restaurant in the capital city in May 2014.[85]

For the majority of Yemenis, the development of war has meant the proliferation of atrocities. In Yemen itself, drone attacks led to the deaths not only of 'bad' Muslims but also of innocent individuals and 'good' Muslims who openly opposed al-Qaeda. In 2013, for example, a drone attack in eastern Yemen killed Ahmad bin 'Ali Jaber, a forty-year-old father of seven who was known for his opposition to al-Qaeda and often preached against it in mosques.[86] His case is not isolated, as numerous civilians have perished as a result of the drone war (see Human Rights Watch, 2013). In the Horn of Africa, the 'war on terror' has entailed a precarious existence, and for some who have been suspected of terrorism it has meant secret detention and extraordinary rendition.

The case of Muhammad 'Abdallah Salih al-Asad illustrates the point. Asad, a Yemeni national, was arrested in Tanzania in 2003 and transferred to Djibouti, where he was held for two weeks before he was given over to a United States rendition team that transferred him to Afghanistan. After he was released in 2006 without any charge of terrorism, Asad's case was brought to the African Commission on Human and People's Rights by the International Centre for the Legal Protection of Human Rights and the Center for Human Rights and Global Justice at New York University.[87] The two organizations filed a case against the Djibouti government, and Asad obtained an opportunity to detail what happened to him to the African Commission. He stated that he was held in several secret prisons operated by the US Central Intelligence Agency (CIA). He claimed that he was abused in prison, purposely isolated and exposed to the cold and to artificial light as well as loud music.[88] The African Commission dismissed the case on the basis of insufficient evidence.[89] However, the United States Senate Select Committee on Intelligence released a report on the CIA's detention and interrogation program in December 2014 that clearly identified Asad as one of the individuals detained by the CIA.[90]

To conclude, because states/empires historically, and to this day, have considered Yemenis to be Muslims, they have developed strategies to counter what is seen as their threat to power. One of the strategies has been to create a distinction between 'good' Muslims and 'bad' Muslims, wherein Arabs are generally considered to be more fanatical than the indigenous population. This has led to a series of attempts to curb Arab influence. As we have seen, however, Yemenis are not just victims; they have participated in the strategies pursued by states/empires and some have also tried to counter empire/state. Being a Muslim Arab has led to particular interactions with states/empires, and it has been a factor in Yemeni social life, one that can both broaden and narrow the individual's options. By being Muslim Arabs, Yemenis have been engulfed in a series of social attitudes that have created hierarchies not only between them and autochthonous groups but also among themselves. This situation has resulted in the proliferation of conflict and the creation of deadlocks between religious groups as well as between the diaspora and state/empire. It has also resulted in human atrocities at all levels.

7. Conclusion

This book began with the story of 'Umar 'Ubayd Ba 'Aqil, my first Yemeni informant, whom I met in 2004 in Dire Dawa. 'Umar is part of the twentieth-century Yemeni migration to the Horn of Africa. At the time of our meeting, he was in trouble after having been found with two passports, which is illegal in Ethiopia. In addition, his cousin had been shot in a Dire Dawa street not long before while helping a French man who had come to study the history of Arabs in the region. 'Umar's story was thus a means of opening up a much wider and deeper examination of the interaction of Yemenis with state/empire in Djibouti and its hinterland.

Using various entry points, including the economy, politics, and religion, the intent of this book has been to show the relevance of state/empire in the lives of Yemenis in the diaspora. I critically engaged with the way diasporic communities have been viewed in Indian Ocean studies, where Yemenis have been represented as people who move freely across national boundaries and seascapes. Indian Ocean migration studies have tended to ignore the ordering power of state/empire and, instead, have looked at social and cultural strategies, including interpersonal networks, as an explanation for Yemeni migration. Abstracted from the context of state/empire in which they live, Yemenis have been regarded by some as free people with a particular set of sociocultural strategies.

Certainly there are diasporic networks and cultural strategies. But the story of Yemeni migration is larger than a set of strategies. Yemeni migrants have also been subject to the structures of state and imperial powers. In this book, I have argued that the archetypal figure of an individual Yemeni with a network is an academic construct that represents only part of the story. Networks and cultural traits have been important in Yemeni migration, but any serious explanation must be contextualized to include the state/empire. An academic engagement on these terms is worth pursuing; it is an ethical approach that attempts to take into account the suffering and challenges that Yemenis have encountered.

In this ethically driven project, the link between space and empire/state becomes useful. In the colonial period, migration by Yemenis was controlled by the enclosures established by sovereign powers. The political, economic, and religious lives of migrants within these closed sovereign spaces were anything but free. This was also the case in the postcolonial nation-state of Djibouti and the hinterland of Ethiopia.

In academic discussions, the current age of neoliberal globalization is characterized as an age of travel where states do not matter and global governance and cosmopolitan culture have triumphed. Equally, although based on different theoretical premises, scholars of the Indian Ocean region have viewed the various spaces of the Indian Ocean, particularly port spaces, as part of a global, cosmopolitan arena marked by the flow of people and commodities. But the port spaces into which Yemenis migrated were not free spaces. They were spaces where Yemenis were incarcerated.

It is not my intention here to deny the presence of interactions that can be viewed as cosmopolitan engagement. Indeed, port spaces have seen multiple movements of people and commodities. Yemenis have multiple relations, and one can rightly claim that they live as cosmopolitan beings. What I am calling for, rather, is a broadening of the discussion by juxtaposing cosmopolitanism with the power that state/empire exercises. Thus, while agreeing that it is possible to search for the cosmopolitan individual and the cosmopolitan scenario in Djibouti, such an exercise results in only part of the story. It does not represent past realities, for example, but only a current global epistemological order, one characterized by the triumph of capitalism and the accompanying rhetoric that emphasizes the flow of commodities and people. Rather than being cultural bricoleurs, Yemenis are clearly state and imperial subjects. In a number of places, we also see them acting as groups that victimize other subjects of empires and citizens of states. It seems reasonable to conclude, then, that the romantic figure of the Yemeni traveler does not exist. Such a figure can only be made to exist if one overemphasizes the natural unity of the Indian Ocean region. The Indian Ocean region has been viewed as a unified system characterized by the presence of monsoon winds. Studies that aim to prove the presence of this unity omit the inconvenient fact that the natural system of the sea has been regularized by the empire/state. This book, while examining the spatial landscape, shows the connectivity between space and state/empire. In doing so, it reveals that the romanticized figure of the Yemeni does not exist, and that the weakness in the dominant paradigm of the Indian Ocean lies in a narrow approach that sees only a flow of people and commodities moving in a natural, rhythmic manner.

Yemenis are not freely moving cosmopolitan beings. Nor are they the chained subjects of empires/states. Their lived experiences defy even the latest constructs of leftist scholarship, particularly that undertaken by Hardt and Negri (2000; 2004), who view migrant groups as heroic actors who are capable of subverting the nation-state and, ultimately, the global empire that supports it. Hardt and Negri assert that the multitude could subvert the empire by breaking through the state's enclosures. For these writers, the mobility of the multitude is a subversive strategy: "A new nomad horde, a new race of barbarians, will arise to invade or overcome empire" (Hardt and Negri, 2000: 213).

Across the Indian Ocean region, there is no better candidate than Yemenis to fill the criteria of a nomadic multitude. The Yemeni "nomad horde," however, is far from being the champions espoused by Hardt and Negri. In old and new circumstances, they have been more than invaders of empires. They have collaborated with state and imperial powers to the detriment of others. They have also been victims of empires and states.

Perhaps, after all, the problem of the representation of Yemenis originates in our characterization of mobile communities. Our enthusiasm to find connections, to identify subversion or opposition, is what has produced the heroic figure of the Yemeni. If, instead, we take on board the multiple stories gained through anthropological investigation, we can begin to correct such generalized elevations, and see the human in the Yemeni: a social being whose complexity can only be partially understood, whose journey has, in some ways, been generalized and oversimplified. The much celebrated network model, in which various sorts of exchanges are celebrated and diasporic capacities are emphasized, only tells us some aspects of the life of the Yemeni diaspora, and in so doing omits many relevant factors.

What we can learn from criticizing the network model, however, supersedes its implication for Indian Ocean studies. It has implications for the sociology of globalization and social analysis in general, as it reflects trends within the broader social sciences. The vision that the network model projects is not new. Its roots can be traced to the Manchester school of anthropology, such as the work of J. Clyde Mitchell (1969), as well as the writings of the Norwegian anthropologist Fredrik Barth (1959), who was interested in looking at the maximizing and rational capacity of the individual.

The outlook the model prescribes also reflects current academic thinking that has become dominant since the triumph of neoliberal capitalism. Presently, as Bruce Kapferer (2005b) affirms, explanations that take societal-level phenomena into account have been in retreat and are increasingly being replaced by reductionist approaches that try to explain society by putting the emphasis on the individual. This "death of the social," to use a phrase of Nicolas Rose's (1996), has become more fashionable than ever with the development of newer theories wherein analyses that take into account "the social" have been explicitly attacked.

The writings of the French social scientist Bruno Latour (2005), in which scholars are called out for reassessing the social, are one example of such an attack. Latour calls for disbanding the category of the social in favor of an explanation that takes into account the actor and its network. The 'actor' he refers to includes not only human beings but also inanimate objects. In this way Latour aims to part ways with the distinction between nature and culture, and in so doing come up with an explanation that shows the natural unity of things.

This Latourian explanation is reflected among those anthropologists who subscribe to what has come to be known as the 'ontological turn.'

This includes scholars such as Eduardo Viveiros de Castro (2004), Martin Holbraad (2007; 2012), and Amiria Henare et al. (2007). The emphasis here is on a greater naturalization of the social sciences perspective by giving primacy to the natural and by broadening the analyses to include not only the relations between human beings but also the networks people have with inanimate objects. The posthumanist Michel Serres (1995) has also advanced processes of naturalization, particularly in relation to globalization. He argues that globalization should be conceived in terms of relations that exist between man and nature.

For Indian Ocean studies, this call for expanding the definition of actors and networks to include inanimate objects, and for looking at the agency or structuring capacity of these inanimate objects, is bound to have an influence. Indian Ocean studies focus on the ocean and look at human mobility as part of the natural rhythm of the ocean. The field's emphasis on exchange makes it prone to adopting the newer theorizations that even stretch the 'traditional' network model. Already, Devleena Ghosh and Stephen Muecke (2007b) have celebrated the new theoretical paradigm and, based on insights gained from Latour and Serres, tried to demonstrate the natural logic of the Indian Ocean.

The network model and its expansion should be readily criticized, as they will not enable us to know how the lives of people around the Indian Ocean have been structured by states/empires. As scholars of the Indian Ocean region, we do not have the luxury of ignoring the impact of states/empires, because this is an arena where thousands of migrants perish to reach this or that corner of the Indian Ocean. As the final pages of this book were being written, some seventy migrants died after their boat sank off the coast of Yemen.[1] Such, then, is the paradox of Indian Ocean spaces: their scholars portray them as a fluid arena marked by intense exchange while its ports have become the graveyards of thousands whose mobility has been effectively hampered by states/empires. When dealing with Indian Ocean spaces, our account must incorporate the issue of power that people face in this corner of the world, and in this endeavor an analysis that focuses on societal dynamics should be given priority over an analytical model that puts the emphasis on the individual.

But what constitutes the social? In the social sciences, particularly among anthropologists, there is a tendency to equate the social with the structural relationships that exist between people or the cultural innovations of natives. The social is, however, not only framed by the presence of horizontal relations or cultural innovations but also by vertical/hierarchical relations (Bourgouin, 2009). States/empires play an important role in generating these societal hierarchies. For this study, such hierarchical processes include issues of class, ethnicity, and citizenship, which are present in the empirical material and form the basis of Yemeni social life. These elements must be addressed and further understood in order to obtain a fuller picture of the relationship between Yemenis and state/empire. The following pages seek to present this fuller picture by looking in turn at class, ethnicity, and citizenship, beginning with the issue of class.

The Relevance of Class

Class was an important analytical tool in the social sciences in the 1960s and 1970s. However, it was eclipsed by other topics and concerns until scholars in the 1990s, such as McNall et al. (1991), John Hall (1997), and Gordon Marshall (1997), called for its reintroduction to social analysis. In examining the role that class plays here, I sympathize with this recent call, especially as it is expressed in the work of Don Kalb (1997), who urges us to avoid the use of a reified concept of class and instead to adopt an understanding that sees class as conditioned by specific developments in a particular region.

Broadly speaking, in the social sciences, there are two ways of looking at class. The first adopts a gradational concept of class, where class corresponds to and describes an income level. This conceptualization has led to the emergence of popular categories such as lower, upper, and middle class. In the second approach, class is explored as a relation. In this approach, with which I will analyze the case of the Yemeni diaspora, two trends can be observed: Weberian and Marxist. The first, developed by the eminent sociologist Max Weber (1978), regards class as a form of relationship that develops within a market situation. For Weber, the determinant of class hierarchy is not income level but the resources (such as production, capital, skills, or labor) that people bring to the market. According to Weber, people's life chances are determined by the types of resources to which they are linked in the market. Thus, an individual who owns machinery will have better life chances and hence a better class position than an individual who merely brings his or her own labor to the market.

While also adopting a relational concept of class, Karl Marx's ([1847]2008) work presents a different position. Class, according to Marx, emanates from an antagonistic relationship that emerged as a result of the differential ownership of the means of production. Thus, Marx locates the issue of class in the arena of production rather than in the market. He identifies two contradictory processes—namely the social nature of production and individual ownership of the means of production—that lead to the alienation of workers and the exploitation of workers by capitalists. It is this contradiction that results in alienation that, for Marx, leads to an irreversible class contradiction and the emergence of two polarized classes: the bourgeoisie and the proletariat ([1847]2008: 29).

In the Horn of Africa, where Yemenis have interacted with empires/states, the Weberian analysis of class can be a useful starting point for discussion. In this corner of the world, Yemenis had various skills that were needed by those who controlled the empire/state machinery. In the market they had different life chances from others, because they had skills that from the perspective of states and empires were more valuable than those held by indigenous people. For example, they had disciplines valued more highly by French companies, as well as language skills that placed Yemenis as negotiators and translators. They also had religious knowledge that was influential in terms of colonial governance, and connections with the outside world that made them more useful than indigenous people.

These resources gave Yemenis better life chances than autochthonous groups, enabling them not only to establish themselves in the region but also to obtain a better class position vis-à-vis the indigenous population. Having said this, not all Yemenis were equally placed. Some had better life chances than others as a result of the resources they had, which resulted in class differentiations within the Yemeni community itself. Resources such as languages, connections, or religious status brought Yemenis closer to power holders, and hence placed them in a better class position in the market.

Class distinctions dependent on various resources, however, did not result in interactions that were only concerned with issues of class. Wealthy Yemenis interacted with those who were less fortunate. In the case of labor recruitment, wealthy Yemenis recruited their own kinsmen, organized them into guilds, and supplied them to European companies, such as Messageries Maritimes. In the market, wealthy Yemenis joined their less fortunate compatriots and united against other ethnic groups, as described in the case of the dock workers' strike of the 1930s (see chapter four). The existence of this kind of relationship, despite the class differentiation, resulted in the development of patron–client relationships within the Yemeni diaspora community. Patron–client relationships, however, did not result in the development of a one-class society in which conflict and contradiction did not exist. Internally, the Yemeni community showed marks of conflict, which became more visible in the second half of the twentieth century alongside the rise of pan-Arab, socialist, and anticolonialist movements.

In this turbulent era, while wealthy Arabs linked with ruling elites supported the status quo, the younger generations, who had not benefited from the system to the same extent, located themselves in the opposite camp and actively engaged in socialist movements and pan-Arab ideology. The changing relationship that developed over time between the Sada religious elite and the rest of the Yemeni diaspora, which had lower status in this stratified system, demonstrates the internal class contradictions that existed among Yemenis. Those who opposed the Sada were not only the poor, they were also the former poor, who had experienced improving life chances as a result of changes in opportunities over time such as the possibility of earning money by engaging in the modern economy.

In looking at the formation of class in the Horn of Africa, it is important to explore beyond the issue of life chances, and beyond the antagonism that developed between privileged and underprivileged people. On the continent of Africa, any discussion of class needs to be seen in the context of the state, as the state forms the main and immediate sphere of influence. Unlike elsewhere, in Africa class does not only emerge as a result of a process of pure accumulation (Sklar, 1979; Schatz, 1984). Rather, class hierarchy is determined by the relationships of power that lead to the manipulation of the state machinery. Those at the top have skills that are suited to colonial and state hierarchies, and colonial powers facilitate class formation. African bourgeoisies thus became an auxiliary figure in alliance with foreign capitalists (Lloyd, 1967). As expressed by Andre Gunder Frank (1971), this is the 'comprador bourgeoisie,' which acts in the service of capital.

This state role is clearly present in the formation of class among Yemenis in the Horn of Africa region. In addition to the resources that Yemenis brought to the market, it was clear that the state determined class structures and formed the bourgeoisie. In Djibouti, the colonial government gave preference to Yemenis until the 1950s, leading to the alienation of indigenous actors in the political field—a fact that could be seen in the ethnic conflict of the 1940s. Yemeni skills and resources were those in which the colonialists and the capitalists were interested. Yemenis were privileged by the French shipping company Messageries Maritimes, for example, in terms of employment in the port of Djibouti, whereas other ethnic people, such as Somalis, had to struggle to gain access to this means of livelihood.

In Ethiopia, the same process can be discerned. Yemenis were protected: those who were at the top and closer to power holders did not reach that position through pure economic accumulation but because they obtained some form of protection from state rulers who were interested in Yemenis because they had useful skills. Sa'id Ba Zar'a and Sheikh Ahmad Salih al-Zahiri in Ethiopia, and Sa'id 'Ali Coubèche in Djibouti, were able to climb the class hierarchy to the top because they were favored by the state machinery and had links to foreign capital.

The literature notes that class formation during the pre-1970s period was different from class formation in the post-1970s period (Carroll, 2010; Cox, 1987; Gill, 1990; Robinson, 2001; Sklair, 2001). After the 1970s, a transnational class and a transnational state developed as a result of the change that occurred between the state and capital. Rather than capital being confined under the control of the state, it freely moved outside the state, leading to the emergence of a transnationalist capitalist class, which, according to Leslie Sklair (2001: 73), is composed of corporate executives, globalizing bureaucrats and politicians, professionals, and a consumerist elite. The post-1970s period was also marked by the emergence of a global labor pool that is not confined to any particular state but, irrespective of national difference, is ready to serve capital across state boundaries wherever it is required in the world (Robinson, 2001: 172). The way global capital and labor operate is different, however. The former is able to move freely while labor, which is now globalized, is juridically controlled. The nation-state now regulates the movement of labor that transnational capitalist needs, and in so doing serves as a population containment zone (see Robinson, 2001; Lefebvre, 1977: 97; Taylor, 1994).

In the case of the Yemeni diaspora in the Horn of Africa, the new theories on the emergence of a transnational class and a transnational state provide a useful context. Both Djibouti and Ethiopia exhibit state structures dominated by a globalized elite. In Djibouti the presidential family dominates state structures, while in Ethiopia this role is performed by the EPRDF ruling elite. These groups have facilitated the opening up of the countries and the operation of corporate capital. The Yemenis with whom we have been concerned here work in relation to this elite—Sa'id 'Ali Coubèche in Djibouti and Muhammad Hussein al-'Amudi in Ethiopia are key examples. In their own right, in and of themselves, Yemenis are also part of this transnational class. Throughout history Yemenis have formed alliances of one sort or another. The alliances they are now forming, however, exist in a situation in which the nature of capital has changed. Yemenis are no longer regional actors working within a single state and regional context but are transnational actors operating in multiple states and in collaboration with companies that are not confined to one nation-state. It is now possible to speak of the emergence of a transnational class among the Yemenis in Djibouti and Ethiopia, which is qualitatively different from the type of class that previously existed.

However, this is not the only discernible difference. There is also a difference in terms of labor. In the 1920s and 1930s the labor force that was moving across the national space was in a sense ethnic labor. In their undertaking Yemenis recruited men from their own region. Yemeni laborers worked in a guild system exclusively composed of their own ethnic groups. In contrast to this, the labor force moving across the national boundaries of Djibouti and Ethiopia by the 1990s was not ethnic but rather atomized and not organized into a guild system of any sort. Ethnic alliances might flourish while on the move, but the framework for organizing labor along ethnic lines no longer exists as a viable option. Thus, at present, we not only see a transnational class of Yemenis but also a globalized labor pool regularized by states across national borders.

The way conflict has evolved, however, does not seem to follow economic realities. In the 1930s labor was organized in terms of ethnic groups, and consequently Yemenis clashed with Somalis. In the 1990s, the main concern, particularly in Ethiopia, was the way in which people such as Muhammad Hussein al-'Amudi were operating. 'Amudi was accused of supporting and being supported by the state. His economic activities were perceived to be a case of state betrayal of the people. The movement of Ethiopian labor to Arab countries was also regarded as part of an overall selling out of the country. If we look at the accusations against 'Amudi, this was actually one of several clashes that occurred in a neoliberal context in which capital indiscriminately violated national boundaries. The neoliberal state, Robinson claims, "retains essential powers to facilitate globalization but it loses the ability to harmonize conflicting social interests within a country, to realize the historic function of sustaining the internal unity of nationally conceived social formation, and to achieve legitimacy" (2003: 46).

The people's challenge to 'Amudi signals this loss of state legitimacy and the clash generated by the operation of transnational capital. The clash was expressed in terms of ethnicity. 'Amudi was not perceived as a leader of transnational corporate capital, in which arena, at one time, nationality did not matter; he was perceived as an Arab, and thus a totalizing argument arose in which all Arabs, irrespective of class background, whether rich or poor, were on an equal footing with 'Amudi.

An Ethnic Game?

This wholesale targeting of ethnic groups suggests that we need to examine the relations among class, ethnicity, and the state. To do so here, I will return to the Africanist literature that explores ethnic and class formations in an African context. A trend in the Africanist literature has been to explain the presence of ethnicity and ethnic conflict by looking at the role the state (such as the colonial state) has played. Scholars such as James S. Coleman (1958) and René Lemarchand (1964) argue that ethnic conflict is a result of the uneven penetration of capital in African countries. The development of roads and port cities in certain areas has resulted from investment by foreign capital, and the lack of such development in other areas is blamed on an absence of capital. It is argued that this has led to uneven development across the region and, thus, to ethnic conflict.

The sociology of colonial hegemony has also been employed to explain ethnic conflict in Africa. State power, it is argued, actively invented the idea of the tribe, which was conceived as having a unique language and a territorial boundary. Thus, ethnicity became a major avenue along which people organized themselves for the purpose of obtaining scarce resources that were controlled and directed by the state. The introduction of political parties to African countries accentuated this ethnicity-based organization and conflict. In short, the danger the state presented made people cling to their own ethnic group, and a kind of patron–client relationship developed within this that helped to protect them from attacks by other groups. In this context, ethnicity became the fundamental idiom of class formation (Breman, 1998: 31).

The relevance of the Africanist literature on class and ethnicity can be discerned in the discussion sections of this book. In Djibouti, ethnic identification became important because of the enforcement of rigid ethnic boundaries and the establishment of institutions such as the Service de Sécurité et des Affaires Indigènes, which enlisted chiefs from each ethnic group. This eventually encouraged the formation of ethnicity-based political parties and the expression of conflict using the language of ethnicity, such as in the 1940s when it was demanded that Arabs should be expelled. In Djibouti, this not only led to the expression of conflict in terms of ethnicity but also to the overlapping of ethnicity and class and the development of patron–client relationships. In postcolonial Djibouti, where the state came to be dominated by 'Issa Somalis, this was clearly discernible, as being at the top of the ethnic structure also meant being at the peak of the class structure. In this context, for Yemenis to succeed, they had to engage in a patron–client relationship as the surest means of remaining at the top of the social structure. A similar process can be observed in the case of Ethiopia, particularly in the 1990s. As success was dependent on being a member of a particular ethnic group in that country, Yemenis also had to engage in a patron–client relationship in order to remain at the top of the class structure.

In both Djibouti and Ethiopia, however, the correspondence between class and ethnicity has never been a matter that concerned the elite. Local people regarded as being lower down the social scale used ethnicity to mobilize against Arabs. This was the case between Arabs and 'Issa in Djibouti, and between Gurages and Yemenis. In the latter case, economic conflict led to the mass expulsion of Yemenis in the 1960s. The practice continues. A continuing interaction of this nature can be discerned, for example, in the accusations leveled against wealthy Yemenis such as Muhammad Hussein al-'Amudi. The accusations of Islamizing Ethiopia or selling Ethiopian girls that are directed against al-'Amudi are also directed against other Yemenis, irrespective of class.

Although it sheds new light on these subjects, looking at ethnicity as an idiom of class does not take us to the core of the matter, as it does not explain why class formation has not proliferated, despite the presence of class. That is, it does not explain why lower-class Yemenis unite with their Yemeni-origin class exploiters against fellow laborers from other ethnic groups. A useful insight and explanation for this can be discerned if we draw attention to the distinction Marx made between 'class in itself' *(Klasse an sich)* and 'class for itself' *(Klasse für sich)*. The former, according to Marx, describes a situation in which class is an abstract category and people lack class consciousness, while the latter is a situation in which people are aware of their class interests (see Evans, 2004: 79–86). For class mobilization to occur, class has to be transformed from an abstract category to a situation of class for itself. What is lacking in the case of Yemenis in the Horn of Africa is this transformation; that is, a situation of *Klasse für sich*. Despite the presence of class, for Yemenis class has not developed at the local level as a principle of social organization.

Citizenship and National Belonging

The lives of Yemenis in the Horn of Africa are not only marked by class and ethnicity. People in the region also belong to the broader framework of the nation-state and, hence, there arises the question of citizenship. It is often assumed in the literature in this area that citizenship in Africa is significantly different from that in the rest of the world, as a result of the differences that arise between African forms of state and North American or European forms of state. The peculiarity of African citizenship has been attributed to factors such as nationalism and the fact that the African state is still under construction (see, for example, Dorman et al., 2007; Peterson, 2012). The deep divisions that colonialism created in African societies have also been seen as a factor in the difference between citizenship in Africa and elsewhere (Mamdani, 1996). The politics of rootedness, wherein a particular group claims an exclusive right to the national territory or part of it, has been identified as another mark of citizenship in Africa (see, for example, Geschiere, 2009; Prestholdt, 2014; Dunn and Bøås, 2013).

The issue of citizenship in Africa is attributable not only to these aspects but also to the logic of the modern state. The African nation-state, like any nation-state, works on the basis of the logics of inclusion/exclusion, in which some are included while others are excluded. To this inclusion/exclusion is added a process of gradation, in which some are ranked higher than others (Bezabeh, 2011). In Africa, the exclusion of some has resulted in struggles of citizenship (Glassman, 1995). As a result, Felicitas Becker and Joel Cabrita (2014), as well as Jonathan Glassman (2014), assert in their refreshingly new analysis of Africa's connection to the Indian Ocean that the matter of inclusion, hence cosmopolitanism, is not the only factor that has existed in this part of the world. Tension, rupture, and exclusion are part and parcel of the citizenship process.

In understanding the presence of Yemenis in Djibouti and Ethiopia, issues of citizenship and national belonging in Africa are certainly significant. Colonial powers in the region, particularly in Djibouti, played a key role, giving tribalism and tribal differences considerable emphasis, which led to the development of an imperfect citizenship upon independence. Yemenis became part of this imperfect form of citizenship in which ethnic/tribal alliances took precedence over being a citizen of the nation-state.

The legacy of the colonial framework has not been the only factor in the region. The exclusion/inclusion logics of the nation-state that come with gradation have been significant. Whether in the colonial or postcolonial period, as well as in the independent state of Ethiopia, Yemenis were trapped by the inclusion/exclusion of the state. In the case of Ethiopia, the cosmological order of the state is linked to the Ethiopian Orthodox Church, which prevails despite the abolition of the monarchical system; indeed, it has been a key factor in processes of exclusion. Yemenis were not regarded as being on equal terms with Ethiopian Orthodox citizens of that state. Similarly, in the current period, Yemeni descendants do not have equal standing compared to indigenous people who are in control of the state machinery. In Djibouti, we can also observe the application of this logic of exclusion. During the colonial period, the status of Yemenis shifted from being excluded natives to being included citizens endowed with political rights. Although in the post independence period Yemenis remained on the inclusion side of the divide, they also remained ranked below autochthonous groups such as 'Issa Somalis, who, in the postcolonial period, became key actors in the national framework.

Citizenship, therefore, was not only a legal issue but also a social concept, like ethnicity, which, as Ann Mische affirms, is "a historically contingent, interactive vehicle of articulation, conflict and dialogue" (1996: 157–58). However, the fact that it should be understood as a facet of the social does not mean that there are no legal consequences. As a legal tool it carries a real power that can lead to incarceration. The experience of my first informant, quoted in chapter one, is an example of what Yemenis have been forced to undergo. It is as a result of this that many Yemenis in Djibouti and Ethiopia play the different identities that they have at hand: Arab, Amhara, Oromo, Somali, and so forth. The various ethnic identities are included in the citizenship game that is played out in a graduated manner. When the Arab identity can be used advantageously, for example during the Italian occupation of Ethiopia or in the social chaos that developed when the EPRDF ousted the Derg, Yemenis have used it extensively. In situations where autochthons controlled the playing field, appearing as one of the locals became a strategy. In this game of citizenship the story of the Yemenis of Djibouti and Ethiopia is not unique. In Indian Ocean Africa, Yemeni diasporas and others who are deemed foreigners have faced similar experiences (see, for example, Glassman, 2014; Brennan, 2012; Desai, 2013).

In addition to its similarity to other contexts in the region, the story of the Yemenis treated in this book informs us how citizenship relates to both ethnicity and class. Those at the top of the state structure are involved in an ethnic game. In both Djibouti and Ethiopia the state has patron–client relationships that radiate from the top of its structure to its base, and back again. This entanglement of ethnicity and the state goes hand in hand with citizenship. Being from the top ethnic groups generally means being at the top of the citizenship ladder, although this is not applicable in all circumstances. Those individuals who are better placed economically are still placed above those who belong to higher-ranked ethnic groups but are financially disadvantaged. Nevertheless, those individuals who are from the top ethnic groups and who are also highly placed in the political sphere have the capacity to contest and dominate the wealthier members of lower-ranked ethnic groups. The gradation of citizenship that lies at the core of the system and is linked with ethnicity is therefore qualified by positionalities within the class structure. This tends to add further complexity to the configuration, which remains unstable in the present day.

A Space for Religion

In looking at citizenship, ethnicity, and class within the state framework, there is a risk in only taking into account these secular phenomena. Among others, Talal Asad (1999) warns against carving out an exclusively secular space distinct from the religious field. He believes that the secular overlaps with the religious. According to other commentators, "The secular is not necessarily outside the religious. The apparent rejection of the religious in much secularism masks the secular subsumption of religious orientation" (Kapferer, Telle, and Eriksen, 2010: 3).

Indeed, if we look at the empirical material it can be seen that religion always figures as part of the secular in this context. In Djibouti and Ethiopia, the categorization of Yemenis by the state has always taken note of religion. The fact that Yemenis are Muslim has always brought them to the attention of state and imperial powers. In the beginning of the twentieth century, for the French, Islam at some point was not a bringer of revolution but of evolution. Some Muslims, however, were regarded as fanatics who needed to be taken care of by spreading Christianity. Almost a century later, global powers' perspective on Islam switched from considering Islam as evolutionary to viewing Islam as a revolutionary element. Again, this stance divided 'bad' Muslims (Salafis/Wahhabis) from 'good' Muslims (Sufis). Hence, the secular has always been concerned about religion in this region.

This has had real consequences for Yemenis. The ways in which empires/states attempted to manage Yemenis made them subject to being categorized (such as being placed in the category of terrorist), and this has created atrocities for Yemenis, particularly those who were accidentally caught up in it, the outstanding example in this case being Muhammad 'Abdallah Salih al-Asad, who found himself in secret CIA prisons.

In addition, social attitudes linked with the state created hierarchies. This has had implications for citizenship and ethnicity, as the hierarchies also depended on the religious field. Thus, for example, the fact that there is a hierarchical relationship between Ethiopian Orthodox Christians and Arabs in Ethiopia relates not only to the latter being foreigners (hence second-class citizens) but also to their being Muslims who are not part of the Orthodox covenant with God. Religion-based social attitudes have also been important for defining and understanding the presence of those who are economically well off. Thus, the attack on 'Amudi, who belonged to a transnational class, was not only about ethnicity or citizenship but also about religion. One of the accusations directed against him was the spread of Islam; another was that he was systematically turning Ethiopia to Islam.

There is a connection between the secular and the religious, and we must recognize this if we are to better understand the lives of diaspora communities. In addition, the secular in and of itself is also deeply religious. The French empire, while officially republican, has been shown in a number of studies to have been deeply connected with the Catholic Church (see, for example, Tudesco, 1980). The Ethiopian state, despite its avowed secularist stance, is still a framework where old religious attitudes are dominant. The United States, the supreme global power of our age, is a place where "religion continues to be important despite the constitutional separation between state and religion" (Asad, 1999: 231). In launching the 'war on terror,' which has continued to lead to civilian atrocities, US president George W. Bush drew extensively on religious principles, particularly on born-again Christianity (Holland, 2013: 53; Murphy, 2003).

In view of this overlap it would be right to assert that theoretical discussions regarding class, ethnicity, and citizenship should be grounded and explained through empirical material. Local realities are always context-dependent and issues such as ethnicity, class formation, or citizenship cannot be generalized to and be applicable in every circumstance. Factors such as class, ethnicity, and citizenship, when the empirical material is taken into account, take different shapes, and this would be the case for each place and each context.

In looking at the complexity present in ethnicity, citizenship, and class, it seems right to ask what lessons we can learn from this discussion. One lesson is the need to produce a more complex picture of the relationship between diasporas and the nation-state. In contemporary theorization of the presence of diasporas in the world, there is a tendency (as shown in the work of Clifford (1994) and Gilroy (1993), for example) to posit the diaspora subject vis-à-vis the state. Diaspora groups are linked with flow, cosmopolitanism, and cultural mixing. A tendency to see a diaspora as an actor in a constant state of networking clouds our understanding, as it hides from view other forms of sociality, particularly hierarchical structures. If we view the existence of diasporas only in terms of networks or cosmopolitanism, we risk displacing political and economic factors, as well as other broader historical and international factors that are relevant in diaspora life. The world cannot be understood through narrowly defined concepts of culture or of sociality but must also be seen in relation to political processes, history, and economics, in which states/empires play an important role.

In arguing for the significance of such an understanding, my position reflects what Aihwa Ong (1999) says in *Flexible Citizenship: The Cultural Logics of Transnationality*. Having criticized a world system perspective for being too mechanical, Ong proceeds to criticize the contemporary anthropological understanding of transnationality. "Anthropologists who are solely concerned with cultural phenomena," she tells us, tend to brush aside political-economic systems and celebrate cultural difference, hybridity, and the social imaginary, which display "native" inventiveness, and sometimes resistance, to homogenizing trends. Seldom is there an attempt to analytically link actual institutions of state power, capitalism, and transnational networks to such forms of cultural reproduction, inventiveness, and possibilities. This is a significant problem of method because it raises hopes that transnational mobility and its associated processes have great liberatory potential . . . for undermining all kinds of oppressive structures in the world (1999: 15).

She goes on to observe,

In our desire to find breaks between the territorially bounded and the deterritorialized, the oppressive and the progressive, and the stable and the unstable, we sometimes overlook complicated accommodations, alliances, and creative tensions between the nation-state and mobile capital, between diaspora and nationalism, or between the influx of immigrants and the multicultural state. Attention to specific histories and geopolitical situations will reveal that such simple oppositions between transnational forces and the nation-state cannot be universally sustained (1999: 16).

In combining anthropological method with historical understanding, and by looking at the working of empires, the operation of capital, and the interactions of Yemenis with colonial and postcolonial states, the present research has shown that there is potential to understand more about Yemenis in the Indian Ocean region by working across a conceptual terrain that does not focus solely on networks and cosmopolitanism. Whatever the imperfections might be in this work, my hope is that the book has made a valuable contribution in opening up critical discussion in the area of Indian Ocean studies.

Notes

1. Introduction

1. For an extensive discussion of the formation of Indian Ocean studies, see Vink (2007).
2. See le Guennec-Coppens (1989), Camelin (2002), and Walker (2011).
3. For a review of the works, see Vink (2007: 46–51).
4. See the works of Campbell (2004), Bose (2006), Metcalf (2007), Tambe and Firt and Lester (2006), Ward (2009), and Harms, Freamon, and Blight (2013).
5. Wink (2010) notes this persistence in his review of Edward Simpson and Kai Kresse's 2008 edited volume. Criticizing Campbell's (2008) lead chapter, which calls for Islam to be viewed as the epitome of historical cosmopolitanism, Wink argues that the emphasis on cosmopolitanism is "the product, largely, of a combination of ignorance, willful distortion, and wishful thinking, [which] naively celebrates the Indian Ocean as the multicultural 'cradle of globalization'—the maritime counterpart of the so-called silk road—and its cosmopolitan Islam as interfaith dialogue."
6. For the interface between space and power, see Foucault (1980; 2004).
7. For early contact and migration, see Hable Selassie (1972).
8. The sixteenth-century war was between the 'Ädalə sultanate, led by Ahmad ibn Ibrahim al Ghazi (popularly known as Gragñ, meaning 'the left-handed'), and the Christian highland kingdom. The war lasted until 1543 and sent the highland king into hiding after Gragñ's army seized most of the Christian kingdom. The army of the 'Ädalə sultanate was eventually defeated, but only after the killing of Gragñ by Portuguese soldiers who were deployed in support of the Ethiopian king. For an account of the war and the reasons behind it, see Aregay (1974).
9. The Queen of Sheba, referred to as Bilqis in the Qur'an, is believed to have lived at the time of King Solomon of Israel. In the Bible we see her paying a visit

to King Solomon, an event also present in the Islamic tradition. In Ethiopia, the visit is considered the key event in the foundation of one of the royal houses of Ethiopia, the Solomonic dynasty. For the legend of the Queen of Sheba, see Lucks (2009). On her connection to Ethiopia, particularly to the mythical foundation of the Solomonic dynasty, see Budge (1922).

10. Dhu al-Qarnayn is a mythical figure mentioned in the Qur'an. Gifted with many talents, he is described as having ruled over a vast territory. Modern-day scholarship connects Dhu al-Qarnayn with Alexander the Great. For an Islamic account and interpretation of Dhu al-Qarnayn, see Abdul-Rahman (2009).
11. Regarding the mythology, see Ibn al Mujawir (2008: 119).
12. Outside the book of Thompson and Adloff (1968) there is an annotated bibliography by Peter J. Schrader (1991) and a dictionary by Daoud Aboubaker Alwan and Yohanis Mibrathu (2000). Rather than being works of history, as their names suggest, the two works are works of reference. Thompson and Adloff have also translated from French into English the work of Robert Tholomier, which mainly focuses on the pre-independence period of Djibouti. For their translation see Tholomier (1981).
13. In addition there are a couple of articles in Amharic published in some of the Ethiopian press, such as *Addis Admass*.
14. See Pankhurst (1968: 448).
15. For a description of these ancient kingdoms, see Hable Selassie (1972).
16. For an interesting discussion of medieval kingdoms, see Tamrat (1972) and Braukämpar (2004).
17. On the consolidation of Ethiopia under Tewodros, see Crummey (1969) and Rubenson (1966).
18. See Imbert-Vier (2011: 40) and Miran (2009: 63–64).
19. On the expansion of Egypt into Sudan, see Hill (1959).
20. On the presence of Egyptians in Massawa and other ports, see Talhami (1979).
21. For a broader discussion of the Egyptian invasion, see Jesman (1959) and Rubenson (1966).
22. On the Italian colonization of Eritrea, see Mesghenna (1988).
23. On the presence of Italians in Somalia, see Hess (1966).
24. Joseph Lambert was at the time twenty-six years old and married to a fifty-year-old woman. He owned a plantation and founded a steamship company that delivered post from Ile Maurice to Aden. In sending out Lambert, Joseph was guided by his business needs. For a more detailed account, see Brunschwig (1978: 36).
25. Abu Bakr Pasha was under Sultan Mohamed Mohamed, the elderly governor of Tajura. Abu Bakr was an influential figure who was able to exert pressure on the regional caravan trade. He was also heavily involved in the Red Sea slave trade. For an account of the history that surrounds Abu Bakr, see Fontrier (2003).
26. Regarding the actions of Lambert, see Simonin (1862: 75) and Daguenet (1992: 176–77).
27. For a detailed account of the death of Lambert, see Simonin (1862) and Daguenet (1992; 2000).
28. Regarding the various agreements made by France, see de Clercq (1884: 418, 423, 429) and Imbert-Vier (2011).
29. On Ethiopian expansion into the south, see Donham and James (2002).

30. This frontier was envisioned as a straight line. For its description, see "M. Waddington to Marquis Salisbury" in Hertslet (1896: 976).
31. "M. Waddington to Marquis Salisbury," quoted in Hertslet (1896: 976).
32. Regarding this agreement, see "Éthiopie et France: Convention pour les frontières, signée à Addis Ababa le 20 mars 1897," *Droit International Public* (1908): 179.
33. For an account of the agreement between Emperor Menelik and the French company, see the concessional agreement of March 9, 1894, in Gilmor (1906: 63–66).
34. "Côte Française des Somali," *Journal des Débat Politiques et Littéraires*, 14 January 1903.
35. For a history of the railway, see Bekele (1982).
36. For a recent perspective on the state, see Hansen and Stepputat (2001), Das and Poole (2004), Steinmetz (1999), and Sharma and Gupta (2006).
37. The interface of space and state is a deep one. The state encloses spaces and exercises power over those spaces. On the relation between space and state, see Lefebvre (1977) and Foucault (1977; 1980; 2004).
38. On the relation between state and economy, see Mitchell (1999).
39. On the relation between state and worldview, see Bourdieu (1999).
40. For a noninstitutional perspective of state that explores the overlapping nature of state, see Steinmetz (1999).
41. For an interesting discussion of the networked relations between state and empire, see Hardt and Negri (2000) and Wood (2003).
42. For the changing relationship between state and capital, see Arrighi (1994; 2007), Robinson (2001), Cox (1987), Carroll (2010), Carroll and Fennema (2002), Sklair (2001), and Kapferer (2004; 2005a).
43. Bollee (2003).
44. The term 'war on terror' was first used by United States President George W. Bush to describe a military campaign by the United States and its allies against extremist Islamist groups considered to be terrorists. For a detailed discussion of the term, see Allen (2009).

2. Disciplining the Natives

1. For an account regarding the vessels of the Indian Ocean, see Agius (2002; 2008; 2014). On seafaring and the social organization of seafarers in the Arabian region, see Hourani (1951) and Simpson (2006).
2. On the first French travel to the Red Sea and the assistance obtained from Arabs in the region, see de la Roque (1732: 14-27).
3. Traditionally, the amir al-bahr played a more important role than controlling the movement of people and checking papers. His duties also included constructing warships and technical inspection of ships. For an account of this role, see Meri (2006: 558).
4. Archive National d'Outre Mer (hereinafter 'ANOM') CFS 2A, Arrêté fixant les limites du port de Djibouti, 14 November 1899.
5. ANOM, 14 November 1899.
6. ANOM, 14 November 1899.
7. *Journal Officiel de la Côte Française des Somali* (hereinafter 'JOCFS'), Arrêté no. 112 fixant les limites du port, 15 February 1943.

8. JOCFS, Arrêté no. 297 réglementant l'embarquement des voyageurs et la sortie des boutres, 10 Novembre 1916.
9. JOCFS, Arrêté no. 297.
10. JOCFS, Arrêté no. 297.
11. JOCFS, Arrêté no. 297.
12. JOCFS, Arrêté no. 297.
13. Djibouti Chamber of Commerce, "Yemeni to the President of Djibouti Chamber of Commerce, 27 May 1922." File: Correspondence of Djibouti Operators (8 January 1907 to 17 June 1957); Box: Correspondence of Economic Operators, 1907 to 1957. Author's translation.
14. Djibouti Chamber of Commerce, "Yemeni to the President of Djibouti Chamber of Commerce, 28 January 1917." File: Correspondence of Djibouti Operators (8 January 1907 to 17 June 1957); Box: Correspondence of Economic Operators, 1907 to 1957. Author's translation.
15. Exposition Nationale Coloniale de Marseille. *Notice Illustrée sur la Côte Française des Somalis* (Marseille: Imprimerie du Sémaphore, Barlatiere, 1922, 33–34).
16. Exposition Nationale Coloniale de Marseille, 33–34.
17. Exposition Nationale Coloniale de Marseille, 33–34.
18. JOCFS, Arrêté réglementant l'immigration dans la Colonie, 15 August 1903.
19. JOCFS, 15 August 1903.
20. Exposition Coloniale Internationale, *Notice illustrée sur la Côte Française des Somalis* (Paris: La Presse Coloniale Illustrée, 1931), 42. See also Poydenot (1889: 67).
21. JOCFS, Arrêté organisant un cadre local d'agents indigènes chargés de la police, 28 August 1900.
22. JOCFS, Arrêté créant des postes de la police rurale, 1 June 1901.
23. JOCFS, 1 June 1901.
24. JOCFS, 1 June 1901.
25. Djibouti Chamber of Commerce, "Undated letter of Yemenis to the President of Djibouti Chamber of Commerce," Djibouti Chamber of Commerce. File: Correspondence of Djibouti Operators (8 January 1907 to 17 June 1957); Box: Correspondence of Economic Operators, 1907 to 1957. Author's translation.
26. Djibouti Chamber of Commerce, "Undated letter of Yemenis to the President of Djibouti Chamber of Commerce."
27. Djibouti Chamber of Commerce, "Undated letter of Yemenis to the President of Djibouti Chamber of Commerce."
28. Djibouti Chamber of Commerce, "Undated letter of Yemenis to the President of Djibouti Chamber of Commerce."
29. Djibouti Chamber of Commerce, "Undated letter of Yemenis to the President of Djibouti Chamber of Commerce."
30. Djibouti Chamber of Commerce, "Undated letter of Yemenis to the President of Djibouti Chamber of Commerce."
31. JOCFS, Arrêté no. 193 fixant les zones urbaine, suburbaines, et rurales, 29 December 1899.
32. Exposition Nationale Coloniale de Marseille (1922 : 29).
33. See JOCFS, Arrêté no. 10 du 5 Janvier 1943 portant réorganisation territoriale de la Côte Française des Somalis.
34. Exposition Coloniale Internationale (1933: 34).

35. JOCFS, Arrêté de police, 23 June 1900.
36. JOCFS, 23 June 1900.
37. JOCFS, 23 June 1900.
38. Djibouti Chamber of Commerce, "Yemeni to the President of Djibouti Chamber of Commerce, 4 August 1921," Djibouti Chamber of Commerce. Box: Autorité Militaire/Haut Commissariat. Author's translation.
39. JOCFS, Arrêté réglementant le droit de répression, par voie disciplinaire, des infractions spécialisé à l'indigénat, 11 September 1912.
40. JOCFS, 11 September 1912.
41. ANOM 1 AFF–POL 697, "Letter of Arab Notables to Monsieur le Procureur de la République Chef du Service Judiciaire," 8 December 1927. File: Affair Barrognes, Farnines, Magistrats.
42. ANOM 1 AFF–POL 697, "Let ter of Arab Notables to Monsieur le Procureur de la Republique Chef du Service Judiciaire."
43. US Department of State, "Addis Ababa American Consulate General to the Secretary of State, 2 January 1929," in *Records of the Department of State Relating to Internal Affairs of Ethiopia (Abyssinia), 1910–1929*. Rol. II (Washington, DC: National Archive and Record Service, 1962).
44. US Department of State, "Addis Ababa American Consulate General to the Secretary of State, 2 January 1929."
45. US Department of State, "Addis Ababa American Consulate General to the Secretary of State, 2 January 1929."
46. US Department of State, "Addis Ababa American Consulate General to the Secretary of State, Visas Required for Travelers to Ethiopia, 24 October 1929," in *Records of the Department of State Relating to Internal Affairs of Ethiopia (Abyssinia), 1910–1929*, Rol. II (Washington, DC: National Archive and Record Service, 1962).
47. US Department of State, "Addis Ababa American Consulate General to the Secretary of State, Visas Required for Travelers to Ethiopia, 24 October 1929."
48. US Department of State, "Addis Ababa American Consulate General to the Secretary of State, Visas Required for Travelers to Ethiopia, 24 October 1929."
49. US Department of State, "Addison E. Southard, Minister and Consul General at Addis Ababa to the Secretary of State, Jurisdiction Regarding Foreigners in Ethiopia, 8 February 1929," in *Records of the Department of State Relating to Internal Affairs of Ethiopia (Abyssinia), 1910–1929*, Rol. II (Washington, DC: National Archive and Record Service, 1962).
50. US Department of State, "Addison E. Southard, Minister and Consul General at Addis Ababa to the Secretary of State, Jurisdiction Regarding Foreigners in Ethiopia, 8 February 1929."
51. US Department of State, "Addison E. Southard, Minister and Consul General at Addis Ababa to the Secretary of State, Jurisdiction Regarding Foreigners in Ethiopia, 8 February 1929."
52. US Department of State, "Addis Ababa American Consulate General to the Secretary of State, Extraterritorial Jurisdiction of the British Consul General in Abyssinia, 9 June 1914," in *Records of the Department of State Relating to Internal Affairs of Ethiopia (Abyssinia), 1910–1929*, Rol. I (Washington, DC: National Archive and Record Service, 1962).

53. US Department of State, "Addis Ababa American Consulate General to the Secretary of State, Extraterritorial Jurisdiction of the British Consul General in Abyssinia, 9 June 1914."
54. US Department of State, "Royal Court of Great Britain Order for the Establishment of Consular Court in Abyssinia, 19 December 1913," in *Records of the Department of State Relating to Internal Affairs of Ethiopia (Abyssinia), 1910–1929*, Rol. I (Washington, DC: National Archive and Record Service, 1962).
55. The Ottomans moved to northern Yemen in the 1830s and made Sanaa their capital in 1870. They withdrew from the region following a series of local insurgencies. For further reading on the Ottoman presence in Yemen, see Kuehn (2011). For research into the challenges that Yemenis faced during the Ottoman period, see Farah (2002).
56. For more on Sayyid Muhammad al-Idrisi and the pro-British 'Asir state, see Bang (1996).
57. "Le blocus des côtes de Yémen," *Correspondance d'Orient*, 16 October 1913, 380–81.
58. On the occupation of Paris and subsequent developemtn, see Paxton (2001).
59. See Paxton (2001).
60. For a further account of the blockade, see Jackson (2006: 211–21).
61. "En juin dernier le gouvernement de la Côte Française des Somalis stigmatisait le blocus britannique," *Journal des Débats Politiques et Littéraires*, 29 August 1941. Author's translation.
62. "En juin dernier le gouvernement de la Côte Française des Somalis stigmatisait le blocus britannique."
63. "En juin dernier le gouvernement de la Côte Française des Somalis stigmatisait le Blocus Britannique."
64. "Le blocus terrestre et maritime de Djibouti continue avec une implacable rigueur," *Journal Des Débats Politiques et Littéraires*, 3 October 1941.
65. "Le blocus terrestre et maritime de Djibouti continue avec une implacable rigueur."
66. "Le blocus terrestre et maritime de Djibouti continue avec une implacable rigueur."
67. "Le blocus terrestre et maritime de Djibouti continue avec une implacable rigueur."
68. "Le blocus terrestre et maritime de Djibouti continue avec une implacable riguer."
69. "Les événements tragiques d'Éthiopie," *Journal des Débats Politiques et Littéraires*, 5 May 1936, 1. Author's translation.
70. "Les événements tragiques d'Éthiopie."
71. "Les événements tragiques d'Éthiopie."
72. British Foreign Office, "Telegram from Mr. Robert, Addis Abba, to Resident at Aden, Italian Policy Regarding Arabs in Ethiopia: Movements of Individuals between Ethiopia and Arabia," FO 371/20202.

3. Nationalized Spaces: Yemeni Mobility in the Second Half of the Twentieth Century

1. For a detailed discussion of political reform after the Second World War, see Grosser (1961).
2. See chapter six.
3. For a discussion of the United Nations mandate in former Italian colonies, see Staford (1949) and Rossi (1980).

4. For a discussion of the incorporation of the Ogaden by the British administration, see Eshete (1991).
5. For a discussion of Somali political movements after the Second World War, see Barnes (2007).
6. See Marcus (1983; 1992).
7. See Ellingson (1978).
8. On the coup d'état, see Clapham (1968).
9. Regarding mass political movements during this period, see Tareke (1991) and Balsuik (1985).
10. On the Ethiopian–Somali war, see Tareke (2000).
11. For a detailed study of this issue, see Agonafer (1979).
12. On United States policy in the Horn of Africa see Jackson (2007) and Woodward (2006). For Soviet involvement in sub-Saharan Africa see Sarris (1985).
13. ANOM FR COM COL 1 AFF POL 2101, "Note de renseignement: Activité de Said Ali Coubeche," 14 Octobre 1953. File: Côte Française des Somalis activités musulmanes.
14. ANOM FR COM COL 1 AFF POL 2101, "Note de renseignement: Activité de Said Ali Coubeche," 14 Octobre 1953.
15. "Retour du calme et contrôle d'identité," *Le Réveil de Djibouti*, 17 September 1966, 2.
16. "Couvre-feu et maintien de l'ordre à Djibouti," *Le Réveil de Djibouti*, 17 September 1966, 1–2. Author's translation.
17. "Couvre-feu et maintien de l'ordre à Djibouti."
18. "Couvre-feu et maintien de l'ordre à Djibouti," 2.
19. "Couvre-feu et maintien de l'ordre à Djibouti."
20. "Couvre-feu et maintien de l'ordre à Djibouti."
21. "Retour du calme et contrôle d'identité," *Le Réveil de Djibouti*, 2. Author's translation.
22. "Retour du calme et contrôle d'identité."
23. "Couvre-feu et maintien de l'ordre à Djibouti," 2.
24. Pompidou was the nineteenth president of the French Republic, 1969 to 1974. For information about his presidency, including his policing tactics, see Bersteil and Rioux (2000).
25. *Le Réveil de Djibouti*, 20 January 1973. Author's translation.
26. "Demain 19 mars, les électeurs de la C.F.S. son appelés à répondre par oui ou par non," *Le Réveil de Djibouti*, 18 March 1967, 1. Author's translation.
27. "Communiqués," *Le Réveil de Djibouti*, 18 March 1967, 2.
28. "Communiqués."
29. "Par 60.6% des suffrages exprimés, la C.F.S. a choisi de demeurer au sein de la République Française avec le statu renouvellé," *Le Réveil de Djibouti*, 25 March 1967, 1.
30. "Djibouti: Au fil de l'actualité," *Le Réveil de Djibouti*, 25 March 1967, 2.
31. Interview with 'Abdallah Mohamed Kamil, former prime minister of Djibouti, Djibouti, November 2009.
32. Interview with Ahmad, a shop assistant who came to Djibouti using an identification card issued by the Ethiopian government, Djibouti, November 2009.

33. On the Red Terror, see Welde-Gyorgis (1989).
34. The Yemeni civil war was fought between royalist forces who sought the return of the monarch, represented by Imam Ahmed, and republicans who sought to end imperial rule. The civil war, which started in 1962, continued until the end of the 1970s and saw the involvement of regional powers, including Saudi Arabia backing the royalists and Egypt supporting the republicans. For further reading on the Yemeni civil war and the general history of modern Yemen, see Dresh (2000).
35. On the general presence of Yemenis in the West, see Friedlander, Kelley, and Pinkel (1988) and Halliday (2000;1992).
36. The Libyan sanctions came after the bombing of airports in Italy and Austria on January 7, 1986. The sanctions, under Executive Orders 12543 and 12544, were imposed by then United States president Ronald Reagan. For further reading on the sanctions, see O'Sullivan (2003).
37. For a discussion of the history of the intervention, see Rutherford (2008).
38. For a discussion of Islamist militant groups in Somalia, see International Crisis Group (2002; 2005).
39. International Crisis Group (2005), 5–8.
40. International Crisis Group (2005), 20.
41. For a discussion on AFRICOM, see Barkely (2009) and Davis and Othieno (2007).
42. For a country-based discussion on the Combined Joint Task Force, see Muhula (2007) and Davis and Othieno (2007).
43. For an extensive analysis of the role of the West in the tightening of borders, see Thiollet (2009).
44. "Djibouti: 100,000 Immigrants to be Expelled," *New York Times*, 2 September 2003.
45. "IOM Opens Office in Djibouti," *MRF Nairobi Bulletin*, June 2009.
46. "IOM Opens Office in Djibouti," 1.
47. "Saudi Urgently Erects New Border Fence to Block 'Massive' Immigration of Shi'ites," *World Tribune*, 15 December 2009.
48. Robert Worth, "Saudi Border with Yemen is Still Inviting for Al Qaeda," *New York Times*, 26 October 2010.
49. "IOM Opens Office in Djibouti," 2.
50. "Sa'id al Batati, Anti-piracy Forces off Yemen Playing Pirates with Fishermen," *Arab News*, 6 May 2010.
51. "Sa'id al Batati, Anti-piracy Forces off Yemen Playing Pirates with Fishermen."
52. "Dutch Forces Free Pirate Captives," *BBC*, 18 April 2009.
53. Regarding labor politics between Saudi Arabia and Yemen within the context of the Gulf War, see Okruhlik and Conge (1997). On the impact of the first Gulf War and the population movement it unleashed, see Adelton (1991) and Okruhlik and Conge (1997).
54. Regarding the revised Ethiopian nationality law, see Ethiopia Nationality Proclamation No. 378/2003, Addis Ababa, December 2003.
55. On the recent conflict in this region, see Boucek (2010).
56. Regarding Saudi Arabia's involvement in the Houthi war, see Joost R. Hiltermann, "Disorder on the Border: Saudi Arabia's War Inside Yemen," *Foreign Affairs*, 16 December 2009.
57. For an excellent analysis of Yemeni protests, see Bonnefoy and Poirier (2012; 2013).

58. For analysis of the involvement of the military, particularly that of Brigadier General Ali Mohsen, see Droz-Vincent (2014).
59. On the role played by the Gulf Cooperation Council and its relationship with the state of Yemen, see Bruke (2012).
60. See "Aides Say Ex-President of Yemen Will Go into Exile in Ethiopia," Fox News, 27 February 2012.
61. Al Jazeera, "Houthi Take Over Yemeni Presidential Palace," 21 January 2015, http://www.aljazeera.com/news/middleeast/2015/01/yemen-ceasefire-collapses-amid-fresh-clashes-2015120144426713527.html
62. BBC, "Yemeni Crisis: President Resign as Rebels Tightened Hold," 23 January 2015, http://www.bbc.com/news/world-middle-east-30936940
63. Al-Arabiya News, "Houthis Take Charge in Yemen," 6 February 2015, http://english.alarabiya.net/en/News/middle-east/2015/02/06/Yemen-s-Houthi-to-issue-constitutional-decree.html
64. *The Guardian*, "Yemen's President Retracts Resignation after Escapes from House Arrest", 24 February 2015.
65. The Daily Star, "Houthi Forces Capture Air Base Near Aden", March 25, 2015, http://www.dailystar.com.lb/News/Middle-East/2015/Mar-25/292098-houthi-forces-capture-air-base-near-aden.ashx
66. *The Guardian*, "Yemen President in 'Safety' as Rebels Advance," 25 March 2015.
67. Felicia Schwartz and Hakim Almasmari, "Saudi Arabia Launches Air Strikes on Houthi Rebels in Yemen," March 25, 2015.
68. On the Yemeni civil war and its context see, Helen Lackner, "The War in Yemen," *Open Democracy*, 6 April 2015, https://www.opendemocracy.net/arab-awakening/helen-lackner/war-in-yemen; Stacey Philbrick Yadav and Seila Carapica, "The Breakdown of GCC Initiatives," *Middle East Information and Research Project*, vol. 44, no. 273; Susane Dahalgreen, "South Yemen After the Fall of Sanna," Middle East Information and Research Project, 7 October 2014; Charles Schmitz, "In Cahoots With the Houthis: Abdullah Saleh's Risky Gamble," *Foreign Affairs*, April 2015, https://www.foreignaffairs.com/articles/yemen/2015-04-19/cahoots-houthis
69. See Yadav and Carapica, "The Breakdown of GCC Initiatives."
70. Michael Pizzi, "Over 250,000 East African Refugees Trapped in Yemen," *Al Jazera America*, 18 April 2015.
71. Pizzi, "Over 250, 000 East African Refugees Trapped in Yemen."
72. On the U.S Policy, see United States Department of State, Bureau of Consular Affairs, Yemen Crisis, 18 May 2015: http://travel.state.gov/travel/english/YemenCrisis.html; John Zarocostas, "U.S Reiterates It Won't Evacuate Americans from Yemen as UN Slams Saudi Attacks," 8 April 2015, http://www.mcclatchydc.com/2015/04/08/262530/us-reiterates-it-wont-evacuate.html
73. Al Jazera America, "Americans Stuck in Yemen File Suit Against State, Defense Departments," 9 April 2015.
74. Civil Action No. 15.-CV-00516-KBJ, United States District Court for the District of Columbia: Emergency Complaint for Mandamus With Request for Injunctive Relief.
75. Civil Action No. 15.-CV-00516-KBJ, United States District Court for the District of Columbia.

76. Council on American-Islamic Relations, "CAIR, ADC Applaud Passage of House Amendment Asking the President to Evacuate US Citizens," 15 May, 2015.
77. International Organization of Migration (IOM). "Yemen Crisis: IOM Regional Response," 30 April 2015.
78. International Organization of Migration (IOM), "Yemen Crisis: IOM Regional Response," 30 April 2015.
79. United Nation High Commissioner for Refugees (UNHCR), "Yemen Situation: UNHCR Crisis update #3," 1 May 2015.
80. See Lyse Doucet, "Yemen Conflict: A Passport out of War," *BBC*, 21 May 2015.

4. Entrepreneurs, Laborers, and Smugglers: Yemenis in the Economy of States/Empires

1. Last Will of Muhammad Yusuf Ba Naji, 16 July 1971 (Author's translation).
2. British Foreign Office, "Confidential Dispatch, Slave Trade No. 7 from Mr. C. Vivian, Cairo, to the Earl of Derby, 22 March 1878, Outlining Mr. G. Malcolm's Tour of the Red Sea Ports, Enclosing 'Notes by Malcolm Pasha' Berbera, 2–7 February 1878; at Zayla', 9–10 February 1878; Jebel Sijam and Ras Dujemerah, 14–15 February 1878; Assab Bay, 16–17 February 1878; Hanfelah, 20 February 1878; Howakil, 21 February 1878; Dahlak Island, 22 February 1878, FO541/22," in Burdett (2006,volume 5).
3. Exposition Coloniale Internationale, 95.
4. Exposition Nationale Coloniale de Marseille, 47–48.
5. Exposition Nationale Coloniale de Marseille, 48.
6. Exposition Nationale Coloniale de Marseille, 46.
7. Djibouti Chamber of Commerce, "Yemeni to the President of Djibouti Chamber of Commerce, 8 May 1920," in File: Correspondence of Djibouti Operators (8 January 1907 to 17 June 1957); Box: Correspondence of Economic Operators, 1907 to 1957. Author's translation.
8. Exposition Coloniale Internationale, 94.
9. Exposition Coloniale Internationale.
10. See Exposition Nationale Coloniale de Marseille, 76-80.
11. Exposition Coloniale Internationale, 106–108.
12. For an account of Bess and his company, see Footman (1986).
13. CO732/78/1 Memorandum, Addenda to Cases of Slavery Previously Reported, undated.
14. British Foreign Office, "Dispatch No. 5 from British Consulate, Harar, to British Minister, Addis Ababa, 28 April 1911, Regarding Sultan Saeed Who is in Prison in Addis Ababa Accused of Abyssinian Slaves in Aden, Enclosing a Copy of Dispatch No. A/882 from Major-General E. de Broth, Political Resident, Aden, to British Consul, Harar, 24 March 1908 (R/20/A/2758)," in Burdett (2006, volume 5).
15. US Department of State, "Aden American Consulate to State Department, Slavery in Abyssinia and the Red Sea Area (Dispatch Number 156)," in *Record of the Department of State Relating to Internal Affairs of Ethiopia (Abyssinia)*, Rol. III (Washington, DC: National Archive and Record Service, 1962).
16. British Foreign Office, "Deputy Governor of Aden to S. S. Colonies, 10 May 1943," in Burdett (2006: vol. 7, 582–86).

17. In the mid-1930s there were around four thousand to five thousand slaves distributed throughout the region. In some parts of the Aden protectorate slaves served as soldiers, agricultural laborers, and domestic workers. There were slaves in the regions of Haushabi, Alawi, Fadhli, Ahl Hasana, Ahl Dathia, Ahl Audhilla, lower Yafa, upper Aulaqi sultanate, lower Aulaqi sultanate, Beidan, Masabi, and Bir Ali sultanate. In the Aden protectorate, slaves also served as soldiers. In this capacity there were four hundred slaves in the country of Ahl Abdul Wahid, five in Hura, a thousand in Qu'ayti, four hundred in Kathiri, and a thousand in Tarim and other parts of Hadramawt. In the same period in northern Yemen there were forty-five hundred slaves. For an account of this issue, see British Foreign Office, "Memorandum on Slavery and the Slave Trade in the Aden Protectorate," in Burdett (2006: vol. 7, 55–60) and British Foreign Office, "H.R. Cowell Esquire, C.M.G. to Colonial Office," in Burdett (2006: vol. 7, 114–17).
18. During the early part of the twentieth century there were a number of arms dealers of Yemeni origin in Djibouti and Ethiopia. In Djibouti the biggest were Hamoudi Ahmed, who died in the 1930s, and Salim Mouti. For a discussion of the region's arms trade in the early nineteenth century, see Pankhurst (1965).
19. US State Department, "Aden American Consulate to the Secretary of State, Present Interest and Relations of Great Britain, France, and Italy in Abyssinia, 22 April, 1919," in *Record of the Department of State Relating to Internal Affairs of Ethiopia (Abyssinia)*, Rol. I (Washington, DC: National Archive and Record Service, 1962).
20. US State Department, "Aden American Consulate to the Secretary of State, Present Interest and Relations of Great Britain, France, and Italy in Abyssinia, 22 April, 1919."
21. US State Department, "Exportation of Arms to Ethiopia," in *Record of the Department of State Relating to Internal Affairs of Ethiopia (Abyssinia)*, Rol. I (Washington, DC: National Archive and Record Service 1962).
22. US State Department, "Exportation of Arms to Ethiopia."
23. US State Department, "Exportation of Arms to Ethiopia."
24. US State Department, "Exportation of Arms to Ethiopia."
25. British Foreign Office, "Consul Jerkins to the British Foreign Affairs, Tension between Arabs and Somalis in French Somaliland," 21 May 1938, FO 371 /22034.
26. On Jimma Aba Jiffar and the importance of Jimma for the trade of Ethiopia, see Abir (1965) and Lewis (1965).
27. AFF-POL 697 (ANOM), A. Lippmann, Adjoint des services civils chef du post du Dikkil à Monsieur le Président du Tribunal Supérieure d'Appelé 9 Juillet 1930. File: Affair Bargone, Farnies, Magistrate.
28. Certificate for the Fourth Honorary Medallion of Ethiopia Awarded to Salim Ba Zar'a.
29. Certificate for the Fourth Honorary Medallion of Ethiopia.
30. King Ahmad bin Hamid al Nasir to Sheikh Ahmad Salih al Zahiri, 25 Safir 1365.
31. King Ahmad bin Hamid al Nasir to Emperor Haile Selassie.
32. Regarding the Suez Canal crisis, see Varble (2009).
33. Djibouti Chamber of Commerce, "Speech of Sa'id 'Ali Coubèche," Procès-verbal du Chambre de Commerce, 1 September 1960.
34. On the traditional attitude of Ethiopians toward manual labor, see Shack (1976).

35. For an account of the migration of Gurages and other southerners to Addis Ababa, see Pankhurst (1961: 113–16).
36. On the nationalization of land and urban houses during the Derg, see Tiruneh (1993: 97–115).
37. Interview with 'Abdallah Mohamed Kamil, former president of Djibouti, Djibouti, April 2010.
38. Interview with 'Abdallah Mohamed Kamil, April 2010.
39. Interview with 'Abdallah Mohamed Kamil, April 2010.
40. Republic of Djibouti, "Accord Franco-Djiboutien: Accord de coopération en matière economique et financière," 27 June 1977.
41. Republic of Djibouti, "Accord Franco-Djiboutien: Stationnement des forces françaises et coopération militaire."
42. For a discussion on the changing relation between state and capital, see Cox (1987), Gill (1990), and Sklair (2001).
43. For a discussion of the emergence of global labor, see Lefebvre (1977) and Robinson (2001).
44. The companies operating in Ethiopia are Addis Home Depot PLC, Addis International Catering PLC, Blue Nile P. P. & Craft Paper Bags Manufacturing PLC, Cabey PLC, East-West Ethio Transport PLC, Elfora Agro-Industries PLC, Lame Dairy PLC, Mamco Paper Products Factory PLC, Midroc Construction Ethiopia PLC, Midroc Energy House Electro-Mechanical Services PLC, MIDROC Ethiopia PLC, Ethiopia Technology Group PLC, Midroc Foundation Specialist PLC, Midroc Gold Mine, Modern Building Industries PLC, Moha Soft Drinks Industry SC, Mugad Travel PLC, National Mining Corp., National Oil Ethiopia PLC (NOC), Pharmacure PLC, Rainbow Exclusive Car Rental and Tour Services PLC, Salam Health Care PLC, Sheraton Addis, Star Soap and Detergent Industries PLC, Summit Engineered PLC, National Motors Corporation PLC, Trans Nation Airways PLC, Trust Protection & Personnel Services PLC, United Auto Maintenance Services PLC, Unity University PLC, Unlimited Packaging PLC, Wamza Furnishing Industries PLC, Equatorial Business Group PLC, Ethio Agri-Ceft PLC, Ethio Leather Industry PLC (ELICO), Huda Real Estate PLC, Kebire Enterprise PLC, Kombolcha Steel Products Industries PLC, Addis Gas and Plastics Factory PLC, Daylight Applied Technologies PLC, Addis Gas, and Plastics Factory PLC.
45. Regarding the bin Laden family history, see Coll (2008).
46. For news coverage of the bridge and the new city, see "The Red Sea: Can It Really Be Bridged? A Fantastic Plan to Span the Red Sea's Troubled Water is Raising Eyebrows," *The Economist*, 31 July 2008.
47. Regarding the Nur city investment, see the company website at http://alnoorcity.com/index.php
48. "The Red Sea: Can It Really Be Bridged?"

5. Colonial Intermediaries, Emperors, Abettors, and Enemies of the People

1. For the anti–African Union position of President Ali Aref, see "Conférence de presse du Président Ali Aref Bourhan," *Le Réveil de Djibouti*, 26 May 1973, 2. For a broad discussion of the presidency of Ali Aref, see Aden (1999).

2. "Ali Aref Bourhan a posé la première pierre de la maison du Club de la Communauté Arabe," *Le Réveil de Djibouti*, 19 January 1974, 3. Author's translation.
3. For a short summary of the initial judiciary setup, see Société de Législation Comparée (1901: 254).
4. French Republic, "Décret portant sur l'organisation du service judiciaire dans le Protectorat Français de la Côte des Somalis," *Journal Officiel de la République*, 4 September 1894.
5. French Republic, "Décret portant sur l'organisation du service judiciaire dans le Protectorat Français de la Côte des Somalis."
6. French Republic, "Décret modifiant le décret du 19 Décembre 1900 réorganisant le Service de la Justice dans la Colonie de la Côte Française des Somalis," *Journal Officiel de la République*, 1 January 1901.
7. French Republic, "Réorganisation du Service de la Justice dans la Colonie de la Côte Française des Somalis," *Journal Officiel de la République*, 10 February 1904.
8. French Republic, "Réorganisation du Service de la Justice dans la Colonie de la Côte Française des Somalis."
9. French Republic, *Côte Française des Somalis et dépendance, budget des recettes et des dépens pour l'exercice 1913* (Marseille: Moullot, 1913).
10. ANOM 1AFF-POL 697, Letter of La Franchi Jean (Président du tribunal de premier instance) à monsieur le président du tribunal supérieur, 21 July 1930. File: Affaire Barrognes, Farnines, Magistrats.
11. ANOM 1AFF-POL 697, 21 July 1930.
12. Archive National d'Outre Mer (ANOM) Cfes 4e 2, 3, 4. L'évolution islamique à la Côte Française des Somalis, 1937. File: Note sur l'Islam en Afrique noire.
13. Archive National d'Outre Mer (ANOM) Cfes 4e 2, 3, 4. L'évolution islamique à la Côte Française des Somalis, 1937
14. Archive National d'Outre Mer (ANOM) Cfes 4e 2, 3, 4. L'évolution islamique à la Côte Française des Somalis, 1937
15. Ali Ba Nabila to Muslims of Djibouti, December 1920, Saigon. File: Correspondence of Djibouti Operators (8 January 1907 to 17 June 1957); Box: Correspondence of Economic Operators, 1907 to 1957. Author's translation.
16. Hassan Ba Nabila to Muslims of Djibouti, December 1920.
17. The names of the founders are Ahmed ben Ahmed, Sa'id 'Ali Coubèche, Hassan Dorani, Nadj Mohamed, Salem Abdelah, Abdourahman Dorani, Sheikh 'Umar Ba Zara, Rached Dallab Hay, Mohamed Delleitah, and Hadj Hussein Nour.
18. ANOM 4e 8–9, Approbation de Statu, le President du Comité, 10 December 1930. File: Association de Bienfaisance Islamique; ANOM 4e 8–9 Règlement de l'Association Islamique de Bienfaisance à Djibouti. File: Association de Bienfaisance Islamique.
19. ANOM 4e 8–9, Approbation de Statu, le Président du Comité, 10 December 1930.
20. ANOM 4e 8–9, La Comité de l'Association Islamique de Bienfaisance a son Excellence Monsieur le Gouverneur de la Côte Française des Somalis, 5 January 1931. File: Association de Bienfaisance Islamique.
21. ANOM 4e 8–9, La Comité de l'Association Islamique de Bienfaisance a son Excellence Monsieur le Gouverneur de la Côte Française des Somalis, 5 January 1931.

22. Mahdist Sudan fought against British colonial rule in Sudan, starting with a revolt that began in the 1880s led by Muhammad Ahmad al Mahdi. On the origin and development of Mahdist Sudan, see Holt (1958).
23. For an interesting discussion of Wilsonian sovereignty, see Smith (2008).
24. US Department of State, "American Consulate at Aden to the State Department, Suggestion as to Possible Method of Reforming Abyssinian Affairs, with Attached Letter of Haj Abdul Kadir Ba Wazir, 23 April 1919," in *Records of the Department of State Relating to Internal Affairs of Ethiopia (Abyssinia), 1910–1929*, Rol. I (Washington, DC: National Archive and Record Service, 1962). Author's translation.
25. US Department of State, "United States Legation of Addis Ababa to the Secretary of State, Report No. 93, November 7, 1928," in *Records of the Department of State Relating to Internal Affairs of Ethiopia (Abyssinia), 1910–1929*, Rol. I (Washington, DC: National Archive and Record Service, 1962).
26. Steen (1936: 8).
27. Steen (1936).
28. See the address of Emperor Haile Selassie I on the occasion of the signing of the Ethiopian empire's constitution in Steen (1936: 5).
29. For a discussion of the invasion of Ethiopia by fascist Italy, see Sbacchi (1997).
30. The seven Hadramis were Muhammad al Mohadar, Muhammad Ba Harun, Ahmad Ba Zar'a, 'Umar al-Sa'adi, Ali Ba Nasir, Aboued Ba Amer, and Ahmad Eljiiro.
31. British Foreign Office, "From H. M. Consul to Secretary of State of Foreign Affairs, Memorandum and Enclosure: Italian Muslim Policy, 18 August 1936," FO /371.20202.
32. British Foreign Office, "From H. M. Consul to Secretary of State of Foreign Affairs, Memorandum and Enclosure: Italian Muslim Policy, 18 August 1936."
33. British Foreign Office, "From H. M. Consul to Secretary of State of Foreign Affairs, Memorandum and Enclosure: Italian Muslim Policy, 18 August 1936."
34. British Foreign Office, "From H. M. Consul to Secretary of State of Foreign Affairs, Memorandum and Enclosure: Italian Muslim Policy, 18 August 1936."
35. British Foreign Office, "From H. M. Consul to Secretary of State of Foreign Affairs, Memorandum and Enclosure: Italian Muslim Policy, 18 August 1936."
36. British Foreign Office, "From H. M. Consul to Secretary of State of Foreign Affairs, Memorandum and Enclosure: Italian Muslim Policy, 18 August 1936."
37. British Foreign Office, "From H. M. Consul to Secretary of State of Foreign Affairs, Memorandum and Enclosure: Italian Muslim Policy, 18 August 1936."
38. British Foreign Office, "From H. M. Consul to Secretary of State of Foreign Affairs, Memorandum and Enclosure: Italian Muslim Policy, 18 August 1936."
39. British Foreign Office, "British Embassy to Foreign Office," 3 September 1936, FO/371.20202.
40. Sheikh Ahmad al Zahiri to Emperor Haile Selassie, typescript, 10 November 1959, Addis Ababa.
41. French Republic, "Ordonnance No. 45–1.874 du 22 aout 1945 fixant le mode de représentation à l'Assemblée Nationale Constituante des territoires d'outre-mer relevant du Ministère des Colonies," *Journal Officiel de la Côte Française des Somalis*, 44 Ann–No. 9, September 1945, 167.

42. French Republic, "Ordonnance No. 45–1.874 du 22 aout 1945 fixant le mode de représentation à l'Assemblée Nationale Constituante des territoires d'outre-mer relevant du Ministère des Colonies."
43. French Republic, "Ordonnance No. 45–1.874 du 22 aout 1945 fixant le mode de représentation à l'Assemblée Nationale Constituante des territoires d'outre-mer relevant du Ministère des Colonies."
44. "Des institutions de la république," *Le Réveil*, 2 October 1946, 2.
45. See *Le Réveil* of 11 March, 1946, and *Le Réveil* of March 26, 1946.
46. "Les résultats des élections," *Le Réveil*, 13 November 1946, 1.
47. Côte Française des Somalis, "Rapport du 12 Janvier 1949" (Archive of Chemin de Fer Djibouti-Éthiopien, Addis Ababa).
48. Côte Française des Somalis, "Rapport du 12 Janvier 1949."
49. Côte Française des Somalis, "Rapport du 12 Janvier 1949." Author's translation.
50. Marchés Coloniaux of 5 November 1949, quoted in Dubois (2007: 83). Author's translation.
51. Doudoub (1962).
52. Doudoub (1962).
53. On the Free Yemeni Movement, see al-Abdin (1979).
54. ANOM CFS YEMEN2, Fondation d'une Association Yéménite à Djibouti, 21 April 1947. File: Parties des Yéménites Libres 1944–1955.
55. ANOM CFS YEMEN2, Fondation d'une Association Yéménite à Djibouti, 21 April 1947.
56. ANOM CFS YEMEN2, Organization du Parti du Yémen Libre. File: Partis des Yéménites Libres 1944–1955.
57. ANOM CFS YEMEN2, "Répercussions des élections au club de la Jeunesse arabe de Djibouti," 11 May 1947. File: Parties des Yéménites Libres 1944–1955.
58. ANOM CFS YEMEN2, "Répercussions des élections au club de la Jeunesse arabe de Djibouti," 11 May 1947.
59. ANOM CFS YEMEN2, "Répercussions des élections au club de la Jeunesse arabe de Djibouti," 11 May 1947.
60. ANOM CFS YEMEN2, "Répercussions des élections au club de la Jeunesse arabe de Djibouti," 11 May 1947.
61. Interview with 'Abdallah Mohamed Kamil, former prime minister of Djibouti, Djibouti, November 2009.
62. Interview with Colonel Fathi Guelleh, a cousin of President Ismail Omar Guelleh, Djibouti, 11 December 2009.
63. Interview with Colonel Fathi Guelleh, 11 December 2009.
64. Interview with Haidar Ali, presently employed by Radio diffusion-Télévision de Djibouti and formerly active in the anti-France movement, Djibouti, December 2009.
65. Interview with 'Abdallah Mohamed Kamil, Djibouti, November 2009.
66. Service Historique de l'Arme de Terre, Château de Vincennes Paris, 10 T 124 Notes des Renseignements, 9 October 1962, quoted in Dubois (1997: 285). Author's translation.
67. "Déclaration des Arabes," *Le Réveil de Djibouti*, 28 September 1963, 3.
68. "Déclaration des Arabes."
69. Interview with 'Abdallah Mohamed Kamil, November 2009.
70. Interview with 'Abdallah Mohamed Kamil, November 2009.

71. Interview with 'Abdallah Mohamed Kamil, November 2009.
72. Interview with 'Abdallah Mohamed Kamil, November 2009.
73. "Soreyan Ena Andand Ye Areb Agerochen Bemekawem Be Meto Shi Yemikoteru Hezbe Selamawi Self Aderege," *Addis Zemen*, 14 March 1961.
74. For a discussion of Arab national strategies, see Erlich (1995).
75. "Soreyan Ena Andand Ye Areb Agerochen Bemekawem Be Meto Shi Yemikoteru Hezbe Selamawi Self Aderege."
76. "Soreyan Ena Andand Ye Areb Agerochen Bemekawem Be Meto Shi Yemikoteru Hezbe Selamawi Self Aderege."
77. "Soreyan Ena Andand Ye Areb Agerochen Bemekawem Be Meto Shi Yemikoteru Hezbe Selamawi Self Aderege."
78. "Soreyan Ena Andand Ye Areb Agerochen Bemekawem Be Meto Shi Yemikoteru Hezbe Selamawi Self Aderege."
79. "Soreyan Ena Andand Ye Areb Agerochen Bemekawem Be Meto Shi Yemikoteru Hezbe Selamawi Self Aderege."
80. "Soreyan Ena Andand Arebochen Bemekawem Ye teklay Gezat Hezbe Selamawi Self Aderege," *Addis Zemen*, 16 March 1961; "Soreyan Be Mekawem Self Endeketele New," *Addis Zemen*, 27 March 1961; "Soreyan Bemekawem Selamawi Self Alabekam," *Addis Zemen*, 28 March 1961.
81. "Soreyan Ena Andand Arebochen Bemekawem Ye teklay Gezat Hezbe Selamawi Self Aderege," *Addis Zemen*, 16 March 1961; "Soreyan Be Mekawem Self Endeketele New," *Addis Zemen*, 27 March 1961; "Soreyan Bemekawem Selamawi Self Alabekam," *Addis Zemen*, 28 March 1961.
82. "Soreyan Ena Andand Ye Areb Agerochen Bemekawem Be Meto Shi Yemikoteru Hezbe Selamawi Self Aderege." Author's translation.
83. "Soreyan Ena Andand Ye Areb Agerochen Bemekawem Be Meto Shi Yemikoteru Hezbe Selamawi Self Aderege." Author's translation.
84. "Rese Ankese: Yeteterakeme Nedet," *Addis Zemen*, 16 March 1961. Author's translation.
85. "Be Eritra Yeminoru Areboch Selaamwi Self Aderegu," *Addis Zemen*, 21 March 1961; "Be Desse Yeminoru Ye Yemen ena Ye Saudi Araboche Soreyan Tekawemu," *Addis Zemen*, 26 March 1961; "Teklay Gezate Yeminoru Ye Yemen Areboch Soreyan Tekawemu," *Addis Zemen*, 23 March 1961.
86. "Janehoye Fite Bemekreb Ye Semen Ena Ye Debub Yemenoch Ye Soryan Adragot Tekawemu," *Addis Zemen*, 20 March 1961.
87. "Janehoye Fite Bemekreb Ye Semen Ena Ye Debub Yemenoch Ye Soryan Adragot Tekawemu." Author's translation.
88. "Janehoye Fite Bemekreb Ye Semen Ena Ye Debub Yemenoch Ye Soryan Adragot Tekawemu."
89. Hassen Gouled Aptidon, "Message à la Nation de Président Hassan Gouled Aptidon à l'Occasion du 8 Mai 1977: Paix–Unité–Fraternité" (Imprimerie Administrative, Djibouti, 1977), 4.
90. Aptidon, "Message à la Nation," 5.
91. Aptidon, "Message à la Nation," 7–8.
92. Aptidon, "Message à la Nation," 8.
93. Aptidon, "Message à la Nation."
94. Aptidon, "Message à la Nation," 9.

95. Aptidon, "Message à la Nation."
96. Aptidon, "Message à la Nation."
97. For a discussion of ethnic politics after independence, see Schraeder (1993).
98. On the position of the 'Afar in newly independent Djibouti, see Shehim and Searing (1980).
99. Interview with 'Abdallah Mohamed Kamil, former prime minister of Djibouti, Djibouti, March 2010.
100. Schraeder (1993: 207).
101. For a discussion of the elections, see Abdallah (2008: 275–77).
102. See Republic of Djibouti, *La Constitution de la République de Djibouti du 15 Séptembre 1992*.
103. Organisation Internationale de la Francophonie, *Rapport de la Mission d'Observation des Élections Législatives du 18 Decembre 1992*, Paris, 1992.
104. Organisation Internationale de la Francophonie, *Rapport de la Mission d'Observation des Élections Présidentielles du 9 Avril 1999*, Paris.
105. For a discussion of the government's war with FRUD, see Kadamy (1996: 512–18).
106. Informal conversation with Aref Mohamed Aref, humanitarian lawyer and a releative of President Ali Aref, 9 November 2009.
107. In the 2011 presidential elections, Ismail Omar Guelleh won for the third time. His election was considered unfair by international observers. For an account of the electoral victory, see "Presidentielles 2011: Les verdicts des urnes," *La Nation*, 1 April 2011. For an analysis of the election, see Berouk Mesfin, "Situation Report: Election, Politics and External Involvement in Djibouti," *Institute for Security Studies*, 14 April 2011.
108. "Le president Coubèche repond au président de la République: Je suis globalement en phase avec le nouveau président de la République," *Djib Ec*, 31 June 1999.
109. For coverage of the death of Sa'id 'Ali Coubèche, see "Adieu, Monsieur Coubèche," *La Nation*, 19 January 2009.
110. "Coubèche hommage posthume," *La Nation*, 5 February 2009.
111. "Adieu, Monsieur Coubèche."
112. "Coubèche hommage posthume." Author's translation.
113. Informal conversation, December 2009.

6. State Vision, Imperial Hierarchies: Being a Muslim Yemeni

1. M. Cadars, "De France en Corée: Journal de route d'une mission," *Les Missions Catholiques* (1913): 407.
2. Louis de Gonzague Lasserre, "Arabie: La mission d'Aden," *Les Missions Catholiques* (1886): 603. Author's translation.
3. de Gonzague Lasserre, "Arabie: La mission d'Aden."
4. de Gonzague Lasserre, "Arabie: La mission d'Aden."
5. On the social stratification of Yemeni society, see Bujra (1971).
6. See Brosselard (1959).
7. R.P. Evangeliste, "Au pays des Somalis," *Les Missions Catholiques*, 1902, 545. Author's translation.

8. For a history of Christianity in Djibouti, see Dubois and Soumille (2004).
9. R.P. Irene, "Au pays des Somali! Fleurs du désert," *Les Missions Catholiques*, 1915, 169.
10. Cadars, "De France en Corée," 406.
11. Evangeliste, "Au pays des Somalis," 169; M. Joseph Bateman, "Une victime de la guerre," *Les Missions Catholiques* (1918): 277.
12. Cadars, "De France en Corée," 406. Author's translation.
13. See the discussion by Triaud (2000: 170).
14. le Chatelier, "Politique Musulmane," *Revue du Monde Musulman*, vol. 12, no. 9 (1910): 79–80. Author's translation.
15. le Chatelier, "Politique Musulmane," 101. Author's translation.
16. le Chatelier, "Politique Musulmane," 102.
17. René Basset, "Opinion," *Questions Diplomatiques et Coloniales*, 1 October 1901, 389. 388. Author's translation.
18. Interview with Aref Mohamed Aref, lawyer and nephew of President Ali Aref, Djibouti, 1 November 2009
19. ANOM CFS 4ᵉ 2, 3, 4, "L'Evolution Islamique a la Côte Française des Somalis," 1937. File: Note sur l'Islam en Afrique noire.
20. ANOM CFS 4ᵉ 2, 3, 4, "L'Evolution Islamique a la Côte Française des Somalis," 1937.
21. ANOM CFS 4ᵉ 2, 3, 4, "L'Evolution Islamique a la Côte Française des Somalis," 1937.
22. ANOM CFS 4ᵉ 2, 3, 4, "L'Evolution Islamique a la Côte Française des Somalis," 1937.
23. For an account of the revolt, see Swedenburg (2003).
24. ANOM CFS 4ᵉ 2, 3, 4, "Le gouverneur de la Côte Française des Somalis et dépendance à Monsieur l'administrateur commandant le cercle de Djibouti," 16 June 1936. File: Note sur l'Islam en Afrique noire.
25. ANOM, CFS 4ᵉ 2, 3, 4, "Le Commissaire de Police de Djibouti à Monsieur le Gouverneur de la Côte Française des Somalis (Sous couvert de M. le Commandant de cercle)," A/S Papiers Vendus en Ville, 9 June 1936. File: Note sur l'Islam en Afrique noire.
26. ANOM, CFS 4ᵉ 2, 3, 4, "Le Commissaire de Police de Djibouti à Monsieur le Gouverneur de la Côte Française des Somalis (Sous couvert de M. le Commandant de cercle)," A/S Papiers Vendus en Ville, 9 June 1936.
27. ANOM, CFS 4ᵉ 2, 3, 4, "Le Commissaire de Police de Djibouti à Monsieur le Gouverneur de la Côte Française des Somalis (Sous couvert de M. le Commandant de cercle)," A/S Papiers Vendus en Ville, 9 June 1936.
28. ANOM, CFS 4ᵉ 2, 3, 4, "Le Commissaire de Police de Djibouti à Monsieur le Gouverneur de la Côte Française des Somalis (Sous couvert de M. le Commandant de cercle)," A/S Papiers Vendus en Ville, 9 June 1936.
29. ANOM CFS 4ᵉ 2, 3, 4, "Extrait du rapport sur la situation politique du mois de janvier 1936, panislamisme et nationalisme." File: Note sur l'Islam en Afrique noire.
30. ANOM CFS 4ᵉ 2, 3, 4, "Extrait du rapport sur la situation politique du mois de janvier 1936, panislamisme et nationalisme."
31. ANOM CFS 4ᵉ 2, 3, 4, "Extrait du rapport sur la situation politique du mois de janvier 1936, panislamisme et nationalisme."

32. ANOM CFS 4ᵉ 2, 3, 4, "Extrait du rapport sur la situation politique du mois de janvier 1936, panislamisme et nationalisme."
33. ANOM CFS 4ᵉ 2, 3, 4, "Extrait du rapport sur la situation politique du mois de janvier 1936, panislamisme et nationalisme."
34. ANOM CFS 4ᵉ 2, 3, 4, "Extrait du rapport sur la situation politique du mois de janvier 1936, panislamisme et nationalisme."
35. ANOM CFS 4ᵉ 2, 3, 4, "Extrait du rapport sur la situation politique du mois de janvier 1936, panislamisme et nationalisme."
36. ANOM CFS 4ᵉ 2, 3, 4, "Extrait du rapport sur la situation politique du mois de janvier 1936, panislamisme et nationalisme."
37. For an English translation of the legend, see Budge (1922).
38. Known in the English-speaking world as the Queen of Sheba.
39. US Department of State, "G.M. Mohamedally & Co. to R.P. Skinner Esqr., London, American Consular Service, Abyssinian Revolution, October 20, 1916," in *Record of the Department of State Relating to Internal Affairs of Ethiopia (Abyssinia), 1910–1929*, Rol. I (Washington, DC: National Archive and Record Service, 1962).
40. For a discussion of internal racism within the facist state, see de Donno (2006).
41. *Manifesto Degli Scienziati Razzisti* (1938), quoted in Gillette (2011: 319).
42. *Manifesto Degli Scienziati Razzisti* (1938).
43. For an interesting discussion of this matter, see Whitford (2009).
44. For a discussion of Mochi's ideas and the later work of Ruggeri, see Caponetto (2008: 49–50).
45. The Sabeans are an ancient people thought to have inhabited what is now known as Yemen.
46. "L'Aïd-el-Fetr," *Le Réveil de Djibouti*, 2 April 1960, 3. Author's translation.
47. "Les Fêtes de l'Aïd el Fitr à Djibouti," *Le Réveil de Djibouti*, 29 January 1966, 1. Author's translation.
48. "Les Fêtes de l'Aïd el Fitr à Djibouti," 3.
49. "L'Aïd el Kebri à Djibouti," *Le Réveil de Djibouti*, 12 June 1960.
50. "L'Aïd el Kebri à Djibouti."
51. "La Fete de l'Aid-el-Kebir," *Le Réveil de Djibouti*, 17 April 1965, 3. Author's translation.
52. For a discussion of divisions in Southeast Asia, see Mobini-Kesheh (1999) and Manger (2010: 20–41). For the effect that the movement in Southeast Asia had in the homeland, see Freitag (2003).
53. On the reaction of the Orthodox community, see Ahmed (1994).
54. Regarding the presence of Ethiopians in Arabia, see Hopper (2006).
55. Leon T. Hadar, "The 'Green Peril': Creating the Islamic Fundamentalist Threat," CATO Institute, http://www.cato.org/pubs/pas/pa-177.html
56. This tendency to classify Muslims represents a wider trend present in many places. For a discussion of this, see Mamdani (2004).
57. US Department of State, "From United States Embassy in Addis Ababa to Secretary of State, Wahhabi in Ethiopia as Cultural Imperialism," 15 July 2009, WikiLeaks, http://wikileaks.org/cable/2009/07/ 09ADDISABABA1674.html
58. For further accounts of the introduction of the Ahbash sect and the controversy that it raised in Ethiopia, see Abbink (2014) and Østebø (2013). For a description of the sect and the way in which it is viewed see Hamzel and Dekmejian (1996); Kabha and Erlich (2006).

59. US Department of State, "From United States Embassy in Addis Ababa to Secretary of State, Ethiopia: Combating Extremism," 25 January 2006, WikiLeaks, http://www.cablegatesearch.net/cable.php?id=06ADDISABABA217
60. US Department of State, "From United States Embassy in Addis Ababa to Secretary of State, Countering Wahabi Influence in Ethiopia through Cultural Programming," 15 July 2009, WikiLeaks, http://wikileaks.org/cable/2009/07/09addisababa1675.html.
61. US Department of State, "From United States Embassy in Addis Ababa to Secretary of State, Countering Wahhabi Influence in Ethiopia through Cultural Programming."
62. US Department of State, "From United States Embassy in Addis Ababa to Secretary of State, Countering Wahhabi Influence in Ethiopia through Cultural Programming."
63. US Department of State, "From United States Embassy in Addis Ababa to Secretary of State, Countering Wahhabi Influence in Ethiopia through Cultural Programming."
64. US Department of State, "From United States Embassy in Addis Ababa to Secretary of State, Countering Wahhabi Influence in Ethiopia through Cultural Programming."
65. US Department of State, "From United States Embassy in Addis Ababa to Secretary of State, Countering Wahhabi Influence in Ethiopia through Cultural Programming."
66. US Department of State, "From United States Embassy in Djibouti to Secretary of State, Islam in Djibouti," 15 February 2005, WikiLeaks, http://leaks.hohesc.us/?view=05DJIBOUTI149
67. US Department of State, "From United States Embassy in Djibouti to Secretary of State, Islam in Djibouti."
68. Comment to "Ethiopian Muslims Celebrate 'Id al Adha," Nazret.com, 27 November 2009, http://nazret.com/blog/index.php/2009/11/27/muslims_in_ethiopia_to_celebrate_a_4768__8206
69. Comment to "Millionaire Sheiks Turning Ethiopia into Their Personal Brothel," *Ethiopian Review*, 18 February 2008, http://www.ethiopianreview.com/content/1922
70. Comment to "Millionaire Sheiks Turning Ethiopia into Their Personal Brothel."
71. US Department of State, "From Addis Ababa United States Embassy to Department of State in Washington, 'Allah in Ethiopia: Mostly Quiet on the Islamic Front,'" 4 January 1997, WikiLeaks, http://wikileaks.org/cable/1997/04/97ADDISABABA2584.html
72. See Maggie Mulvihill et al., "Slick Deals, the White House Connection: Saudi Agents Close Bush Friends," *Boston Globe*, 11 December 2001; Adam Zagorin, "Blaming the Saudis," *Time*, 25 November 2002.
73. Mulvihill et al., "Slick Deals, the White House Connection."
74. Zagorin, "Blaming the Saudis."
75. For an account of 'Amudi, see pages 134 and 290 of Thompson 2004.
76. Mulvihill et al., "Slick Deals, the White House Connection."
77. Thompson, "Correction to Time Line Entries Containing Erroneous Information about Mohammed Hussein al Amoudi," 24 January 2008, http://www.historycommons.org/essay.jsp?article=al-amoudi_correction

78. Regarding the perspective that he advanced, see US Department of State, "From Addis Ababa United States Embassy to Department of State, Washington, Ethiopia: Traditional Islam under Threat According to Sheikh," 8 August 2006, WikiLeaks, http://wikileaks.org/cable/2006/08/06ADDISABABA2352.html
79. A number of scholarly works address the emergence of Muslim intellectuals who defend Islam using media. These include Larkin (2008), Sadouni (1999), and Westerlund (2003).
80. On Islamic polemical discourse in Ethiopia, see Abbink (2011).
81. See Atnatewos (2001).
82. Craig Whitlock, "U.S. Drone Base in Ethiopia is Operational," *Washington Post*, 27 October 2011.
83. On the threat of al-Zawahari see: Dr. Ayman al-Zawahari Addressed to Muslims: "Set Out and Support Your Brothers in Somalia," http://www.Counterterrorismblog.org/site-resources/images/SITE, 4 January, 2007
84. Regarding bin Laden's characterization of Ethiopia, see Office of the Directorate of National Intelligence (ODNI), 2015, "Osama bin Laden Letter to Mujahedin in Somalia," http://www.dni.gov/files/documents/ubl/english2/Letter%20to%20Mujahidin%20in%20 Somalia%20dtd%2028%20 December%202006.pdf
85. On the Djibouti bombing see *BBC*, "Deadly Attack on Djibouti Restaurant," 24 May 2014.
86. Robert F. Worth, Mark Mazzetti, and Scott Shame, "Drone Strikes Risked to Get Rare Moment in the Public Eye," *New York Times*, 5 February 2013.
87. Centre for the Legal Protection of Human Rights and Centre for Human Rights and Global Justice, "African Commission Urged to Take on Ground Breaking Extraordinary Rendition Case," 28 February 2011.
88. Communication No. 383/2010, "Declaration of Mohamed Abdulah Saleh al-Asad before the African Commission for Human and People's Rights, 49 Ordinary Session: April– May 2011."
89. Communication No. 383/2010, "Mohamed Abdulah Saleh al-Asad V.: The Republic of Djibouti."
90. US Senate Select Committee on Intelligence, "Committee Study of the Central Intelligence Agency's Detention and Interrogation Program," December 2014.

7. Conclusion
1. BBC, "Yemen Migrant Boat Carrying Ethiopians Sinks Killing 70," 7 December 2014.

Bibliography

Aalen, Lovise. 2002. *Ethnic Federalism in a Dominant Party State: The Ethiopian Experience, 1991–2000*. Bergen: Chr. Michelsen Institute.
———. 2011. *The Politics of Ethnicity in Ethiopia: Actors, Power and Mobilisation under Ethnic Federalism*. Leiden: Brill.
Abbink, Jon. 2011. "Religion in Public Spaces: Emerging Muslim–Christian Polemics in Ethiopia." *African Affairs* 110, no. 439: 253–74.
———. 2014. "Religious Freedom and the Political Order: The Ethiopian 'Secular State' and the Containment of Muslim Identity," *Eastern African Studies*, 8, no. 3 : 346–65.
Abdallah, Abdo A. 2008. "State Building, Independence and Post-conflict Reconstruction in Djibouti." In *Post-conflict Peace-building in the Horn of Africa: A Report of the 6th Annual Conference on the Horn of Africa*, edited by Ulf Johansson, 269–79. Lund: Media-Tryck Sociologen.
al-Abdin, A.Z. 1979. "The Free Yemeni Movement (1940–48) and Its Ideas on Reform." *Middle Eastern Studies* 15, no. 1: 36–48.
Abdul-Rahman, Mohammad Saeed. 2009. *Tafsir Ibn Kathir Juz 16 (Part 16): Al-Kahf 75 to Ta-Ha 135*. London: MSA Publications.
Abebe, Berhanou. 2001. "Le coup d'état du 2 Septembre 1916 ou le dénouement d'une décennie de crise." *Annales d'Ethiopie* 17, no. 17: 307–57.
Abegaz, Berhanu. 2001. "Aid and Reform in Ethiopia." In *Aid and Reform in Africa: Lessons from Ten Case Studies*, edited by Shantayanan Devarajan, David R. Dollar, and Torgny Holmgren, 167–226. Washington, DC: World Bank.
Abir, Mordechai. 1965. "The Emergence and Consolidation of the Monarchies of Enarea and Jima in the First Half of the Nineteenth Century." *Journal of African History* 6, no. 2: 207.
Adelton, Jonathan S. 1991. "The Impact of the Gulf War on Migration and Remittances in Asia and the Middle East." *International Migration* 29, no. 4: 509–26.

Aden, Mohamed. 1999. *Sombloloho: Djibouti la chute du Président Ali Aref (1975–1976)*. Paris: L'Harmattan.
Agius, Dionisius. 2002. "Classifying Vessel-types in Ibn Baṭṭuta's *Rihla*." In *Ships and the Development of Maritime Technology in the Indian Ocean*, edited by David Parkin and Ruth Barnes, 174–208. London: Routledge Curzon.
———. 2008. *Classic Ships of Islam: From Mesopotamia to the Indian Ocean*. Leiden: Brill.
———. 2014. *The Life of the Red Sea Dhow: A Cultural History of Islamic Seaborne Exploration*. London: I.B. Tauris.
Agonafer, Fantu. 1979. "Djibouti's Three Front Struggle for Independence, 1975–77." PhD diss., University of Denver.
Ahmed, Hussein. 1994. "Islam and Islamic Discourse in Ethiopia (1973–1993)." In *New Trends in Ethiopian Studies*, vol. 1, edited by Harold G. Marcus, 775–801. Lawrenceville, NJ: Red Sea Press.
———. 1997. "A Brief Note on the Yemeni Arabs in Ethiopia." In *Ethiopia in Broader Perspective: Papers of the XIIIth International Conference of Ethiopian Studies*, vol. 1, edited by Katsuyoshi Fukuki, Eisei Kurimoto, and Masayoshi Shigeta, 339–348. Kyoto: Shokado Book Sellers.
———. 2000. "Archival Sources on the Yemeni Arabs in Urban Ethiopia: The Dessie Municipality." *History in Africa* 27: 31–37.
———. 2001. *Islam in Nineteenth-century Wallo, Ethiopia*. Leiden: Brill.
Allain, Jean. 2006. "Slavery and the League of Nations: Ethiopia as a Civilised Nation." *Journal of the History of International Law* 8: 213–44.
Alexanderson, Kris. 2014. "A Dark State of Affairs: Hajj Networks, Pan Islamism, and Dutch Colonial Surveillance during the Inter War Period," *Journal of Social History* 47, no. 4 :1021–41.
Allen, Neal. 2009. "The Fight against Terrorism in Historical Context: George W. Bush and the Development of Presidential Foreign Policy Regimes." In *America's War on Terror*, edited by Tom Lansford, Robert P. Watson, and Jack Covarrubias, 37–48. Farnham: Ashgate.
Allen, Richard. 1999. *Slaves, Freedmen, and Indentured Laborers in Colonial Mauritius*. Cambridge: Cambridge University Press.
Allievi, Stefano. 1996. "Muslim Organisations and Islam–State Relations: The Italians' Case." In *Muslim in the Margin: Political Responses to the Presence of Islam in Western Europe*, edited by W.A.R. Shadid and P.S. van Koningsveld, 181–201. Kampen: Kok Pharos.
Alpers, Edward. 2009. *East Africa and the Indian Ocean*. Princeton, NJ: Markus Wiener.
———. 2014. *The Indian Ocean in World History*. Oxford: Oxford University Press.
Alwan, Daoud Aboubaker, and Yohanis Mibrathu. 2000. *A Historical Dictionary of Djibouti*. Metuchen, NJ: The Scarecrow Press.
Aminzade, Ronald. 2013. *Race, Nation and Citizenship in Post-colonial Africa: The Case of Tanzania*. New York: Cambridge University Press.
Amrith, Sunil. 2013. *Crossing the Bay of Bengal: The Furies of Nature and the Fortunes of Migrants*. Cambridge, MA: Harvard University Press.
Anderson, Benedict. 1983. *Imagined Communities: Reflections on the Origin and Spread of Nationalism*. London: Verso.
Anderson, Clare. 2000. *Convicts in the Indian Ocean: Transportation from South Asia to Mauritius, 1815–53*. Basingstoke: Palgrave Macmillan.

———. 2012. *Subaltern Lives: Biographies of Colonialism in the Indian Ocean World, 1790–1920*. Cambridge: Cambridge University Press.
Angoulvant, Gabriel, and Sylvain Vignéras. 1902. *Djibouti, Mer Rouge, Abyssinie*. Paris: Librairie Africaine et Colonial.
Anthony, Ross. 2013. "Infrastructure and Influence: China's Presence on the Coast of East Africa." *Journal of the Indian Ocean Region* 9, no. 2: 134–49.
Antonsich, Marco. 2000. "Signs of Power: Fascist Urban Iconography in Ethiopia (1930s–1940s)." *Geo Journal* 52: 325–38.
Appadurai, Arjun. 1996. *Modernity at Large: Cultural Dimensions of Globalization*. Minneapolis, MN: University of Minnesota Press.
Aregay, Merid Wolde. 1974. "Population Movement as a Possible Factor in the Christian–Muslim Conflict of Medieval Ethiopia." *Symposium Leo Frobenius*. Munich: Pullach.
Arrighi, Giovanni. 1994. *The Long Twentieth Century: Money, Power and the Origins of Our Times*. London: Verso.
———. 2007. *Adam Smith in Beijing: Lineages of the Twenty-First Century*. London: Verso.
Asad, Talal. 1999. "Religion, Nation-State, Secularism." In *Nation and Religion: Perspectives on Europe and Asia*, edited by Peter van der Veer and Hartmut Lehmann, 178-196. Princeton, NJ: Princeton University Press.
Atnatewos, A. 2001. "Allah Yemilew Semena Ye kuran Mesehaf Tarikawi Ametattchew Sifetesh." *Hamere Tewahedo*. Addis Ababa: Amanuel Printing Press.
Awad, Haidar Abdallah. 2000. *Wyaam: Recueil de Poésies et Chansons Variées*. Djibouti: Imprimerie Nationale.
Balsuik, Randi. 1985. *Haile Selassie's Students: The Intellectual and Social Background to Revolution, 1952–1977*. East Lansing, MI: Michigan State University Press.
Balzacq, Thierry, and Sergio Carrera. 2006. *Security versus Freedom? A Challenge for Europe's Future*. Burlington: Ashgate.
Bang, Anne K. 1996. *The Idrisi State in Asir: Politics, Religion and Personal Prestige as State Building Factor in Early Twentieth-century Arabia*. Bergen: University of Bergen Press.
———. 2003. *Sufis and Scholars of the Sea: Family Networks in East Africa, 1860–1925*. London: Routledge Curzon.
———. 2008. "Cosmopolitanism Colonised? Three Cases from Zanzibar 1890–1920." In *Struggling with History: Islam and Cosmopolitanism in the Western Indian Ocean*. New York: Columbia University Press.
———. 2014. *Islamic Sufi Networks in the Western Indian Ocean (c. 1880–1940): Ripples of Reform*. Leiden: Brill.
Bardey, Alfred. 1897. "Notes sur le Harar." *Bulletin de Géographie Historique et Descriptive* 12: 130–80.
Barkely, Russell. 2009. *AFRICOM: Security, Development, and Humanitarian Functions*. Hauppauge, NY: Nova Science Publishers.
Barnes, Cedric. 2007. "The Somali Youth League, Ethiopian Somalis and the Greater Somalia Idea, c. 1946–48." *Journal of East African Studies* 1, no. 2: 277–91.
Barth, Fredrik. 1959. *Political Leadership among Swath Pathans*. London: Athlone Press.
Basset, René. 1893. "Les inscriptions de l'île de Dahlak." *Journal Asiatique* 9: 77–111.
Becker, Felicitas, and Joel Cabrita. 2014. "Introduction: Performing Citizenship and Enacting Exclusion on Africa's Indian Ocean Littoral." *Journal of African History* 55, no. 2: 161–71.

Beckerleg, Susan. 2009. "From Ocean to Lakes: Cultural Transformation of Yemenis in Kenya and Uganda." *African and Asian Studies* 8: 288–308.
Bekele, Shiferaw. 1982. "The Ethiopian Rail Road and British Finance Capital, 1896–1902." MA thesis, Addis Ababa University.
———. 1989. "Aspects of the History of Dire Dawa (1902 to 1936)." Proceedings of the Fourth Seminar of the Department of History, Awassa, Ehiopia, 8–12 July 1987.
———. 1994. "The People of Dire Dawa: Towards a Social History (1902–1936)." In *Étude des Éthiopiennes: Actes de la Xe Conférence Internationale des Etudes Éthiopiennes, Paris, 24–28 Août 1988*, edited by Claude Lepage. Paris: Société Française pour les Études Éthiopiennes.
Bersteil, Jean, and Jean-Pierre Rioux. 2000. *The Pompidou Years, 1969–1974*. translated by Christopher Woodall. Cambridge: Cambridge University Press.
Bertz, Ned. 2003. "Indian Ocean World Travelers: Moving Models in Multi-sited Fieldwork." *Africa Current* 22, no. 35: 46–76.
Betts, Alexander. 2009. *Forced Migration and Global Politics*. London: Wiley-Blackwell.
Bezabeh, Samson A. 2011. "Citizenship and the Logics of Sovereignity in Djibouti." *African Affairs* 110, no. 441: 587–606.
Bhabha, Homi K. 1990. *Nation and Narration*. London: Routledge.
Bird, James Harold. 1971. *Seaports and Seaport Terminals*. London: Hutchinson.
Bollee, Amedee. 2003. "Djibouti from French Outpost to US Base", *Review of African Political Economy*, 30,97 :481-484.
Bonnefoy, Laurent, and Marine Poirier. 2012. "La structuration de la révolution Yéménite." *Revue Française de Science Politique* 62: 895–913.
———. 2013. "Dynamics of the Yemeni Revolution: Contextualizing Mobilization." In *Social Movements, Mobilization and Contestation in the Middle East and North Africa*, edited by Joel Beinin and Frederic Vairel, 228–45. Stanford, CA: Stanford University Press.
Borelli, Jules. 1890. *Éthiopie méridional: Journal de mon voyage aux pays Amhara, Oromo et Sidama*. Paris: Librairies-Imprimeries Réunies.
Borsa, Giorgio. 1990. *Trade and Politics in Indian Ocean: Historical and Contemporary Perspectives*. New Delhi: Manohar Publisher.
Bose, Sugata. 2006. *A Hundred Horizons: The Indian Ocean in the Age of Global Empire*. Cambridge, MA: Harvard University Press.
Boswell, Christina. 2003. *European Migration Policies in Flux: Changing Patterns of Inclusion and Exclusion*. Oxford: Blackwell/Royal Institute of International Affairs.
Botman, Selma. 1991. *Egypt from Independence to Revolution 1919–1952*. Syracuse, NY: Syracuse University Press.
Boucek, Christopher. 2010. "War in Saada: From Local Insurrection to National Challenge." In *Yemen on the Brink*, edited by Christopher Boucek and Marina Ottaway, 45-60. Washington, DC: Carnegie Foundation for International Peace.
Bouchard, Christian, and William Crumplin. 2010. "Neglected No Longer: The Indian Ocean at the Forefront of World Geopolitics and Global Geostrategy." *Journal of Indian Ocean Region* 6, no. 1: 260–81.
Bourdieu, Pierre. 1999. "Rethinking the State: Genesis and Structure of the Bureaucratic Field." In *State/Culture: State-Formation after the Cultural Turn*, edited by George Steinmetz, 53–75. Ithaca, NY: Cornell University Press.
Bourgouin, France. 2009. *From Network to Class? Towards a More Complex Conception of Connection and Sociability*. Copenhagen: Danish Institute of International Studies.

Bowen, H.V., Elizabeth Mancke, and John G. Reid. 2012. *Britain's Oceanic Empires: Atlantic and Indian Ocean Worlds, c. 1550–1850*. Cambridge: Cambridge University Press.

Braudel, Fernand. 1972. *The Mediterranean and the Mediterranean World in the Age of Philip II*. Translated by Siân Reynolds. London: Collins.

Braukämpar, Ulrich. 2004. *Islamic History and Culture in Southern Ethiopia: Collected Essays*. Münster: Lit Verlag Münster.

Breman, Bruce. 1998. "Ethnicity, Patronage and the African State: The Politics of Uncivil Nationalism." *African Affairs* 97, no. 338: 305–41.

Brennan, James, 2008. *Lowering the Sultan's Flag: Sovereignty and Decolonization in Coastal Kenya, Comparative Studies in Societies and History* 50: 831-861.

———. 2012. *Taifa: Making Nation and Race in Urban Tanzania*. Athens, OH: Ohio University Press.

Brenner, Louis. 2001. *Controlling Knowledge: Religion, Power and Schooling in a West African Muslim Society*. Bloomington, IN: Indiana University Press.

Brisard, Jean-Charles. 2002. *Terrorism Financing: Roots and Trends of Saudi Terrorism Financing: Report Prepared for the President of Security Council, United Nations*. Paris: JCB Consulting.

Brosselard, M. Charles. 1859. *Les Khouan: De la constitution des ordres religieux Musulmans en Algérie*. Paris: Imprimerie d'A. Bourget.

Bruce, James. 1790. *Travels to Discover the Source of the Nile*, vol. 1. Edinburgh: George Ramsay and Co.

Bruke, Edward. 2012. *"One Blood and One Destiny"? Yemen's Relations with the Gulf Cooperation Council*. London: Kuwait Programme on Development, Governance and Globalisation in the Gulf States.

Brunschwig, Henri. 1978. "Une colonie Inutile: Obock (1862–1888)." *Cahier d'Études Africaines* 8, no. 29: 32–47.

Budge, E.A. Wallis. 1922. *The Kebra Nagast: The Queen of Sheba and Her Only Son Menyelek*. London: Forgotten Books.

Bujra, Abdallah. 1967. "Political Conflict and Stratification in Hadramaut." *Middle East Studies* 3, no. 1: 355–75.

———. 1971. *The Politics of Stratification*. Oxford: Oxford University Press.

Burdett, A., ed. 2006. *The Slave Trade into Arabia, 1820–1973*. Cambridge: Cambridge University Press.

Burton, Richard. 1856. *First Foot Steps in East Africa*. London: Longman, Brown, Green, and Longmans.

Camelin, Sylvaine. 2002. "Du Hadramaout aux Comores . . . et retour." *Journal des Africanistes* 72, no. 2: 123–37.

———. 2004. "Le territoire du politique: Quartiers et lignages dans la Ville de Shihr (sud du Yémen)." *Journal des Africanistes* 74, nos. 1–2: 413–33.

Campbell, Gwyn. 2004. *Structure of Slavery in Indian Ocean Africa and Asia*. London: Frank Cass.

———. 2008. "Islam in Indian Ocean Africa Prior to the Scramble: A New Historical Paradigm." In *Struggling with History: Islam and Cosmopolitanism in the Western Indian Ocean*, edited by Edward Simpson and Kai Kress, 43–92. New York: Columbia University Press.

Capponeto, Rosetta. 2008. "Going Out of Stock: Mulattos and Levantines in Italian Litreature and Cinema of the Fascist Period." PhD diss., University of Connecticut.

Carroll, William. 2010. *The Making of a Transnational Capitalist Class: Corporate Power in the Twentieth Century*. New York: Zed Books.
Carroll, William, and M. Fennema. 2002. "Is There a Transnational Business Community?" *International Sociology* 17, no. 3: 393–419.
Caulk, R.A. 1970. "Menelik and the Ethio-Egyptian War of 1875–1876: A Reconsideration of Source Material." *Rural Africana* 11: 63–69.
Chaudhuri, K. N. 1985. *Trade and Civilization in the Indian Ocean: An Economic History from the Rise of Islam to 1750*. Cambridge: Cambridge University Press.
———. 1990. *Asia before Europe: Economy and Civilization of the Indian Ocean from the Rise of Islam to 1750*. Cambridge: Cambridge University Press.
Christopher, W. 1844. "Extract from a Journal by Lieutenant W. Christopher, Commanding the H.C. Brig of War Tigris." *Journal of Royal Geographical Society of London* 14: 76–103.
Clapham, Christopher. 1968. "The Ethiopian Coup d'État of December 1960." *Journal of Modern African Studies* 6, no. 4: 495–507.
Clifford, James. 1994. "Diasporas." *Cultural Anthropology* 9, no. 3: 1–50.
Coetzee, J.M.1980. *Waiting for the Barbarians*. London: Vintage.
Coleman, James S. 1958. *Nigeria: Background to Nationalism*. Berkeley, CA: University of California Press.
Coll, Steve. 2008. *The Bin Ladens: An Arabian Family in the American Century*. London: Penguin.
Cooper, Frederick. 2001. "What is the Concept of Globalization Good for? An African Historian's Perspective." *African Affairs* 100, no. 399: 189–213.
Cordner, Lee. 2010. "Rethinking Maritime Security in Indian Ocean Region." *Journal of the Indian Ocean Region* 6, no. 1: 67–85.
Cortese, Guido. 1938. *Problemi dell Impero*. Rome: Pinciana.
Coubba, Ali. 1993. *Djibouti: Une Nation en Otage*. Paris: L'Harmattan.
Cox, Robert. 1987. *Production, Power and World Order*. New York: Columbia University Press.
Crummey, Donald. 1969. "Tewodros as Reformer and Modernizer." *Journal of African History* 10, no. 3: 457–69.
Cunningham, Hilary, and Josiah Heyman. 2004. "Introduction: Power Mobilities and Enclosures at Borders." *Identities: Global Studies in Culture and Power* 11, no. 3: 289–302.
Cuoq, Joseph. 1981. *L'Islam en Ethiopie: Des origines au XVIe siècle*. Paris: Nouvelles Editions Latins.
D'Abbadie, Arnauld. 1808. *Douze ans dans la Haute Éthiopie (Abyssinie)*. Paris: Librairie Hachette.
Daguenet, Roger Joint. 1992. "Le meurtre d'Henry Lambert, agent consulaire de France à Aden (1855–1865)." *Journal of the Royal Asiatic Society of Great Britain* 3, no. 2: 175–90.
———. 2000. *Aux origines de l'implantation française en Mer Rouge: Vie et mort d'Henry Lambert consul de France à Aden*. Paris: L'Harmattan.
Das, Veena, and Deborah Poole. 2004. "State and Its Margin: Comparative Ethnographies." In *Anthropology in the Margins of the State*, edited by Veena Das and Deborah Poole, 3–34. Santa Fe, NM: School of American Research Press.
Davis, John, and Andrew Othieno. 2007. "Djibouti's Pre-eminent Role in the War on Terror." In *Africa and the War on Terrorism*, edited by John Davis, 27–37. Aldershot: Ashgate.

De Clercq, Jules. 1884. *Recueil des traités de la France, publié sous les auspices du ministère des affaires étrangères*. Paris: A. Durant et Pedone-Lauriel.
De Donno, Fabrizio. 2006. "La razza Ario-Mediterranea." *Intervention: International Journal of Postcolonial Studies* 8, no. 3: 394–412.
De Jong, Huub. 1997. "Dutch Colonial Policy Pertaining to Hadrami Migrants." In *Hadrami Traders, Scholars and Statesmen in the Indian Ocean, 1750s–1960*, edited by Ulrike Freitag and William G. Clarence-Smith, 94–111. Leiden: Brill.
———. 2002. "Contradictory and Against the Grain: Snouck Hurgronje on the Hadramis in the Dutch East Indies, 1889–1936." In *Transcending Borders: Arabs, Politics, Trade and Islam in Southeast Asia*, edited by Huub de Jonge and Nico Kaptain, 219–234. Leiden: KITLV Press.
De la Roque, Jean. 1732. *A Voyage to Arabia Felix through the Eastern Ocean and the Straight of the Red Sea, being first made by the French in the Year 1708, 1709 and 1710*. Anonymous translator. London: E. Symon.
Desai, Gaurav. 2013. *Commerce with the Universe: Africa, India, and the Afrasian Imagination*. New York: Columbia University Press.
Donham, Donald L., and Wendy James. 2002. *The Southern Marches of Imperial Ethiopia: Essays in History and Social Anthropology*. Oxford: James Currey.
Donnan, Hastings, and Thomas M. Wilson, eds. 2010. *Borderlands: Ethnographic Approaches to Security, Power, and Identity*. Lanham, MD: University Press of America.
Dorman, Sara, Daniel Hammett, and Paul Nugent. 2007. "Introduction: Citizenship and Causalities in Africa." In *Making Nations, Creating Strangers: State and Citizenship in Africa*, edited by Sara Dorman, Daniel Hammett, and Paul Nugent. Leiden: Brill.
Doudoub, I.A. 1962. *Esquisse Ethnique de Divers Groupement Autochtones de Djibouti*. École National de la France d'Outre-Mer, Mémoire No. 1110.
Dresh, Paul. 2000. *A History of Modern Yemen*. Cambridge: Cambridge University Press.
Droit International Public. 1908. *Document: Éthiopie et France, convention pour les frontières, signée à Addis Ababa le 20 mars 1897*. Paris: A. Pedone Libraire-Editeur.
Droz-Vincent, Philippe. 2014. "The Military amidst Uprisings and Transitions in the Arab World." In *The New Middle East: Protest and Revolution in the Arab World*, edited by Fawaz A. Gerges, 180–208. Cambridge: Cambridge University Press.
Dubois, Colette. 1997. *Djibouti 1888–1967: Héritage ou Frustration?* Paris: L'Harmattan.
———. 2007. *Saïd Ali Coubèche, la passion d'entreprendre: Témoin du XXe siècle à Djibouti*. Paris: Karthala.
Dubois, Colette, and Pierre Soumille. 2004. *Des chrétiens à Djibouti en terre d'Islam*. Paris: Karthala.
Dunn, Kevin, and Morten Bøås. 2013. *Politics of Origin in Africa: Autochthony, Citizenship and Conflict*. London: Zed Books.
Edward, John. 1982. "Slavery, the Slave Trade and Economic Reorganisation of Ethiopia, 1916–1935." *African Economic History* 11: 3–14.
Ellingson, Lyod. 1978. "The Origin and Development of the Eritrean Liberation Front." In *Proceedings of the Fifth International Conference of Ethiopian Studies*, edited by Robert L. Hess, 613–628. Chicago, IL: Session B.
Erlich, Haggai. 1983. *The Struggle over Eritrea, 1962–1978: War and Revolution in the Horn of Africa*. Stanford, CA: Hoover Institute Press.
———. 1995. *Ethiopia and the Middle East*. Boulder, CO: Lynne Rienner.

———. 2007. *Saudi Arabia and Ethiopia: Islam, Christianity and Politics Entwined*. Boulder, CO: Lynne Rienner.

———. 2014. "From Wello to Harer: Lïj Iyasu, the Ottomans and the Somali Sayyid." In *The Life and Times of Lïj Iyasu of Ethiopia*, edited by Éloi Ficquet and Wolbert G.C. Smidt, 135–147. Berlin: Lit Verlag.

Eshete, Tibebe. 1991. "The Root Causes of Political Problems in the Ogaden, 1942–1960." *Northeast African Studies* 13, no. 1: 9–29.

Evans, Michael. [1975]2004. *Political Thinkers: Karl Marx*. London: Routledge.

Ewald, Janet, and William G. Clarence-Smith. 1997. "The Economic Role of the Hadrami Diaspora in the Red Sea and the Gulf of Aden." In *Hadrami Traders, Scholars and Statesmen in the Indian Ocean, 1750s–1960*, edited by Ulrike Freitag and William G. Clarence-Smith, 281–296. Leiden: Brill.

Farah, Caesar. 2002. *The Sultan's Yemen: Nineteenth-century Challenges to Ottoman Rule*. London: I.B.Tauris.

Ferry, Edmond. 1905. *La France en Afrique*. Paris: Librairie Armand Colin.

Fiquet, Éloi. 2006. "Flesh Soaked in Faith: Meat as Markers of the Boundary between Christian and Muslims in Ethiopia." In *Muslim–Christian Encounters in Africa* edited by Benjamin Soares, 39-56. Leiden: Brill.

Fontrier, Marc. 2003. *Abou-Bakr Pacha de Zayla, marchand d'esclaves*. Paris: L'Harmattan.

Footman, David. 1986. *Antonin Bess of Aden*. London: Macmillan.

Foucault, Michel. 1977. *Discipline and Punish: The Birth of the Prison*. London: Penguin.

———. 1980. "Questions on Geography." In *Power/Knowledge: Selected Interviews and Other Writings, 1972–1977*, edited by Colin Gordon, 63–77. New York: Pantheon Books.

———. 2004. *Security, Territory, Population: Lectures at the College de France 1977–1978*. London: Palgrave Macmillan.

Frank, Andre Gunder. 1971. *Capitalism and Underdevelopment in Latin America: Historical Studies of Chile and Brazil*. Harmonsworth: Penguin.

Freitag, Ulrike. 2003. *Indian Ocean Migrants and State Formation in Hadramout: Reforming the Homeland*. Brill: Leiden.

Freitag, Ulrike, and Achim von Oppen. 2010. *Translocality: The Study of Globalising Processes from a Southern Perspective*. Leiden: Brill.

Freitag, Ulrike, and W.G. Clarence-Smith, eds. 1997. *Hadhrami Traders, Scholars and Statesmen in the Indian Ocean, 1750s–1960s*. Leiden: Brill.

Frennelet, Weiss André. 1894. *Pandectes française: Nouveau répertoire de doctrine, de législation et de jurisprudence*. Paris: Librairie Marescq Aine et Librairie Plon.

Friedlander, Jonathan, Ron Kelley, and Sheila Pinkel. 1988. *Sojourners and Settlers: The Yemeni Immigrant Experience*. Salt Lake City, UT: University of Utah Press.

Furber, Holden. 1976. *Rival Empires of Trade in the Orient, 1600–1800*. Minneapolis, MN: University of Minnesota Press.

Geschiere, Peter. 2009. *The Perils of Belonging: Autochthony, Citizenship and Exclusion in Africa and Europe*. Chicago, IL: University of Chicago Press.

Ghazal, Amal N. 2010. *Islamic Reform and Arab Nationalism: Expanding the Crescent from the Mediterranean to the Indian Ocean (1880s–1930s)*. London: Routledge.

Ghosh, Devleena, and Stephen Muecke. 2007a. *Cultures of Trade: Indian Ocean Exchange*. Newcastle: Cambridge Scholar Publication.

———. 2007b. "Natural Logics of the Indian Ocean." In *Cultures of Trade: Indian Ocean Exchange*, edited by Devleena Ghosh and Stephen Muecke, 150-163. Newcastle: Cambridge Scholar Publication.
Gill, Stephen. 1990. *American Hegemony and the Trilateral Commission*. Cambridge: Cambridge University Press.
Gillette, Aaron. 2011. "The Origin of the 'Manifesto of Racial Scientists.'" *Journal of Modern Italian Studies* 6, no. 3: 305–23.
Gilmor, T. Lenox. 1906. *Abyssinia: The Ethiopian Railway and the Powers*. London: Alston Rivers.
Gilroy, Paul. 1993. *The Black Atlantic*. London: Verso.
Girault, Arthur. 1904. *Principes de colonisation et de législation coloniale*. Paris: L. Larose.
Glassman, Jonathan. 1995. *Feasts and Riots: Revelry, Rebellion, and Popular Consciousness on the Swahili Coast, 1856–1888*. Portsmouth, NH: Heinemann.
———. 2014. "Creole Nationalists and the Search for Nativist Authenticity in Twentieth Century Zanzibar: The Limits of Cosmopolitanism." *Journal of African History* 55, no. 2: 161–71.
Gray, Randal. 1980. "Bombing the 'Mad Mullah'—1920." *RUSI Journal* 125, no. 4: 41–47.
Gregory, Shaun. 2000. "The French Military in Africa: Past and Present." *African Affairs* 99, no. 396: 435–48.
Grosser, Alfred. 1961. *La Quatrième République et sa politique extérieure*. Paris: Armand Colin.
Gupta, Akhil, and James Ferguson. 1997a. *Anthropological Location: Boundaries and Grounds of Field Science*. Berkeley, CA: University of California Press.
———. 1997b. *Culture, Power and Place: Explorations in Critical Anthropology*. Durham, NC: Duke University Press.
Gupta, Ashin Das. 2004. *India and the Indian Ocean World: Trade and Politics*. New Delhi: Oxford University Press.
Hable Selassie, Sergew. 1972. *Ancient and Medieval Ethiopian History to 1270*. Addis Ababa: United Printers.
Hall, John R. 1997. *Reworking Class*. Ithaca, NY: Cornell University.
Hall, Richard. 1996. *Empires of the Monsoon: A History of the Indian Ocean and Its Invaders*. London: Harper Collins.
Hall, Stuart. 1991. "The Local and the Global: Globalization and Ethnicity." In *Culture, Globalization and the World-System*, edited by Anthony D. King, 19–40. Binghamton, NY: State University of New York.
Halliday, Fred. 1992. *Arabs in Exile: Yemeni Migrants in Urban Britain*. London: I.B.Tauris.
———. 2000. *Britain's First Muslims: Portraits of an Arab Community*. London: I.B Tauris.
Hamzel, A Nizar and R. Hrair Dekmejan. 1996. A Sufi Response to Political Islam : Al-Ahbash of Lebanon, *International Journal of Middle Eastern Studies*, 8, no. 2 : 217-229.
Hansen, Stig Jarle. 2013. *Al-Shabaab in Somalia: The History and Ideology of a Militant Islamist Group 2005–2012*. London and New York: Hurst.
Hansen, Thomas Blom, and Finn Stepputat. 2001. "Introduction." In *States of Imagination: Ethnographic Explorations of the Postcolonial State*, edited by Thomas Blom Hansen and Finn Stepputat, 1–38. Durham, NC: Duke University Press.
Hardt, Michael, and Antonio Negri. 2000. *Empire*. Cambridge, MA: Harvard University Press.

———. 2004. *Multitude: War and Democracy in the Age of Empire.* New York: Penguin Press.
Harms, Robert, Bernard K. Freamon, and David W. Blight. 2013. *Indian Ocean Slavery in the Age of Abolition.* New Haven, CT: Yale University Press.
Harris, W. Cornwallis. 1844. *The Highland of Æthiopia*, vol. 1. London: Brown, Green, and Longmans.
Harrison, Christopher. 1988. *France and Islam in West Africa, 1860–1960.* Cambridge: Cambridge University Press.
Harvey, David. 1989. *The Condition of Postmodernity.* Oxford: Blackwell.
———. 2001. *Spaces of Capital: Toward a Critical Geography.* New York: Routledge.
———. 2010. *The Enigma of Capital and the Crises of Capitalism.* Oxford: Oxford University Press.
al-Haymi, Hasan B. Ahmad. [1650]1986. *Sirat al-Habesha.* Translated by E.J. Van Donzel as *A Yemenite Embassy to Ethiopia, 1647–1649: al-Haymi's Sirat al-Habasha.* Stuttgart: Steiner Verlag Wiesbaden.
Henare, Amiria, Martin Holbraad, and Sari Wastell, eds. 2007. *Thinking through Things: Theorizing Artefacts Ethnographically.* New York: Routledge.
Hertslet, Sir Edward. 1896. *The Map of Africa by Treaty*, vol. 3. London: Harrison and Sons.
Hess, Robert. 1964. "The 'Mad Mullah' and Northern Somalia." *Journal of African History* 5, no. 3: 415–33.
———. 1966. *Italian Colonialism in Somalia.* Chicago, IL: Chicago University Press.
Hill, Richard. 1959. *Egypt in the Sudan, 1820–1881.* Oxford: Oxford University Press.
Ho, Engseng. 2002. "Names Beyond Nations: The Making of Local Cosmopolitanism." *Etudes Rurales* 3–4, nos. 163–64: 215–31.
———. 2004. "Empire through Diasporic Eyes: A View from the Other Boat." *Comparative Study of Society and History* 46, no. 2: 210–46.
———. 2006. *The Graves of Tarim: Genealogy and Mobility across the Indian Ocean.* Berkeley, CA: University of California Press.
Holbraad, Martin. 2007. "The Power of Powder: Multiplicity and Motion in the Divinatory Cosmology of Cuba Ifá (or *Mana* Again)." In *Thinking through Things: Theorizing Artefacts Ethnographically*, edited by Amiria Henare, Martin Holbraad, and Sari Wastell, 189–225. New York: Routledge.
———. 2012. *Truth in Motion: The Recursive Anthropology of Cuban Divination.* Chicago, IL: Chicago University Press.
Holcomb, Bonnie K., and Sisai Ibssa. 1990. *The Invention of Ethiopia: The Making of a Dependent Colonial State in Northeast Africa.* Trenton, NJ: Red Sea Press.
Holland, Jack. 2013. *Selling the War on Terror: Foreign Policy Discussion after 9/11.* New York: Routledge.
Holt, P.M. 1958. *The Mahdist State in the Sudan, 1881–1898.* London: Oxford University Press.
Hopper, Matthew Scott. 2006. "The African Presence in Arabia: Slavery, the World Economy, and the African Diaspora in East Arabia, 1840–1940." PhD diss., University of California.
Horden, Peregrine, and Nicholas Purcell. 2006. "The Mediterranean and 'the New Thalassology.'" *American Historical Review* 111, no. 3: 722–40.
Hourani, George Fadlo. 1951. *Arab Seafaring in the Indian Ocean in Ancient and Early Medieval Times.* Princeton, NJ: Princeton University Press.

Human Rights Watch. 2013. *Between a Drone and al-Qaeda: The Civilian Cost of US Targeted Killings in Yemen*. New York: Human Rights Watch.
Ibn al-Mujawir, Yusuf ibn Yaqub. 2008. *A Traveler in Thirteenth-Century Arabia: Tarik al-Mustabsir*. Translated by G. Rex Smith. Farnham: Ashgate.
Ibn Battuta. 1966. *The Travels of Ibn Battuta A.D. 1325–1354*. Translated by H.A.R. Gibb. Cambridge: Cambridge University Press.
Imbert-Vier, Simon. 2011. *Tracer des frontières à Djibouti: Des territoires et des hommes aux XIX et XX siècles*. Paris: Karthala.
International Crisis Group. 2002. "Somalia: Countering Terrorism in a Failed State." Africa Report No. 45. Brussels: International Crisis Group.
———. 2005. "Somalia's Islamists." Africa Report No. 100. Brussels: International Crisis Group.
Jackson, Ashley. 2006. *The British Empire and the Second World War*. London: Continuum.
Jackson, Donna R. 2007. *Jimmy Carter and the Horn of Africa: Cold War Policy in Ethiopia and Somalia*. Jefferson, NC: McFarland and Co.
Jesman, Czeslaw. 1959. "Egyptian Invasion of Ethiopia." *African Affairs* 58: 75–81.
Kabha, Mustafa, and Haggai Erlich. 2006. "Al-Ahbash and Wahhabiyya: Interpretation of Islam." *International Journal of Middle East Studies* 38, no. 4: 519–38.
Kadamy, Mohamed. 1996. "Djibouti: Between War and Peace." *Review of African Political Economy* 23, no. 70: 511–21.
Kalb, Don. 1997. *Expanding Class: Power and Everyday Politics in Industrial Communities, the Netherlands, 1850–1950*. Durham, NC: Duke University Press.
Kalb, Don, and Heman Talk. 2005. *Critical Junctions: An Anthropological History beyond the Cultural Turn*. Oxford: Berghahn Books.
Kapferer, Bruce. 2004. "Old Permutations, New Formations? War, State and Global Transgression." In *State, Sovereignty, War*, edited by Bruce Kapferer, 1–15. Oxford: Berghahn Books.
———. 2005a. *Oligarchs and Oligopolies: New Formation of Global Power*. Oxford: Berghahn Books.
———. 2005b. "Introduction: The Social Construction of Reductionist Thought in Practice." In *The Retreat of the Social: The Rise and Rise of Reductionism*, edited by Bruce Kapferer, 151–161. Oxford: Berghahn Books.
Kapferer, Bruce, Kari Telle, and Annelin Eriksen. 2010. *Contemporary Religiosities: Emergent Socialities and the Post-Nation-State*. Oxford: Berghahn.
Kathirithamby-Wells, Jeyamalar. 2009. "'Strangers' and 'Stranger-Kings': The Sayyids in Eighteenth-century Maritime Southeast Asia." *Journal of East Asian Studies* 40, no. 3: 567–91.
Khalid, Mansour. 2010. *War and Peace in Sudan: A Tale of Two Countries*. New York: Routledge.
Killion, Thomas. 1985. "Workers, Capital and the State in the Ethiopian Region 1919–1974." PhD diss., Stanford University.
Krapf, Rev. Dr. J. Lewis. 1860. *Travels, Research, and Missionary Labors during an Eighteen Years' Residence in East Africa*. London: Trubner and Co.
Kresse, Kai. 2007. *Philosophising in Mombassa: Knowledge, Islam and Intellectual Practice on the Swahili Coast*. Edinburgh: Edinburgh University Press.

Kuehn, Thomas. 2011. *Empire, Islam and Politics of Difference: Ottoman Rule in Yemen, 1849–1919*. Leiden: Brill.
Lambert, David, and Alan Lester. 2006. *Colonial Lives across the British Empire: Imperial Careering in the Long Nineteenth Century*. Cambridge: Cambridge University Press.
Larkin, Brian. 2008. "Ahmed Deedat and the Form of Islamic Evangelism." *Social Text* 26, no. 3: 101–121.
Larson, Pier M. 2009. *Ocean of Letters: Language and Creolization in an Indian Ocean Diaspora*. Cambridge: Cambridge University Press.
Latour, Bruno. 2005. *Reassembling the Social: An Introduction to Actor-Network-Theory*. New York: Oxford University Press.
Le Guennec-Coppens, Françoise. 1989. "Social and Cultural Integration: A Case Study of the East African Hadramis." *Africa* 59, no. 2: 185–95.
Le Pointe, Henri. 1914. *La colonisation française au pays des Somali*. Paris: Anmeldelsen.
Lefebvre, Henri. 1977. *De l'état: Le mode de production étatique*. Paris: Union Générale d'Éditions.
Legum, Colin, and Bill Lee. 1979. *The Horn of Africa in Continuing Crisis*. New York and London: Africana Publishing Company.
Lejean, Guillaume. 1865. *Voyage aux deux Nils*. Paris: Librairie Hachette.
Lemarchand, René. 1964. *Political Awakening in the Belgian Congo*. Berkeley, CA: University of California Press.
Lévi-Strauss, Claude. 1992/1995. *Tristes tropiques*. Translated by John and Doreen Weightman. New York: Penguin Books.
Lewis, Herbert. 1965. *A Galla Monarchy: Jimma Abba Jifar, 1830–1932*. Madison, WI: University of Wisconsin Press.
Lloyd, P.C. 1967. *Africa in Social Change*. Harmondsworth: Penguin.
Lucks, Naomi. 2009. *Queen of Sheba*. New York: Infobase Publishing.
Machado, Pedro. 2014. *Ocean of Trade: South Asian Merchants, Africa and the Indian Ocean, c. 1750–1850*. Cambridge: Cambridge University Press.
Mamdani, Mahmood. 1996. *Citizen and Subject: Contemporary Africa and the Legacy of Late Colonialism*. Princeton, NJ: Princeton University Press.
———.2004. *Good Muslim/Bad Muslim: America, the Cold War and the Roots of Terror*. New York: Pantheon.
Manger, Leif. 2010. *The Hadrami Diaspora: Community-Building on the Indian Ocean Rim*. Oxford: Berghahn Books.
Marcus, Harold. 1968. "Menelik II." In *Leadership in East Africa: Six Political Biographies*, edited by Norman R. Bennett, 3-62. Boston, MA: Boston University Press.
———. 1975. *The Life and Times of Menelik II: Ethiopia, 1844–1914*. Oxford: Clarendon Press.
———. 1983. *Ethiopia, Great Britain and the United States, 1941–1974: The Politics of Empire*. Berkeley, CA: University of California Press.
———. 1992. "The United States and the Ethiopian Recovery of the Ogaden in 1948." In *Proceedings of the First International Conference of Somali Studies*, edited by Hussein M. Adam and Charles L. Geshekter. Atlanta, GA: Scholars Press.
———. 2002. *A History of Ethiopia*. Berkeley, CA: University of California Press.
Markakis, John. 2011. *Ethiopia: The Last Two Frontiers*. Oxford: James Currey.

Marshall, Gordon. 1997. *Repositioning Class: Social Inequalities in Industrial Societies*. London: SAGE Publications.
Martin, B.G. 1975. "Mahdism, Muslim Clerics and Holy Wars in Ethiopia, 1300–1610." In *Proceedings of the First United States Conference on Ethiopian Studies*. East Lansing, MI: Michigan State University.
Marx, Karl, and Frederick Engels. [1847]2008. *The Communist Manifesto*. New York: Pathfinder Press.
McNall, Scott, Rhonda Levine, and Rick Fantasia. 1991. *Bringing Class Back In: Contemporary and Historical Perspectives*. Boulder, CO: Westview Press.
McPherson, Kenneth. 1993. *The Indian Ocean: A History of People and the Sea*. Oxford: Oxford University Press.
Meri, Josef. 2006. *Medieval Islamic Civilization, an Encyclopedia*, vol. 1. New York: Routledge.
Mesghenna, Yemane. 1988. "Italian Colonialism: A Case Study of Eritrea, 1869–1934: Motives, Praxis and Result." PhD diss., University of Lund.
Metcalf, Thomas R. 2007. *Imperial Connections: India in the Indian Ocean Arena, 1860–1920*. Berkeley, CA: University of California Press.
Middleton, John. 1992. *The World of the Swahili: An African Mercantile Civilization*. New Haven, CT: Yale University Press.
Miers, Suzanne. 1997. "Britain and the Suppression of Slavery in Ethiopia." *Slavery and Abolition: A Journal of Slave and Post-slave Studies* 18, no. 3: 257–88.
Milkias, Paulos. 2006. "Mussolini's 'Civilizing Mission,' and Fascist Political Socialization in Occupied Ethiopia 1936–1941." In *Proceedings of the XVth International Conference of Ethiopian Studies*, edited by Siegbert Uhlig, 328–36. Wiesbaden: Harrassowitz Verlag.
Miran, Jonathan. 2009. *Red Sea Citizens: Cosmopolitan Society and Cultural Change in Massawa*. Bloomington, IN: Indiana University Press.
———. 2012. "Space, Mobility, and Translocal Connections across the Red Sea Area since 1500." *Northeast African Studies* 12, no. 1: ix–xxvi.
Mische, Ann. 1996. "Projecting Democracy: The Construction of Citizenship across Youth Networks in Brazil." *International Review of Social History* 40, no. 3: 131–58.
Mitchell, Clyde. 1969. *Social Networks in Urban Situations: Analyses of Personal Relationship in Central African Towns*. Manchester: Manchester University Press.
Mitchell, Timothy. 1999. "Society, Economy and the State Effect." In *State Culture: State Formation after the Cultural Turn*, edited by George Steinmetz, 76–97. Ithaca, NY: Cornell University Press.
Mobini-Kesheh, Natalie. 1999. *The Hadrami Awakening: Community and Identity in the Netherlands East Indies, 1900–1942*. Ithaca, NY: Southeast Asia Program, Cornell University.
Monfreid, Henry de. 1932. *Aventures de Mer*. Paris: Bernard Grasset.
———. 1938. *Le trésor du Perline*. Paris: Bernard Grasset.
———. 2002. *Mer Rouge*. Paris: Bibliothèque Grasset.
———. 2007. *Aventures extraordinaires, 1911–1921*. Paris: Arthaud.
Moorthy, Sharti, and Ashraf Jamal. 2010. "Introduction: New Conjectures in Maritime Imaginaries." In *Indian Ocean Studies: Cultural, Social, and Political Perspectives*, edited by Sharti Moorthy and Ashraf Jamal, 1–31. New York: Routledge.

Morin, Didier. 2008. "Saïd Ali Coubèche, la passion d'entreprendre. Témoin du 20e siècle à Djibouti, Djibouti: Lions Club de Djibouti ; Paris: Karthala, 2007." *Pount: Cahiers d'études Corne de l'Afrique – Arabie du Sud* 2: 139–47.

Muhula, Raymond. 2007. "Kenya and the Global War on Terrorism: Searching for a New Role in a New Year." In *Africa and the War on Terrorism*, edited by John Davis, 43-60. Farnham: Ashgate.

Murphy, John. 2003. "'Our Mission and Our Moment': George W. Bush and September 11." *Rhetoric and Public Affairs* 6, no. 4: 607–32.

al-Muqaddasi, Muhammad ibn Ahmad Shams al-Din. 2001. *The Best Divisions for Knowledge of the Regions: Ahsan al-Taqasim fi Ma'rifat al-Aqalim*. Translated by Basil Anthony Collins. Reading: Garnet.

National Commission on Terrorist Attacks upon the United States. 2004. *The 9/11 Commission Report*. Washington: Government Printing Office.

Nogno, Paulos. 1989. *Dagmawi Ate Menelik*. Addis Ababa: Berehanena Selam.

Okruhlik, Gwen, and Patrick Conge. 1997. "National Autonomy, Labor Migration and Political Crisis: Yemen and Saudi Arabia." *Middle East Journal* 51, no. 4: 554–65.

Ong, Aihwa. 1999. *Flexible Citizenship: The Cultural Logics of Transnationality*. Durham, NC: Duke University Press.

Orsi, Robert. *The Madonna of 115th Street: Faith and Continuity in Italian Harlem, 1880–1950*. New Haven, CT: Yale University Press.

Østebø, Terje. 2011. "Local Reformers and the Search for Change: The Emergence of Salafism in Bale, Ethiopia." *Africa* 81, no. 4: 628–648.

———. 2012. *Localising Salafism: Religious Change among the Oromo Muslims in Bale, Ethiopia*. Leiden: Brill.

———. 2013. "Postscript." In *Muslim Ethiopia: The Christian Legacy, Identity Politics and Islamic Reformism*, edited by Patrick Despalt and Terje Østebø, 241–258. New York: Palgrave Macmillan.

O'Sullivan, Meghan. 2003. *Shrewd Sanctions: Statecraft and State Sponsors of Terrorism*. Washington, DC: Brookings Institute.

Pankhurst, Richard. 1961. "Menelik and the Foundation of Addis Ababa." *Journal of African History* 2, no. 1: 103–17.

———. 1965. *The Trade of Southern and Western Ethiopia and the Indian Ocean Port in the Nineteenth and Early Twentieth Centuries*. *Journal of Ethiopian Studies*, 3: 33–74.

———. 1968. *Economic History of Ethiopia, 1800–1935*. Addis Ababa: Haile Selassie University.

Parkyns, Mansfield. [1966]1853. *Life in Abyssinia: Being Notes Collected during Three Years' Residence and Travels in That Country*. London: Frank Cass and Co./New Impression.

Paxton, Robert. 2001. *Vichy France: Old Guard and New Order*. New York: Columbia University Press.

Pearson, Michael. 1998. *Port Cities and Intruders: The Swahili Coast, India, and Portugal in the Early Modern Era*. Baltimore, MD: Johns Hopkins University Press.

———. 2003. *The Indian Ocean*. London: Routledge.

———. 2005. *The World of the Indian Ocean, 1500–1800: Studies in Economic, Social and Cultural History*. Burlington: Ashgate.

Penrad, Jean-Claude. 1994. "Societies of the Ressac: The Mainland Meets the Ocean." In *Continuity and Autonomy in Swahili Communities: Inland Influences and*

Strategies of Self-Determination, edited by David Parkin, 41–48. London: School of Oriental and African Studies.

Péroz, Etienne. 1907. *Le chemin de fer éthiopien et le port de Djibouti*. Paris: Comité de l'Afrique Française.

Peterson, Derek. 2012. *Ethnic Patriotism and the East African Revival: A History of Dissent, c. 1935–1972*. New York: Cambridge University Press.

Piombo, Jessica. 2007. Terrorism and US Counter-Terrorism Programs in Africa : An Overview. *Strategic Insights*, Vol, 6, no. 1.

Plowden, Walter. 1868. *Travels in Abyssinia and the Galla Country: With an Account of a Mission to Ras Ali in 1848*. London: Longmans, Green and Co.

Poinsard, Léon. 1894. *Études de Droit international conventionnel: Transport, transmission, relation economique international, propriété intellectuelle*. Paris: Librairie Cotillon.

Poulantza, Nicos. 1978. *State, Power, Socialism*. London: Verso.

Poydenot, G. 1889. *Obock: Station de ravitaillement pour la marine française*. Paris: Imprimer Charles Blot.

Prakash, Om. 2004. *Bullion of Goods: Europe and Indian Merchants in the Indian Ocean Trade, 1500–1800*. New Delhi: Manohar.

Prestholdt, Jeremy. 2008. *Domesticating the World: African Consumerism and Genealogies of Globalization*. Berkeley, CA: University of California Press.

———. 2014. "Politics of the Soil: Separatism, Autochthony and Decolonization at the Kenyan Coast." *Journal of African History* 55, no. 2: 161–71.

Reese, Scott. 2012. "Salafi Transformations: Aden and the Changing Voices of Religious Reform in the Interwar Indian Ocean." *International Journal of Middle Eastern Studies* 44, no. 1: 71–75.

Robinson, David. 1988. "French Islamic Policy and Practice in Late Nineteenth Century Senegal." *Journal of African History* 29, no. 3: 415–35.

———. 1999. "France as a Muslim Power in West Africa." *Africa Today* 46, no. 3–4: 105–27.

Robinson, William. 2001. "Social Theory and Globalization: The Rise of a Transnational State." *Theory and Society* 30, no. 2: 157–200.

———. 2003. *Transnational Conflicts: Central America, Social Change and Globalisation*. London: Verso.

Rose, Nicolas. 1996. "The Death of the Social? Re-figuring the Territory of Government." *Economy and Society* 25, no. 3: 282–300.

Rossi, Gianluigi. 1980. *L'Afrique Italiana verso l'indipendenza (1941–1949)*. Varese: Giuffrè Editore.

Rotberg, Robert I. 2005. "The Horn of Africa and Yemen: Diminishing the Threat of Terrorism." In *Battling Terrorism in the Horn of Africa*, edited by Robert I. Rotberg, 1–22. Washington: Brookings Institution Press.

Rubenson, Sven. 1966. *King of Kings Tewodros of Ethiopia*. Addis Ababa: Haile Selassie I University.

Rutherford, Ken. 2008. *Humanitarianism under Fire: The US and UN Intervention in Somalia*. Bloomfield, CT: Kumarian Press.

Sadouni, Samadia. 1999. "Le minoritaire Sud-Africain Ahmed Deedat, une figure originale de la Da'wa." *Islam et Société au Sud du Sahara* 12: 89–108.

Sarris, Louis George. 1985. "Soviet Military Policy and Arms Activities in Sub-Saharan Africa." In *Arms and the African: Military Influences on Africa's*

International Relations, edited by William J. Foltz and Henry S. Bienen, 29–57. New Haven/London: Yale University Press.

Sbacchi, Alberto. 1985. *Ethiopia under Mussolini: Fascism and the Colonial Experience*. London: Zed Books.

———. 1997. *Legacy of Bitterness: Ethiopia and Fascist Italy, 1935–1941*. Lawrenceville, NJ: Red Sea Press.

Scarr, Deryck. 1998. *Slaving and Slavery in the Indian Ocean*. Basingstoke: Palgrave Macmillan.

Schatz, S. P. 1984. "Pirate Capitalism and the Inert Economy of Nigeria." *Journal of Modern Africa Studies* 32, no. 1: 45–58.

Schiller, Nina Glick, and Noel B. Salazar. 2013. "Regimes of Mobility across the Globe: Imaginaries and Relationalities of Power." *Journal of Ethnic and Migration Studies* 39, no. 2: 1–18.

Schraeder, Peter. 1991. *Djibouti*. Oxford: Clio Press.

———. 1993. "Ethnic Politics in Djibouti: From 'Eye of the Hurricane' to 'Boiling Cauldron.'" *African Affairs* 92: 203–21.

Serjeant, Robert. 1978. "Wards and Quarters of Towns in South West Arabia." *Storia della Citta* 2, no. 11: 43–48.

Serres, Michel. 1995. *The Natural Contract*. Translated by Elizabeth MacArthur and William Paulson. Ann Arbor, MI: University of Michigan Press.

Shack, William. 1976. "Occupational Prestige, Status, and Social Change in Modern Ethiopia." *Africa* 46, no. 2: 166–81.

Shamir, Ronen. 2005. "Without Borders? Notes on Globalization as a Mobility Regime." *Sociological Theory* 23, no. 2: 197–217.

Sharma, Aradhana, and Akil Gupta. 2006. *The Anthropology of the State*. Oxford: Blackwell Publishing.

Shehim, Kassim, and James Searing. 1980. "Djibouti and the Question of Afar Nationalism." *African Affairs* 79, no. 315: 209–26.

Sheriff, Abdul. 1987. *Slaves, Spices and Ivory in Zanzibar*. London: James Currey.

———. 2010. *Dhow Cultures of the Indian Ocean: Cosmopolitanism, Commerce and Islam*. London: C. Hurst and Co.

Sheriff, Abdul, and Engseng Ho. 2014. *The Indian Ocean: Connections and the Creation of New Societies*. London: C. Hurst and Co.

Shipman, John. 2006. "In the Lion's Paw: Henry de Monfreid and the British at Aden (1916–1922)." *Journal of the British-Yemeni Society* 14, http://www.al-bab.com/bys/articles/shipman06.htm.

Simonin, L. 1862. "Voyages de M. Henri Lambert, agent consulaire de France à Aden 1855–1859." In *Le tour du monde: Nouveau journal des voyages*, edited by Edouard Charton, 68. Paris: Librairie Hachette.

Simpson, Edward. 2006. *Muslim Society and the Western Indian Ocean: The Seafarers of Kachchh*. London: Routledge.

Simpson, Edward, and Kai Kresse, eds. 2008. *Struggling with History: Islam and Cosmopolitanism in the Western Indian Ocean*. New York: Columbia University Press.

Sklair, Leslie. 2001. *The Transnational Capitalist Class*. Oxford: Blackwell Publishing.

Sklar, R. L. 1979. "The Nature of Class Domination in Africa." *Journal of Modern African Studies* 17, no. 4: 531–32.

Smart, Alan, and Josephine Smart. 2008. "Time–Space Punctuation: Hong Kong's Border Regime and Limits on Mobility." *Pacific Affairs* 81, no. 2: 175–93.

Smith, Leonard. 2008. "Wilsonian Sovereignty in the Middle East: The King–Crane Commission Report of 1919." In *The State of Sovereignty: Territories, Laws, Population*, edited by Douglas Howland and Louise S. White, 56–74. Bloomington, IN: Indiana University Press.

Soares, Benjamin F. 2005. *Islam and the Prayer Economy: History and Authority in a Malian Town*. Edinburgh: Edinburgh University Press.

Soares, Benjamin F., and René Otayek. 2007. "Introduction: Islam and Muslim Politics in Africa." In *Islam and Muslim Politics in Africa*, edited by Benjamin Soares and René Otayek, 1–16. New York: Palgrave Macmillan.

Société de Législation Comparée. 1901. *Annuaire de législation française*. Paris: Librairie Cotillon.

Sohier, Estelle. 2011. *Portraits controversés d'un prince éthiopien, Iyasu (1997–1935)*. Montpellier: L'Archange Minotaure.

Soulé, Aramis Houmed. 2014. "Lïj Iyasu's Asylum among the Afar in Awsa, 1916–1918." In *The Life and Times of Lïj Iyasu of Ethiopia*, edited by Éloi Ficquet and Wolbert G.C. Smidt, 165–176. Berlin: Lit Verlag.

Staford, F.E. 1949. "The Ex-Italian Colonies." *International Affairs* 25, no. 1: 47–55.

Steen, William M., ed. 1936. *The Ethiopian Constitution*. Washington, DC: Ethiopian Research Council.

Steinmetz, George, ed. 1999. *State/Culture: State Formation after the Cultural Turn*. Ithaca, NY: Cornell University Press.

Subrahmanyam, Sanjay. 2005. *Explorations in Connected History: From the Tagus to the Ganges*. New Delhi: Oxford University Press.

Swedenburg, Ted. 2003. *Memories of Revolt: The 1936–1939 Rebellion and the Palestinian National Past*. Fayetteville, AR: University of Arkansas Press.

Täkəlämariyamə, Fitawurari Täkəlähäwariyatə. 2006. *Ye Hiwote Tarik*. Addis Ababa: Addis Ababa University Press.

Talhami, Ghada Hashem. 1979. *Suakin and Massawa under Egyptian Rule, 1865–1885*. Washington, DC: University Press of America.

Tambe, Ashwini, and Harald Fischer-Tiné. 2009. *The Limits of British Colonial Control in South Asia: Spaces of Disorder in the Indian Ocean Region*. New York: Routledge.

Tamrat, Tadesse. 1972. *Church and State in Ethiopia, 1270–1527*. Oxford: Oxford University Press.

Tareke, Gebru. 1991. *Ethiopia Power and Protest: Peasant Revolt in the Twentieth Century*. Cambridge: Cambridge University Press.

———. 2000. "The Ethiopia–Somalia War of 1977 Revisited." *International Journal of African Historical Studies* 33, no. 3: 635–67.

Taylor, Peter. 1994. "The State as a Container: Territoriality in the Modern World System." *Progress in Human Geography* 18, no. 3:151–62.

Thiollet, Hélène. 2009. "La mobilité dans la Corne de l'Afrique: Entre urgence humanitaire et contrainte sécuritaire." *Migrations Société* 21, no. 121: 75–88.

Tholomier, Robert. 1981. *Djibouti Pawn of the Horn of Africa*. Trans. Virginia Thompson and Richard Adloff. Metuchen, NJ : The Scarecrow Press.

Thompson, Paul. 2004. *The Terror Timeline: Year by Year, Day by Day, Minute by Minute: A Comprehensive Chronicle of the Road to 9/11—and America's Response*. New York: Harper Collins.

Thompson, Virginia, and Richard Adloff. 1968. *Djibouti and the Horn of Africa*. Stanford, CA: Stanford University Press.

Tiruneh, Andargachew. 1993. *The Ethiopian Revolution, 1974–1987*. Cambridge: Cambridge University Press.

Triaud, Jean-Louis. 2000. "Islam in Africa under French Colonial Rule." In *The History of Islam in Africa*, edited by Nehemia Levtzion and Randall L. Pouwels, 169–87. Athens, OH: Ohio University Press.

Trimingham, J. Spencer. 1952. *Islam in Ethiopia*. London: Oxford University Press.

Tudesco, James Patrick. 1980. "Missionaries and French Imperialism: The Role of Catholic Missionaries in French Colonial Expansion, 1880–1905." PhD diss., University of Connecticut.

Turton, David. 2006. *Ethnic Federalism: The Ethiopian Experience in Comparative Perspective*. London: James Currey.

Ullendorff, Edward. 1969. "Two Letters from the Emperor Yohannes of Ethiopia to Queen Victoria and Lord Granville." *Bulletin of the School of Oriental and African Studies* 32, no. 1: 135–42.

United States Department of State. 2004. *Patterns of Global Terrorism*. Washington, DC: United States Department of State Publication Office.

———. 2010. *Country Report on Terrorism 2009*. Washington, DC: United States Department of State Publication Office.

Van Dijk, Kees. 2002. "Colonial Fears, 1890–1918: Pan Islamism and the Germano-Indian Plot." In *Transcending Borders: Arabs, Politics, Trade and Islam in Southeast Asia*, edited by Huub de Jonge and Nico Kaptain, 53–89. Leiden: KITLV Press.

Varble, Derek. 2009. *The Suez Crisis*. New York: Rosen Publishing Group.

Vianello, Alessandra. 2012. "One Hundred Years in Brava: The Migration of Umar Ba Umar from Hadhramaut to East Africa and Back, c. 1890–1990." *Journal of East African Studies* 6, no. 4: 655–71.

Vignon, Louis. 1919. *Un programme de la politique coloniale: Les questions des indigènes*. Paris: Plon-Nourrit.

Vink, Markus P.M. 2007. "Indian Ocean Studies and 'the New Thalassology.'" *Journal of Global History* 22, no. 1: 41–62.

Viveiros de Castro, Eduardo. 2004. "Perspectival Anthropology and the Method of Controlled Equivocation." *Tipitií: Journal of the Society for the Anthropology of Lowland South America* 2, no. 1: 2–20.

Walker, Iain. 2008. "Hadramis, Shimalis and Muwalladin: Negotiating Cosmopolitan Identities between the Swahili Coast and Southern Yemen." *Journal of Eastern African Studies* 2, no. 1: 44–59.

———. 2011. "Hybridity, Belonging and Mobilities: The Intercontinental Peripatetics of a Transnational Community." *Population, Space, and Place* 17, no. 2: 167–78.

———. 2012. "Comorians and Hadramis in the Western Indian Ocean: Diasporic Practices in a Comparative Context." *Social Dynamics: A Journal of African Studies* 38, no. 3: 435–53.

Walter, Dostal. 2005. "Saints of Hadramawt." In *Shattering Tradition: Custom, Law and the Individual in the Muslim Mediterranean*, edited by Walter Dostal and Wolfgang Kraus, 233–53. New York: I.B.Tauris.

Ward, Kerry. 2009. *Networks of Empire: Forced Migration in the Dutch East India Company*. Cambridge: Cambridge University Press.

Weber, Max. [1924]1978. *Economy and Society*. Berkeley, CA: University of California Press.

Welde-Gyorgis, Dawit. 1989. *Red Tears: War, Famine and Revolution in Ethiopia*. Lawrenceville, NJ: Red Sea Press.

West, Deborah. 2005. *Combating Terrorism in the Horn of Africa and Yemen*. Cambridge, MA: Belfer Center for Science and International Affairs.

Westerlund, David. 2003. "Ahmed Deedat's Theology of Religion: Apologetics through Polemics." *Journal of Religion in Africa* 33, no. 3: 263–78.

Whitford, David M. 2009. *The Curse of Ham in the Early Modern Era: The Bible and the Justifications for Slavery*. Farnham: Ashgate.

Williams, Paul D. 2014."The African Union Mission and the Next Stage in the War against al-Shabab." *The RUSI Journal* 159, no. 2: 52–60.

Wills, Justin. 1993. *Mombassa, the Swahili, and the Making of the Mijibenda*. Oxford: Clarendon Press.

Wink, André. 2010. "Cosmopolitanism and Xenophobia." Review of *Struggling with History: Islam and Cosmopolitanism in the Western Indian Ocean*, by Edward Simpson and Kai Kresse. *H-Asia*, October 2010, http://www.h-net.org/reviwes/showrev.php?id=30792.

Wood, Ellen Meiksins. 2003. *Empire of Capital*. London: Verso.

Woodward, Peter. 2006. *US Foreign Policy and the Horn of Africa*. Aldershot and Burlington: Ashgate.

Zellelew, Tilahun. 2015. "The Semiotics of the Christian/Muslim Knife: Meat and Knife as Markers of Religious Identity in Ethiopia." *Signs and Society* 3, no. 1, 44–70

Zewde, Bahru. 2005. "The City Center: A Shifting Concept in the History of Addis Ababa." In *Urban Africa: Changing Contours of Survival in the City*, edited by Abou Maliq Simone and Abdelghani Abouhani, 120–1137. Dakar: Codesria Books.

Zewdu, T. 1995. "A Social History of Arada, 1890–1935." MA thesis, Addis Ababa University.

Index

Page numbers followed by f indicate a figure.

A

Abu Bakr, Dini 18
Abu Bakr Pasha 18
Addis Ababa: bureaucratization of 44–47; as federal city 140; during occupation 54–55; and railway 19; residential areas in 43–44. *See also* Ethiopia
Aden 46, 50, 110
Adloff, Richard 16
'Afar 91, 128, 129, 135–36
Afghanistan 6
African Commission on Human and People's Rights 178–79
AFRICOM (United States African Command) 69
al-Ahbash 169–70
Ahmad, Ahmad bin 111, 123
Ahmad bin Hamid al Nasir, King 97
al-Ahmar, Ali Mohsen 77
Ahmed, Hussein 16
Alexanderson, Kris 6
Algeria 149
Alhoumekani, Muhammad Saleh 138–39
'Ali Jaber, Ahmad bin 178
Alpers, Edward 3, 15
American Muslim Council 67–68
American-Arab Anti-Discrimination Committee (ADC) 79

Amhara 74, 139–41, 166
amir al-bahr (commander of maritime frontier) 32, 42
Al-amoudi, Abdurahman 67–68
al-'Amudi, Muhammad Hussein 102, 103, 142–43, 173–75, 191, 193, 197
Anderson, Benedict 10
Ansar Allah 78
anthropology to support racism 156–57
Aptidon, Hassan Gouled 126, 133–34, 135
'Aqil, Salim Ubad 121–22
Arab Club (Aden) 110
Arab Club (Djibouti) 126–27
Arab League 78, 100
Arab Satellite Communication Organization 176
Aref, Ali 105–106
Ark of the Covenant 153
Armenians 115–17
arms trade 90–91, 97
Arrighi, Giovanni 85
Arta agreement 129
al-Asad, Muhammad 'Abdallah Salih 178–79, 197
Asad, Talal 196
*'askari*s (native soldiers) 35, 38. *See also* police forces
Asmara 131–32

al-Asnag, Sa'id 151
al Asnaj, Ahmad Muhammad 110–11
assassination plot, Libyan 68
assassinations 127, 170
assembly, prohibition of 63–64
Association Islamique de Bienfaisance 111
associations of mutual assistance 91–92
attitudes toward traditional social roles, challenges to 162–63
authorities, traditional 42
'Awad, Haydar 'Abdallah 134–35

B
Ba 'Aqil, 'Umar 'Ubayd 1–2, 181
Ba Magad, 'Awad 'Abdallah 74–75
Ba Makhrama, Rifki Abdulkader 136, 150
Ba Nabila, Hassan 110–11, 150
Ba Naji, Muhammad Yusuf 83–85
Ba Wazir, Abd al-Qadir 'Umar 113–15
Ba Zar'a, Abd al-Hamid Sa'id 47–48
Ba Zar'a family 89, 94–95
Ba Zar'a, Sa'id 47–48, 48f, 94
Ba Zar'a, Salim 94–95, 95f
Baath Party 59, 130–31
Balzacq, Thierry 70
Bang, Anne 9, 10, 12
al Bar, 'Abdallah Mahajus 121
barricades 62–64
Barth, Fredrik 184
Barəyas (darker-skinned people) 152
Basset, René 149–50
Berbera 30, 31
Bertz, Ned 12
Betts, Alexander 70
Bin Laden, Osama 5–6, 8, 174
Bin Laden, Tarek 102–103
Bin Mahfuz, Khalid 174–75
blind sheikh 110, 150
blockades, naval 48–53
border controls 70–72
Boreh, Abdourahman 103
Borelli, Jules 32
Borrel, Bernard 138
Boswell, Christina 70
Braudel, Fernand 2, 7
Brisard, Jean-Charles 174
British protectorate in Yemen 46, 120
British Somaliland 18, 57–58
British–Ottoman conflict 50–51

Bruce, James 112
Bujra, Abdallah 12
Burton, Richard 30, 32–33

C
Cadars, M. 146
capital–state relationship. *See* states/empires, relationship with capital
caravan routes 31, 32
Carrera, Sergio 70
Catholic Church 146, 148–49
Central Intelligence Agency (CIA) 178–79
Cerulli, Enrico 157
challenges to traditional social attitudes 162–63
Chaudhuri, Kirti N. 3, 15
Chefneux, Léon 19
Christian–Muslim relations in Djibouti 145–46, 148–51, 158–59, 196–97
Christian–Muslim relations in Ethiopia. *See* Orthodox Christians
citizenship: as condition for work 97–98; denied to non-Europeans 105–107, 109; dual 2, 76; granted to subjects 122–23; as social and legal concept 193–95, 196
civil wars: Djibouti 135–36; Houthi revolt 78–80; Somalia 68–69
Clarence-Smith, William G. 6
class, relevance of 186–90
classifications of people. *See* hierarchies and classifications
clientage. *See* patron–client relationships
Clifford, James 198
Cold War 59
Coleman, James S. 192
colonial administration, collaboration with 107–109
colonial powers, wars 48–50
colonization 17–19, 46
Combined Joint Task Force–Horn of Africa (CJTF-HOA) 69
commander of maritime frontier (amir al-bahr) 32, 42
Communauté Financière Africaine (CFA) 21
Compagnie Maritime de l'Afrique Orientale 86–88
competition: with colonial-based capital 86–89; for jobs 91–93
conferences, pan-Islamic 151

conflicts, ethnic. *See* ethnic conflicts
conflicts, religious. *See* religious conflicts
connections, political and economic 93–97, 101, 151
constitutions 116–17, 158
consular courts 45–46
Cooper, Frederick 11
Coptic community. *See* Orthodox Christians
Cornwallis, M. 30
Coubèche, 'Ali 151
Coubèche, Magda Sa'id 'Ali 137–38
Coubèche, Sa'id 'Ali 60, 98, 123, 125, 129–30, 136–38
Coubèche family 101, 136–38
Council on American-Islamic Relations (CAIR) 79
counterterrorism. *See* terrorism and counterterrorism
courts: consular 45–46; sharia 121–22, 157–58
curfews 46–47, 60–61
customs duties 35–36, 87

D
d'Abbadie, Arnauld 30, 32
de Champloret 30, 32
de Gaulle, Charles 52, 61, 159
De Jong, Huub 6
de la Merveille, Godefroy Gollet 30, 32
decolonization 127–30
demonstrations: anti-Arab 99, 131–32; anti-colonial 61; anti-ELF 132–33; anti-EPRDF 170; labor 93; for Muslim rights 163; pro-Italian 118–20
Derg regime 58, 64–65, 99–100, 164–65
dhows: attacks on 74–76; competition with European shippers 86–88; made illegal 90–91; regulations on 35–36
diaspora, Islamic 5–6
diaspora studies 198. *See also* Indian Ocean studies
Dini, Ahmed 135
Dire Dawa: ethnic conflict in 140–41; murders of foreigners in 1–2; under occupation 55; religious leaders in 121–22; rise of 19, 33; segregation in 42–43
disarming of natives 39–40

discrimination: ethnic 166; against Muslims 111–13; racial 152–53; against Somalis 91–93; against Yemenis 115–17, 143–44. *See also* judicial systems; segregation
Djama, Ali 123, 125
Djibouti: barricades within 62–63, 64; blockades of 52–53; books on 16; border controls in 71–72; civil war 135–36; currency of 21; defense pact with France 59; earlier names for 24–25; economic agreement with France 101; elections in 135, 136; independence referendum 63–64; nationalism in 98; political reforms in 57, 59–64, 122–26; tribalism 133–34, 135; US military base in 21, 69
Djibouti, political positions of Yemenis in: during decolonization 127–30; effect of divisions in Yemen on 126–27; moral revival 109–111; participation 107–109; post-independence 133–39; under reform policies 122–26; subjects versus citizens 105–107, 109
Djibouti civil war 135–36
Dorani, 'Abd al-Karim 150, 151
drone attacks 177–78
Dubois, Colette 137–38
Dutch empire 6

E
economic influence of Yemeni diaspora 162–63
economic reforms in Ethiopia 98–99
education 108, 148–49, 150
Egypt 17, 59–60, 97. *See also* Nasserite ideology
elections: in Djibouti 135, 136; in Ethiopia 142–43
Eritrea 18, 57–58, 68, 131–32
Eritrean Liberation Front (ELF) 130–33
Ethiopia: administrative divisions 139–40; attempts to overthrow government 113–15; books on 16; claims in Eritrea 57–58; during Cold War 59; consular courts in 45–46; economic reforms in 98–99; elections in 142–43; under EPRDF rule 139–42; European presence in 18–19, 22; expansion

Index | 245

of 21; guerrilla wars in 68; under Italian occupation 53–56, 117–22, 155–57; liberalization of travel in 69–70; nationalism in 98–101; racial discrimination in 152–53; Red Terror 64–65; restoration of monarchy 157–58; state cosmology 152–55, 195; suppression of Muslims in 111–13; suppression of slavery in 90; ulama in 169–70; Yemeni interactions with state 163–64. *See also* Addis Ababa; Dire Dawa; Orthodox Christians

Ethiopia, political positions of Yemenis in: anti-Arab sentiments 130–33; attempts to overthrow government 113–15; under EPRDF rule 139–42; under Italian occupation 117–22; suppression of Muslims 111–13; vulnerability 115–17

Ethiopian People's Revolutionary Democratic Front (EPRDF) 68, 139–42

ethnic conflicts 125–26, 129, 139–42, 191–92. *See also* demonstrations; discrimination; ethnicity; tribalism

ethnic groups: 'Afar 91, 128, 129, 135–36; Amhara 74, 139–42, 166; Gadabursi 125; Gurage 99, 104, 193; Oromo 1–2, 74, 139–42, 166; Somali 91–93, 100, 123–25

ethnicity 193, 195–96. *See also* ethnic conflicts

European Union 70–71

expulsions, mass: from Djibouti 60, 62, 71, 97–98, 103, 138; from Ethiopia 130–33, 143; from Saudi Arabia 76

F

fanaticism, countermeasures to 145–51, 168–75

Farah, Rachad 139

federalism 139–40

First World War 50–51

fishermen, attacks on 74–76

foreigners: early presence in Djibouti 30–31; Europeans 39–40; murders of 1–2; registration of 44–46; under suspicion 60–61. *See also* identity cards; passports and travel permits

France: attitude toward Islam 145–46, 147–51; colonization by 18–19; defense pact with Djibouti 59; economic agreement with Djibouti 101

Frank, Andre Gunder 189

free agency, myth of 3–4, 5–6, 31, 182–83

Free Yemeni Movement 126–27

Freitag, Ulrike 6, 10

Front for the Restoration of Unity and Democracy (FRUD) 135–36

Frontex (European Agency for the Management of Operational Cooperation at the External Borders of the Member States of the European Union) 70–71

G

Gadabursi 125
Gaddafi, Muammar 68
genealogy studies as strategy 9–10
Getu (Ethiopian informant) 73–74
al-Ghashmi, Ahmad bin Hussein 67
al-Ghazi, Ahmad ibn Ibrahim (Gragñ) 112
Ghosh, Devleena 185
Gilroy, Paul 198
globalization of labor 190–91
globalization theories 10–11, 15, 182
Graziani, Rodolfo 119–21
Guelleh, Ismail Omar 135, 138
Gulf Cooperation Council 77, 78
Gulf states 66
Gulf war, first 76
Gurage 99, 104, 193

H

Hadi, Abd Rabbuh Mansur 77, 78
Hadramis, defined 24
Haile Selassie I 58, 59, 64, 94–95, 97, 115–17, 131–32
Ham (biblical character) 156–57
al-Hamdi, Ibrahim 66–67
Harar 17, 18, 30, 32–33, 154–55
al-Harari, Abdallah Muhammad 169–70
Hardt, Michael 85, 183
Harris, W. Cornwallis 31–32
Harvey, David 85
al-Hasan, Muhammad 'Abdallah ("Mad Mullah") 147–48
health regulation 36–37
Henare, Amiria 185
hierarchical processes 12–13, 186

hierarchies and classifications: among Muslims 165–67; among Yemenis 146–47, 165, 166; challenged 162–63; in Ethiopia 153–54; 'good' and 'bad' Muslims 167–69, 172–73; moral 165–66; racist/mythical 155–57; religion-based 197. *See also* citizenship
hinterland, defined 24
history: anthropological use of 22; early European presence 17–19, 30–31; early periods 14, 17, 29; suppression of 2
Ho, Engseng 5–6, 7, 8–10
Holbraad, Martin 185
Horden, Peregrine 3
al-Houthi, Hussein Badreddin 76–77
Houthi revolt 76–80
Houthi revolt/civil war 78–80
human trafficking. *See* trafficking

I
identity cards: in Djibouti 62–63, 92; in Ethiopia 65, 140, 141, 142; falsified 64, 76; in Yemen 67. *See also* passports and travel permits
Idris, Ahmad bin 'Abdallah 118
Idris, Salah 174–75
al Idrisi, Muhammad 50
Ilg, Alfred 19
Imam Yahya 109, 126–27
immigration: illegal 73–74, 76, 78–79; restrictions on 37, 41–42. *See also* migration
imperialism, defined 21
impurity, ritual 153–54
inclusion/exclusion. *See* citizenship; hierarchies and classifications
independence movements 59–61. *See also* separatist movements
Indian Ocean 3, 29–31
Indian Ocean studies: methodologies 8–13, 16; myth of free agency 3–4, 5–6, 31, 182–83; network model 3–4, 6–7, 12, 181–82, 183–85; unity/disunity model 2–3, 183
Institute of Ethiopian Studies 171
insurgency groups, sponsorship of 162. *See also* independence movements; Islamist groups; separatist movements
intermarriage 141, 146, 165

International Monetary Fund (IMF) 101–102
International Organization of Migration (IOM) 71–72, 79
investment and clientage 101–104
IOM (International Organization of Migration) 71–72, 79
Iran, proxy war 78
al-Iryani, Abdul Rahman 66
ISIS (Islamic State in Iraq and Syria) 78
Islam: "black" versus Arab 145–46; defense of 175–76; French strategies for 148–51; and relations with west 5–6, 53–54, 55
Islamic Affairs Supreme Council (Ethiopia) 169
Islamic Court (Ittihad al-Mahakim alaaa-Islamiya) 69
Islamic diaspora 5–6
Islamic Front for the Liberation of Oromia (IFLO) 1–2
Islamic State in Iraq and Syria (ISIS) 78
Islamist groups 1–2, 68–69, 78, 109–111
Israel 152–53
'Issa Somalis 123–25. *See also* discrimination; ethnic conflicts
Italian Somaliland 18, 57
Italy: colonization by 17–19; former colonies of 57; occupation of Ethiopia by 53–56, 117–22, 155–57
Ittihad al-Islamiya 68

J
jihad 175–79
judicial systems 40–41, 107. *See also* courts
justice de paix 107

K
Kamil, Abdallah 135
Kapferer, Bruce 184
Kebra Nagast 152–53
Khedive Ismail 17
Krapf, Lewis 30
Kresse, Kai 15

L
labor: competition 91–93; globalization of 190–91; restrictions on 97–98; shortages 51
Lambert, Henry 18
Latour, Bruno 184–85

Index | 247

law, maritime 33–34
le Chatelier, Alfred 149
Lefebvre, Henri 85
legations, colonial 46, 48
legends 14, 152–53
Lejean, Guillaume 112
Lemarchand, René 192
letters of protest: to Chamber of Commerce 35–36, 87–88; on disarmament 39–40; to district attorney 40–41; to Haile Selassie I 116–17; on trains 38; to US consular office 113–15
Libyan assassination plot 68
Lij Iyasu 116, 154–55
lighthouses 33
Lippmann, Alphonse 94
Luqman, Muhammad 'Ali 110–11

M

"Mad Mullah" (Muhammad 'Abdallah al-Hasan) 147–48
Mahebere Kedusan 176
Mäkonənə Rasə 46
Mandatory Palestine 150–51
Manger, Leif 6, 16
marginalization of Yemenis, political 128–30, 135, 136, 142
Marill, Paul 35–36
maritime law 33–34
Marshal Shaposhnikov (ship) 75
Martine, Jean 123, 125
Marx, Karl 187, 193
Massawa 31
McPherson, Kenneth 3
media, use of 175–76
mediating roles of Yemenis 129–30, 136
Menelik I 153
Menelik II 18, 19, 33, 44, 99, 116
Mengistu Haile Mariam 65
merchant class 85, 93–97
Messageries Maritimes 91, 93
Metcalf, Thomas R. 3
Middleton, John 15
migrant groups as heroic actors 183
migration 54–55. *See also* immigration
al Mihdar, Muhammad 118–20
Miran, Jonathan 7
Mische, Ann 195
missionaries: Christian 146; Muslim 168–69

Mitchell, J. Clyde 184
mobility. *See* movement
Mochi, Aldobrandino 157
Mollat, Michael 7
Monfreid, Henry de 42, 43, 51, 89
monopolization: of labor recruitment 91–92; of transportation 89
monsoons 31–32
moral revival 109–111
mosques 121–22
movement: in colonial period 33–34; control and adaptation 13–14; liberalization of travel in Ethiopia 69–70; myth of free travel 3–4, 5–6, 31, 182–83; in precolonial period 31–33; as threat 15, 70–72. *See also* immigration; migration; movement restrictions; passports and travel permits; railway; regulation
movement restrictions: barricades 62–64; curfews 46–47, 60–61; in Ethiopia 45–47; naval blockades 48–53; in occupied Ethiopia 53–56; segregation 38–40, 54–55
Muecke, Stephen 185
Muhammad (informant) 177
Muhammad, descendants of. *See* Sada
Muhammad al-Badr, Imam 66
al-Muqaddasi, Muhammad ibn Ahmad Shams al-Din 29
Muslim Brotherhood 110
Muslim–Christian relations in Djibouti 158–59
Muslim–Christian relations in Ethiopia. *See* Orthodox Christians
Muslims: discrimination against 111–13; under Italian occupation 117–22; seen as threats 164–65, 167–69. *See also* Islam; religious leaders; states/empires, relationships with Muslims
Mussolini, Benito 155
Muti, Salim 89
mutual assistance associations 91–92

N

Nasser, Gamal Abdel 97, 128–29, 130. *See also* Nasserite ideology
Nasserite ideology 128–29, 161–62. *See also* Nasser, Gamal Abdel; pan-Arabism
nationalism: in Djibouti 98; in Ethiopia 98–101

nationalization: under Derg regime 100; of Suez Canal 97
native soldiers ('*askari*s) 35, 38. *See also* police forces
natives, disarming of 39–40
natural forces 31–32
naturalization of social sciences 184–85
naval attacks on fishermen 74–75
naval blockades 48–53
navigation practices 30, 31–32, 33–34, 74, 86–88
Negri, Antonio 85, 183
network model 3–4, 6–7, 12, 181–82, 183–85
El Nour, Ashraf 71–72

O
Obock 18, 19, 25, 33, 37
Ong, Aihwa 198–99
ontological turn 184–85
Oppen, Achim von 10
Oromo 1–2, 74, 139–41, 166
Orthodox Christians: anti-Arab demonstrations by 131–32; cosmology of 152–55, 195; under Italian occupation 118, 120–21; in Muslim moral hierarchy 166; opposition to Yemenis 163–64, 165, 173–74, 176–77, 197; T-shirt incident 176–77; website comments from 173–74
Ottoman Empire 17, 50–51
Ottoman–British war 50–51

P
Palestine 150–51
Palestine Liberation Organization (PLO) 131
pan-Arabism 59–60, 109–110, 128–29, 130–33, 161–62, 163–64
pan-Islamism 109–110, 147–48, 151
Parkyns, Mansfield 30
passports and travel permits 41, 46–49, 65–66, 92. *See also* identity cards
patron–client relationships 101–104, 139, 142–43, 144, 188–89, 192–93, 196
Pearson, Michael 3, 15
penal system 40–41
penal systems 107. *See also* courts
People's Democratic Republic of Yemen (south) 66–67

Pétain, Philippe 52
Piombo, Jessica 70
pirates 75–76
Plowden, Walter 112
police forces: in Addis Ababa 46–47; in Dire Dawa 43; in Djibouti 35–38
Police Sanitaire Maritime-Lazaret 37
political parties 135, 140
political positions of Yemenis. *See* Djibouti, political positions of Yemenis in; Ethiopia, political positions of Yemenis in
political reforms in Djibouti 57, 59–64, 122–26
Pompidou, George 62–63
ports and vessel traffic regulation 32, 33–37
post–Cold War 101–103
post-independence Djibouti 133–39
privatization in Djibouti and Ethiopia 101–102
prostitution 110–11
Purcell, Nicholas 3
puritanism 161–62

Q
qadis: under French rule 53–54, 149–50, 158, 161f; under Italian occupation 121. *See also* al Saqqaf, 'Ali Abu Bakr
al-Qaeda 78, 174, 177–78
al Qaiti, 'Abdullah 121, 147
quarantines 36–37

R
racism 152–53, 156–57, 167. *See also* discrimination; ethnic conflicts; segregation
radicalization and countermeasures 145–51, 168–76
Radman, Elias 175
railway: construction of 19, 20f, 33; monopolization of transportation by 89; policing of 37–38; restrictions of travel on 45, 46; segregation on 38–39; travel passes 46
Rasə Täfari 116
Red Sea: blockades in 50–51; early European presence 30; Egyptian expansion in 17; navigation practices 30, 31–32; in network model 7
Red Terror 64–65

referendum for independence 63–64
reforms, economic, in Ethiopia 98–99
reforms, political, in Djibouti 57, 59–64, 122–26
refugees from Houthi revolt/civil war 78–80
Reglement Concernant les Règles établies pour Prévenir les Abordages 34
regulation: of health 36–37; of immigration 37, 41–42; of ports and vessel traffic 33–37; of zones 39–40
religious conflicts 154–55. *See also* Orthodox Christians
religious leaders 121–22, 158–60, 169–70. *See also* Muslims
rescue missions for returning Yemenis 66–67
revolts 150–51
riots 93. *See also* demonstrations; ethnic conflicts
Robinson, William 191
Rose, Nicolas 184
Ruggeri, Giuffrida 157
Russian navy attacks 74–75

S
Sabeans 157
Sada (descendants of Prophet Muhammad) 4, 9, 146–48, 149–50, 158, 162–63
*säfär*s (occupation-based areas) 43–44
Saget, Louis 61
Said Bey, Abdel Hamid 151
Saleh, Ali 'Abd Allah 77, 78
Salih, Ali Tahir 129
Sapeto, Giuseppe 17
al Saqqaf, 'Ali Abu Bakr 150, 158–60
Saudi Arabia: border controls in 72; export of puritanism 161–62; Gulf war 76; migrants in 66, 73–74; proxy wars 78
schools 148–49, 150
Second World War 52–54, 57–59
secular–religious connection 197–98
security efforts 70–72
segregation: in Djibouti 39–40; in occupied Ethiopia 54–55; on trains 38–39
separatist movements 1–2, 59–60, 130–31
sermons 176
Serres, Michel 185

Service de Sécurité et des Affaires Indigènes 107, 108, 192
al-Shabab (Harakat al-Shabaab al-Mujahidin) 69
Shamir, Ronen 15
sharia courts 121–22, 157–58
Sheriff, Abdul 7, 15
slave trade 89–90
smugglers 66, 73–74, 90–91
social stratification. *See* hierarchies and classifications
socialism 66–67, 164–65
soft politics 111
soft power 72
Somali 91–93, 100, 123–25
Somali civil war 68–69
Somalia 17–18, 64, 68
Somalia–Ethiopia war 58
sovereignty, Wilsonian 113–15
Soviet Union 59
space and spaces: cities 32–33, 54–55; hinterland cities 42–44; nature of 9–11, 23; ports 32, 34–37, 182–83; during wars 50–56
states/empires: control of mobility by 13–14, 182, 185; hierarchies generated by 186; nature of 20–21; structuring role of 8
states/empires, relationship with capital: competition with colonial-based capital 86–89; example of Ba Naji 83–85; investment and clientage 101–104, 188–89; labor competition 91–93; merchant class with connections 93–97; nationalism and socialism 97–101; outlawing of traditional trade 89–91
states/empires, relationships with Muslims: countering fanaticism and radicalization 145–51, 168–75; enduring attitudes and hierarchies 165–67; enemies of state 164–65; Ethiopian state cosmology 152–55, 195; jihad and counterterrorism 175–79; new interpretations of Islam 161–63; racist/mythical hierarchy 155–57; religious leaders associated with state 158–60; subjects of state 157–58; threat to United States and allies 167–68
subjects versus citizens 105–107, 109
Sudan 6

Suez Canal crisis 97
Sufis 12, 147, 169–70
Sultan Saʻid 89
Sumayt, Ahmad ibn 9
surveillance by governments 60, 63, 65

T
Täfari Mäkonənə 115–16
Tajura 30, 32
Tajura, Gulf of 52
taxation 99. *See also* customs duties
Teferi Benti 65
terrorism and counterterrorism 70–72, 175–79
Tewodros II 17, 112
TFAI (Territoire Français des Afars et des Issas) 25
Thompson, Paul 174–75
Thompson, Virginia 16
torture 178–79
trade, traditional 89–91
traders: competition with Europeans 86–89; under Derg regime 99–100
traditional attitudes, challenges to 162–63
traditional authorities 42
trafficking: of arms 90–91, 97; of humans 66, 73–74, 89–90
transnational class 101–103
transnationality 198–99
travel permits. *See* passports and travel permits
tribalism 133–34, 135, 194–95. *See also* discrimination; ethnic conflicts
T-shirt incidents 176–77

U
ulama, sponsorship of 149, 169–70
United States: appeal to by Yemenis in Ethiopia 113–15; attacks in Yemen 78–79; Bin Laden and 6; Cold War and 59; cultural programming 170–72; drone attacks 177–78; embassy correspondence 168–69; embassy personnel 45; military aid to Yemen 72; military base in Djibouti 21, 175; Muslims in 67–68; religious principles in 197–98; troops in Somalia 68–69; use of torture by 178–79
United States African Command (AFRICOM) 69

unity, Islamic 109–110, 147–48, 151
unity/disunity model 2–3, 183

V
Van Dijk, Kees 6
vessel traffic and ports: competition with Europeans 86–88; regulation of 32, 33–37
Viveiros de Castro, Eduardo 185

W
Wahhabism 150, 161–62, 168–69, 171–72, 173–74
wars: Cold War 59; between colonial powers 48–50; Djibouti civil war 135–36; drone attacks 177–78; first Gulf war 76; First World War 50–51; Houthi revolt/civil war 78–80; Ottoman–British 50–51; Second World War 52–54, 57–59; Somali civil war 68–69; Somalia–Ethiopia 58; Yemeni civil war 66–67
Wavell, Archibald 52
Weber, Max 186–88
websites, Ethiopian 173–74
wills 83–85
Wills, Justin 15
Wilsonian sovereignty 113–15
al-Wizir, Al-Sayyid Abdallah bin Ahmad 127
Wood, Ellen Meiksins 85
World Bank 101–102
World War I 50–51
World War II 52–54, 57–59
Worth, Robert 72

Y
Yamamoto, Donald 171–72
Yemen: civil war 66–67; divisions within 126–27, 166–67; Houthi revolt 76–80; return to 66–67, 165; US military aid to 72
Yemen Arab Republic (north) 66–67
'Yemeni,' use of term 24
Yemeni civil war 66–67
Yemenis: respected among Muslims 146–47; seen as throwbacks 8–9; seen as unclean 153–54
Yohannes I 112
Yohannes IV 113
Young Muslim Association 110

Index | 251

Z

al Zahir, 'Abd al Rahman b. Muhammad 5, 8–9
al-Zahiri, Sheikh Ahmad Salih 96–97, 96f, 122
al-Zawahari, Ayman 178
Zayla' 30, 31, 32, 52
zonal control 39–40, 54–55